PENGUIN BOOKS

OPPORTUNITIES

Edward de Bono was born in Malta and after his initial education at St Edward's College, Malta, and the Royal University of Malta, where he obtained a degree in medicine, he proceeded as a Rhodes Scholar to Christ Church, Oxford, where he gained an honours degree in psychology and physiology and then a D.Phil. in medicine. He also holds a Ph.D. from Cambridge. He has had faculty appointments at the universities of Oxford, London, Cambridge and Harvard.

Dr de Bono runs the largest curriculum programme for the direct teaching of thinking in schools. Some countries, like Venezuela, have made it compulsory in all schools, and there is a growing use in Canada, the USA, China and the USSR. Dr de Bono's instruction in thinking has also been sought by such well-known corporations as NTT (Japan), Du Pont, Ericsson, United Technologies, American Standard, Exxon and Shell. His 'Six Hats' method is now used in many corporations, such as Prudential and IBM. He has also worked for governments, including the Government of California on toxic waste problems. He may be teaching senior executives of multi-national corporations one day and nine-year-olds in a primary school the next.

Dr de Bono has been invited to address such meetings as The Institute of Institutional Investors, The Commonwealth Law Conference, The American Bar Association, The World Congress on Emergency and Disaster Medicine, The World Economic Forum (Davos) and The Society of Information Managers. In 1989 he chaired a meeting of Nobel Prize laureates in Seoul, Korea.

He is the founder and director of the Cognitive Research Trust (1969) and the Centre for the Study of Thinking, and the founder of SITO (Supranational Independent Thinking Organisation), which was set up as a sort of intellectual Red Cross to provide additional and creative thinking on problems and issues. He has also set up a Task Force on Thinking in Washington.

Dr de Bono has been invited to lecture and work in forty-five countries. He has written over thirty books and there are translations available in twenty-four languages, including Chinese, Korean, Japanese, Russian, Arabic, Hebrew, Urdu, Bahasa and all major languages. He has made two television series, *De Bono's Course in Thinking* for the BBC and *The Greatest Thinkers* for WDR, Germany. He runs a newsletter which is published ten times a year and is the inventor of the classic L-Game, which is said to be the simplest real game ever invented. He is perhaps best known for originating the term 'lateral thinking', which now has an entry in the Oxford English Dictionary.

OTHER TITLES PUBLISHED BY PENGUIN:

Atlas of Management Thinking
Children Solve Problems
Conflicts: A Better Way to Resolve Them
Edward de Bono's Masterthinker's Handbook
The Five-Day Course in Thinking
Future Positive
The Happiness Purpose
I Am Right You Are Wrong
Lateral Thinking
Lateral Thinking for Management
Letters to Thinkers
The Mechanism of Mind
Po: Beyond Yes and No
Practical Thinking
Six Thinking Hats
Teaching Thinking
The Use of Lateral Thinking
Wordpower

Edward de Bono

Opportunities

A Handbook of
Business Opportunity Search

Penguin Books

PENGUIN BOOKS

Published by the Penguin Group
Penguin Books Ltd, 27 Wrights Lane, London w8 5tz, England
Viking Penguin, a division of Penguin Books USA Inc.
375 Hudson Street, New York, New York 10014, USA
Penguin Books Australia Ltd, Ringwood, Victoria, Australia
Penguin Books Canada Ltd, 2801 John Street, Markham, Ontario, Canada l3r 1b4
Penguin Books (NZ) Ltd, 182–190 Wairau Road, Auckland 10, New Zealand

Penguin Books Ltd, Registered Offices: Harmondsworth, Middlesex, England

First published by Associated Business Programmes 1978
Published by Pelican Books 1980
Reprinted in Penguin Books 1991
10 9 8 7 6 5 4 3 2 1

Printed in England by Clays Ltd, St Ives plc
Set in Linotype Juliana

Introduction 7
The opportunity search 10
Form of the book 12
Lateral thinking and opportunity search 14

Part I: *People, attitudes and opportunities* 19
The distinction between
  what is urgent and what is important 20
Problem-solving and problem-finding 22
Executive styles 28
The opportunity-negative structure 31
Obstacles to opportunity search 33
Cultural attitude towards opportunity 38
Corporate attitude towards opportunity 40
Executive attitude towards opportunity 46
What is an opportunity? 53
Levels of opportunity 64
Benefits and motivation 68
The opportunity dilemma 72

Part II: *The Opportunity Audit and
  the Opportunity Team* 75
Status of the opportunity search exercise 76
Elements of the opportunity search exercise 79
The Opportunity Audit 82
Opportunity space 87
Idea-sensitive areas and general opportunities 92
The specific opportunity objective 97

Progress reports   102
Opportunities in other areas   104
The Opportunity Manager   106
The Opportunity Team   110
Opportunity Task Force   123

Part III: *Thinking for opportunities*   127
Review of fundamental thinking processes   128
'Moving-in' and 'moving-out' as modes of thinking   137
Starting point check-list   140
End-point check-list   169
The treatment of ideas   189
'If-box' maps   204
Action structure for opportunity   213
Dealing with risk and uncertainty   220
Evaluation   228

Summary of Terms   243

Introduction

'An opportunity is as real an ingredient in business as raw material, labour or finance – but it only exists when you can see it.'

For the small sum of $100,000 Alexander Graham Bell offered to sell all his telephone patents to the giant Western Union Telegraph Company. He had no choice because his backers had run out of funds. Without any hesitation William Orton, then president of Western Union, turned the offer down. Today Bell Telephone makes as much profit as General Motors.

Many, many years before, the British Admiralty had similarly turned down the invention of wireless telegraphy because the noble Sea Lords were quite content with their system of using men on hilltops to signal to each other by semaphore.

The Xerox corporation does more copier business than all its rivals combined. Yet mighty IBM with its superb record of innovation turned down the Xerox process when it was offered to them. In contrast, the Rank Organisation in England, a film and entertainment company set up by a flour miller, acquired the Xerox rights outside the USA simply because the chairman John Davies could see the opportunity. Today the profits from the Xerox operation sustain the whole organization.

The Bekaert company in Belgium is one of the largest wire-makers in the world. For decades much of its profits have come from a product invented on the shop-floor by a foreman. In barbed wire the strands of wire are twisted and the barbs are held between the twists. Usually the twist was continued in the same direction throughout the length of the wire. The result was wire that tended to coil around and was awkward to handle. The foreman's suggestion was that the wire should twist clockwise between two barbs and then anti-clockwise between the next two and so on – reversing the twist each time a barb was passed. The result is a wire that does not coil and lash and is therefore much easier to handle.

In the airline business a few per cent increase in the number of passengers flown can make a huge difference to profitability because the fixed costs have to be covered in any case. For example, in 1976 both Air Canada and Canadian Pacific Airways made a loss with a sixty-three-per-cent occupancy but would have made a profit with a sixty-six-per-cent occupancy of their planes. When British Airways introduced the 'shuttle' concept on their London to Glasgow route the occupancy went up by a massive thirty-two per cent.

Although it occupies the best site in town, the land for the erection of the prestigious James Cook Hotel in Wellington, New Zealand, cost only a fraction of what it should have cost. The developers seized the opportunity of purchasing the air rights above a municipal car-park and erected the hotel above it. As a guest in the hotel one is not even aware that the car-park exists.

Between 1975 and 1977 the US Postal Service trimmed its workforce by 57,000 and cut expenses by $800 million. Cost-cutting is as much an opportunity as technical innovation.

In July 1972, Ned Cook called on the head of a Russian grain-buying mission which had arrived in New York. The follow-up to that call resulted in his selling vast amounts of wheat and soyabean to the Russians. The pre-tax profits of Cook Industries rose from $4 million in 1972 to $75 million in 1974.

Hindsight

It is easy to point to opportunities that were missed. As everyone knows hindsight is perfect or '20/20' as the saying goes. Writers of books such as this rarely point to the apparent opportunities that were rightly dismissed. Nor do they point to the apparent opportunities that were taken up and proved disastrous. We know that Du Pont spent $100 million trying to launch the artificial leather 'Corfam' before dropping the project. Over recent years several companies such as RCA and the Xerox Corporation have seen an opportunity in the rapidly expanding computer field and have bought their way in. But the opportunity has turned out not to be an opportunity and they have retreated with heavy losses.

In setting forth the examples my purpose was not to castigate Western Union for turning down the Bell patents and IBM for turning down the Xerox process. My purpose was to show the *reality* of opportunities. I wanted to show the reality of opportunities that were missed and the reality of those that were taken. I wanted to show that a new idea, a new way of doing things or a new way of looking at things can make a huge difference to an organization.

Most of the examples I gave referred to large corporations but opportunities exist at all levels. In this book I shall be dealing with opportunity search both at senior management and at middle management level. Everyone is surrounded by opportunities. But they only exist once they have been seen. And they will only be seen if they are looked for.

The cleaning bill for Britain's hospitals is £55 million a year. An attempt is being made to seek out cost-cutting opportunities at all levels. In one hospital £14,000 was saved by cutting out extra cleaning services to staff quarters. Another hospital saved £30,000 on window-cleaning alone by employing one man for the job instead of contracting out the work.

Some years ago I wanted to build a raised platform at one end of the living-room in my London flat. I obtained various quotes from builders and these were in the region of £500 with a four-months' delay before they could handle the job. I then thought of exhibition contractors who were used to erecting platforms in a hurry and in any case did not have steady work. The platform was completed within twenty-four hours at a cost of £200.

'We can take it for granted that every corporation is environment-conscious, progressive, humane, creative and opportunity-conscious – or can we?'

The opportunity search

We must take note of the pious executive waffle that appears in the corporate image advertising in magazines like *Fortune*. But we must realize that saying something on the advice of an image-building consultant and even feeling the emotional truth of what we are saying is not always the same as doing it. Over the years I have worked as lecturer, instructor, problem-solver or consultant with a large number of corporations including Shell, BP, Unilever, Proctor and Gamble, IBM, 3M, Merck Sharpe and Dohm, American Airlines, the Prudential Company and Kodak. I have been invited to talk at a large number of conferences and meetings such as those of the Young Presidents' Organisation (YPO) and the Institute of Institutional Investors. I have travelled all over Europe, to Canada, the United States and Argentina, to Australia and New Zealand, and to Japan. Yet I have never come across a corporation that operated a systematic approach to opportunity-seeking. This is not to say that such an approach does not exist but merely that I have not come across it even though I have looked for it in a wide variety of areas.

Many organizations look to the R & D division to generate or develop new opportunities. Others operate New Business divisions or even Venture divisions. It is often assumed that opportunity seeking is the concern of the Corporate Strategy team or the Diversification programme. A large number of corporations operate suggestion schemes at lower levels. The calling in of consultant groups for cost-cutting exercises or feasibility studies is also a common practice. All of these activities have to do with opportunity-seeking but each of them only covers part of the field. Many parts of the field are left out. And even in the case of those parts that are covered there is no integrated approach.

We know that in 1975 the Swiss watch industry lost a colossal twenty-two per cent in sales because the industry was too slow to get into the quartz and electronic technology.

The chemical progesterone is the basis of the birth control pill now taken by 70 million women world-wide. In the beginning progesterone could only be produced as an extract from pig ovaries. As a result it was very expensive, costing up to $100 for a microgramme. Dr Russel Marker went off to Mexico and discovered how to make progesterone out of the roots of the wild Mexican yams. In a short time he had produced three kilogrammes. But none of the major pharmaceutical companies were interested in his discovery so he went his own way and set up the very successful Syntex Corporation. I do not think the situation has changed much today. On two occasions I have suggested to major pharmaceutical companies that there is a product idea – which if it is not already in the pipeline somewhere would have a huge market potential – that I would like to discuss with their 'opportunity reception' division. The idea is still undivulged.

Objective

My objective in writing this book is to focus attention on the area of opportunity search. I shall set forth a systematic approach which covers opportunity-seeking both at the corporate level and also at the level of individual executives. This book is the *handbook* for the operation of this systematic approach. The book is designed in such a way that it may also be used by someone who is operating outside the executive framework.

I am well aware that there are people who have demonstrated their brilliance at spotting opportunities. I am also aware that there are others who are highly motivated to look for opportunities. In addition there are those who for sound logical reasons do not wish to be distracted by opportunities. In a subsequent section I shall be discussing attitudes to opportunities and why so many executives find it difficult to be opportunity-conscious. Nevertheless what I shall be proposing is a formal framework within which a variety of different attitudes can operate – and in operating pay deliberate attention to opportunity search. Without such a formal framework opportunity search will always remain a matter of mood, chance and individual motivation.

'To get something done we need to combine method and motivation. Motivation without method is ineffective. Method without motivation sits on a libarary shelf.'

Form of the book

If executives are to be motivated to look for opportunities they must be given a reason for doing so. There are many sound logical reasons why someone should not look for opportunities and these must be discussed honestly. Persuasion through exhortation has only a short-term effect. The first part of the book will be devoted to people, motivation, the need to look for opportunities and some of the difficulties involved. I shall be dealing with the different attitudes towards opportunity. I shall also be dealing with different types or styles of executive and how they see their role: the train-driver type, the doctor type, the farmer type and the fisherman type.

In this first part of the book we shall need to distinguish between problem-solving and problem-finding. What are we trying to do when we look at a problem? What are we trying to do when we look at an opportunity? The key distinction between *import-ant* and *urgent* must be made.

I shall do my best to spell out quite clearly the real dilemma of opportunity search: opportunities involve risk, effort, hassle and dilution of effort, yet we cannot afford not to look for them. There is a secondary dilemma: an executive can function very well without ever looking for opportunities and yet a corporation made up of such executives will stagnate to disaster. Having set up these dilemmas I shall propose a concrete solution.

In the second part of the book I shall put forward a corporate structure for opportunity search. This structure will operate on two levels. The basic level is that of each executive who will be required to examine his own 'opportunity space'. This concept will be discussed. At regular intervals an executive will be given the opportunity to carry out an 'Opportunity Audit'. This is a formal exercise designed to sanction initiative on the part of the executive: he is encouraged to say where he sees the opportunities and what he would like to do about them as distinct from being told what to do.

At the corporate level a group is given responsibility for opportunity search and is designated the 'Opportunity Team'. This team will have a liaison function with other established divisions such as R & D or Corporate Planning but will have the centralized responsibility for focusing directly on opportunities. This opportunity team will also have the responsibility for collecting the input from the opportunity audits carried out by each executive. These inputs will be integrated and assessed by the team. The team will also be responsible for arranging the help and support that an executive may require in following up an opportunity that he has put forward in his audit return.

This second section will also discuss the role of outside consultants in terms of organization, feasibility studies, and the value of a fresh look from outside. The training and instruction involved in setting up the opportunity search framework will be indicated.

The morale-boosting value of the opportunity search procedure will be discussed. It is likely that this will be even more important than the actual opportunities discovered.

The third and final part of the book will cover the methods used for discovering opportunities. I shall go in detail into the thinking methods that an executive would employ when he sets out to find opportunities. These methods include both analysis and provocation. I shall introduce the concept of an 'idea-sensitive area' (i.s.a.) in which the pay-off from a change of idea can be considerable.

Sometimes in our thinking we need to 'move-in' towards a goal or objective. At other times we need to 'move-out' from an existing asset in order to see how best to employ it. The distinction between 'moving-in' and 'moving-out' will be made in this third part of the book. A check-list of areas for attention will be provided. For example, the better we become at doing something the more likely we are to leave behind us an area of opportunity. The concept of 'de-averaging', although an ugly word, is useful in opening up opportunities.

I shall be introducing the notation of an 'opportunity map' as a help in making external our thinking about opportunities. The opportunity map will be made up of 'if-boxes' and 'action-channels'. In this way risk and uncertainty can be crystallized so that they may be dealt with more effectively.

The important areas of benefit, assessment and evaluation will be examined in this part of the book.

The third part of the book can be used, on its own, by anyone who is looking for a methodology of opportunity search but is not concerned with the corporate structure suggested in the second part of the book.

'You cannot dig a hole in a different place by digging the same hole deeper.'

Lateral thinking and opportunity search

Imagine that you are attracted by tall blondes and that you are at a party and spot a tall blonde at the other end of the room. The room is crowded. You move about the room asking your friends whether any one of them knows the blonde well enough to introduce you. It is a tiresome process. Yet had you looked around you before starting off on the quest you would have seen that standing just behind you was an even more attractive blonde conversing with a good friend of yours. The moral is that opportunities may not be difficult to see in themselves but they remain impossible to see if we happen to be looking in the wrong direction.

The excellence of our brains as information-processing systems lies in their ability to make sense of the outside world. This the brain does by allowing the incoming information to *organize itself* into channels or tracks. Once these channels have been set up we can find our way around because as soon as we spot something we can follow the established channel and so have access to all our knowledge about that thing. This is an immensely useful system but it does have the disadvantage that the brain achieves its excellence by establishing fixed ways of looking at things. Sometimes we may need to break out of these fixed ways in order to find new and better routes.

It is this switching of channels, this breaking away from a fixed approach, this moving sideways in order to change concepts that I called 'lateral thinking'. The term is now officially recognized in the *Oxford English Dictionary* which operates the final acceptance of new expressions.

Though I shall touch upon it briefly in the third part of this book, I do not intend to go into the details of lateral thinking here. Both the way the brain handles information and the process of lateral thinking are described in other books of mine.* The response to these books has suggested that many people are aware of the type of thinking required to switch from one way of looking at things to another. The books have been translated into seventeen languages including Hebrew and Japanese. In fact the sales in Japan of my first book exceeded (on a per head basis) those of the famous novel *Love Story* in the USA. The explanation is that the Japanese are conscious that theirs is a rigidly patterned culture. As a result they are interested in methods of switching patterns other than the traditional Western method of polarization, opposition, clash and change – which they regard as inefficient and wasteful.

Lateral thinking is rather different from creative thinking. I have done quite a lot of work with art colleges, and creative thinkers in the artistic sense are are not especially good at lateral thinking. An artist may be valuable to society because he has a perception that is different from everyone else's but the artist may be stuck quite firmly within the channel of that perception. He does not have the flexibility of the lateral thinker who is forever switching concepts and putting things together in new ways.

Information and ideas

In our management thinking we tend, quite rightly, to rely heavily on information. A good financial reporting system leads to profits. A speedy sales reporting system results in effective marketing. Detailed market analysis information brings about the correct product choice. An examination of trends and forecasts provides the information required for planning. It could be said that the size of any decision is proportional to the inadequacy of the reason for making it. If our information was complete then the information would make its own decisions. If a shipowner for instance

* For the way the brain works see *The Mechanism of Mind*, published by Penguin in the UK and Penguin Inc. in the USA; for lateral thinking see *Lateral Thinking for Management*, published by McGraw-Hill in the UK and the American Management Association in the USA.

had complete information about oil transport requirements, future cost of finance, the firm plans of his competitors, knowledge of political and labour stability, information about government subsidies and regulations and so on, he could feed all this into a computer and the decision would be produced for him. It is only when our information is inadequate that we have to make a human decision. And the greater the inadequacy of information the bigger the decision will seem.

Our hunger for information should not, however, blind us to the fact that information alone is insufficient. In addition to information we need ideas. Ideas are the spectacles through which we look at information. I once gave the following problem to a group of chief executives:

'A man buys a dog as a watch-dog. He then finds that the dog does not bark. What should he do?'

I got the following suggestions:

'Buy another.'

'Take it back and complain. Report the matter to the Consumers' Association.'

'Train it to fetch its handler.'

'Train the dog to press an alarm button.'

'Switch on a photo-electric beam across the dog's kennel at night so when the dog leaves his kennel he will break the beam and activate an alarm.'

'Have a sensing device strapped to the dog's back so that his rising hackles will trigger the device and activate an alarm.'

'Train the dog to switch on a tape-recording of a dog barking.'

'Find out why it does not bark and put matters right.'

'Install burglar alarms as well.'

There is a wide variety of different ideas here. But there is still room for more. We could actually treat the silence of the dog as an opportunity. We would erect an illuminated sign stating: BEWARE OF SILENT WATCH-DOG. The idea of a vicious dog creeping up quietly and attacking might be even more frightening than a barking dog.

The Nigerian Government intends to introduce universal primary education into the country by 1980. This means increasing the number of children in school from four million to eighteen million and the number of primary teachers from 150,000 to 450,000. This could be done by building teacher training colleges and training student teachers in the same way as is done in most industrialized countries. An alternative idea, which arose in the course of a lateral thinking exercise I conducted with some Nigerians, would be to give each existing teacher two assistants who would follow the teacher around wherever he went (almost to the bathroom). The assistants would sit in on every lesson and then take over half an hour of a lesson or a whole lesson or a whole day. They would be trained in an apprenticeship manner. It is estimated that this approach would save $300 million. The new teachers could always be sent on to college for further training when the training colleges had been established.

Ideas without information are pretty worthless. Information without ideas can still be useful. The best of all is abundant information supplemented by ideas. The mistake, which so many people make, is to assume that collecting more information will do away with the need for ideas.

The need for ideas

In the course of my seminars I often ask the participants to write down an area or problem to which they would like to apply lateral thinking. The response is always poor. These executives are trained to solve problems as they arise. They are not trained to pick out areas in which the generation of ideas could be useful. That is why deliberate creative effort is so rarely used outside the world of advertising. An advertising Creative Director *knows* that he has to produce an idea to win or to service an account. Other executives like the idea of creative thinking in the abstract but never seem to have an actual need for it in their day-to-day lives.

But when an executive consciously sets out to find opportunities he quickly finds areas that are in need of ideas. In this way the opportunity search provides a framework that excites and focuses the creativity of executives.

Ideas thrown up for no good reason are rarely used. But ideas generated to satisfy the idea-hunger of an opportunity search are more valuable because they fulfil a need.

Many years ago I was working to design a safer cigarette. The

17

usual approach might be to make a stronger filter that would extract more particles from the inhaled smoke. Using a lateral provocation I decided to 'add' something to the smoke. The obvious thing to add was air. This could be done by making tiny holes through the cigarette paper near the butt end so that air would be drawn in and would dilute the smoke. Since the deposition of smoke particles in the lungs is by Brownian motion which depends on the concentration of particles, the air dilution reduces the particle deposition in the lungs. At that time no cigarette manufacturer was very interested in the process because there was no obvious need for milder or less harmful cigarettes. Today several brands (notably Benson and Hedges in the UK) use the 'ventilated filter' process.

We know that market-pull innovation is much more effective than technology-push innovation. So it is with the generation of ideas. The first stage is to generate a need for an idea. The second stage is to generate the idea to fit that need. That is what opportunity search is about.

Part I: People, attitudes and opportunities

The most important thing about an opportunity is the person who sets out to look for it. Even the most obvious opportunity can be ignored by a person who is not motivated to see it. In this part of the book we shall examine attitudes towards opportunity-search. There is no point in pretending that opportunities are wonderful and that everyone should be out looking for them. An honest appraisal of the difficulties, problems and risks is required. There are 'opportunity-negative' structures within which it is madness for an executive to look for opportunities.

'Thank goodness the sun has gone in and I do not have to go out and enjoy it,' is a common attitude towards opportunities which are seen to bring hassle, risk and distraction. Through selection, training, inclination, performance pressures and a logical assessment of the best survival strategy, executives are rarely opportunity-seekers. In this part of the book we shall distinguish between problem-solving and problem-finding. We shall also make the vital distinction between what is urgent and what is important.

We shall look at cultural attitudes towards opportunity-seeking, at corporate attitudes and at individual attitudes. We shall see why many corporations are content to 'ride the business cycle' and others are fearful of an 'opportunity war'.

Finally we shall look directly at the nature of opportunities and at their benefits – which is the only way of motivating people to want to look for them.

'Repairing the leaks in an old boat will not build a new one.'

The distinction between what is urgent and what is important

Some executives never learn to make this distinction. The more senior such executives become in a corporation the more disastrous it is likely to be. Putting out a fire is urgent. Planning sensible fire regulations is important. It is no use sitting down to work out the best way to re-finance the payments on your house when the upstairs bathroom tap is leaking and flooding the house. The re-finance decisions are much more important but turning off the tap at the stop-cock is urgent.

It is obvious that whatever is urgent must come first. An executive may have to deal urgently with an impending strike or a serious loss of quality control or an expected rise in raw material supplies. Such matters have to be dealt with as soon as possible. They have priority over everything else. They are more 'important' than anything else. It is urgent that a fisherman repairs the leaks in his old boat otherwise he will be unable to go fishing.

Because something must be done at once it becomes more 'important' than anything else. But in the long term it may not be more important at all.

New Zealand depends very heavily on its exports of agricultural products – for instance, butter. Lately there has been a substantial loss of the butter market to the margarine-makers. This is not just a matter of price because even margarine that is more expensive than butter has increased its market share. It is felt that the margarine makers have been cleverly using that section of medical opinion that proclaims that the cholesterol in butter increases the danger of heart attacks. The matter is urgent so in 1977 the Butter Information Council were given $NZ2 million to fight off this challenge by the use of counter-propaganda. Yet it is far more *important*, in the long run, that the butter-producers should spend thinking-time and money re-packaging and re-marketing their product so that it is treated as a branded product not a commodity. I have seen housewives in New Zealand use margarine in preference to butter simply because it is easier to spread and the housewife has to make sandwiches for her children. There is spreadable butter and there are refrigerators with special butter compartments, but in terms of convenience these do not compete with margarine. I would like to see all butter being as easily spreadable as margarine. There could then be 'Family Butter' marketed for wives and children with an emphasis on the natural product. In addition there would be 'Butter Plus' with the addition of polyunsaturated sunflower oil for the man in the family.

Minding the store

If you run a store you have to serve the customers as they come in. That takes priority over everything else. It is urgent. Stock control and ordering may be more important but they are not urgent. All executives are aware of the danger of getting so caught up in 'minding the store' that they have no time to devote to anything else. But few do anything about it. In these days of increasing problems there is even less time to spare. There are increasing problems connected with labour relations, with inflation and pricing, with government regulations and almost everything else. In a survey in the USA in the early 1970s chief executives claimed that they spent as much as forty per cent of their time on public relations: countering ecological attacks and presenting their case to government and public alike.

It is bad enough that urgent problems are increasing all the time. On top of this an executive can also increase his load of 'urgent' matters by refusing to delegate and a concern with detail. There was a time when executives prided themselves on working eighteen hours a day. Then someone realized that a man who had to work so long was in a job that was too big for him. Today it is more fashionable to work short hours, delegate the urgent and reserve one's thinking for the important.

I have always felt that if an executive works right through the day to five o'clock there is no way of telling how well he is doing his job. He may have needed to work until seven or eight o'clock to complete the job. If, on the other hand, an executive was allowed to leave for home as soon as he had finished his work then he could make an effort to improve his efficiency. A worker who left at 4.55 p.m. under this new scheme would be in a totally different situation from one who left at 5.00 p.m. – even though the actual difference was only five minutes. The first worker would be declaring that he had done his work; the second might have needed another two or three hours.

The test is quite simple and it takes the form of a self-administered question: How much of my time do I spend on urgent matters and how much on important matters? The question is easy enough to ask but it is rarely answered honestly. The usual escape is to protest that the 'urgent' matters are also actually 'important'.

An opportunity search attitude relies very heavily on the distinction between what is urgent and what is important. An executive who fills his life with urgent matters is going to have no time to devote to the important matter of seeking out opportunities. Yet in no way can the pressure of urgent matters make it unnecessary to look for opportunities. An increase in the number of influenza cases that have to be treated urgently does not make unnecessary the search for a better anti-flu vaccine.

'Problem-finding is just as important as problem-solving but much more difficult and much more rare.'

Problem-solving and problem-finding

A few years ago with the help of a grant from the Perstorp company in Sweden, I ran a national 'inventions' competition in the United Kingdom. The response was good because the prizes were good. There were over five thousand entries and the standard in some cases was high. That is to say the standard of problem-solving was high. But the standard of problem-finding was surprisingly low. Most of the inventors were inventing things that did not need inventing – over fifteen per cent of the entries were for rotary internal combustion engines.

We find problem-solving much easier than problem-finding because in our thinking we like to have something to 'react' to. We like to have in front of us some information and some desired goal. Then we work to achieve that goal through skilled use of the information.

With the Cognitive Research Trust (Cambridge, UK) I run what is now the largest curriculum programme in the world for the direct teaching of thinking as a school curriculum subject. It is fascinating to see how the emphasis in education is on 'reactive' rather than 'projective' thinking. In reactive thinking we analyse and sort the information that is presented to us. However, in projective thinking we, ourselves, have to generate the information and even create the context as we try to bring something about. We get the 'Everest effect'. An able child will love to have his mind stretched by a difficult problem. Like Mount Everest the problem is there in front of the child and he sets off to scale it. But give the same child a simple problem around which he has to generate the context and he feels uncomfortable. Such children plead: 'Please give us the information and the problem so that we can solve it.' They are unable to find the problem in a situation.

Reactive thinking includes problem-solving and it includes judgement. Most executives have got where they are because they are good at both these skills. There is a problem to be solved. There is something to be judged. In both cases there is something out front – something that you can look at and tackle. But if you were to say to an average executive: 'I think there is an opportunity somewhere in that situation, can you find it?' the performance would be less impressive.

A problem is something you want to do but cannot.

An opportunity is something you do not yet know that you want to do – and can.

By training, inclination and expectancy executives tend to be problem-solvers. This is because they are able, intelligent and sensible. Any deficiency in the smooth running of an organization is a problem and it is the executive's business to solve the problem and keep things running smoothly until the next problem arises. An executive is somewhat in the position of a forest fire control team. As soon as a brush fire appears he has to rush out and extinguish it. Between fires he spends his time watching over his domain so as to spot a fire as soon as it breaks out. Executives are expected by their superiors to behave in this fashion. Executives are also expected to overcome the problems that may arise in the course of implementing a policy decision that is handed down to them. If they want to get promoted they have to be good problem-solvers and trouble-shooters. A problem is always urgent. An opportunity is only important.

I was once having lunch with Sir Arnold Weinstock, the much respected chief executive of the General Electric Company in the UK. He it was who made a successful company out of an odd assortment of relatively unsuccessful companies that had been lumped together. In the course of lunch he said that he was happiest when there were no problems in any of his divisions: when things were running along smoothly. At first sight this would suggest that he saw himself as a problem-solver not as an opportunity-seeker. But to be fair we can consider some alternative explanations. Opportunity-seeking may have been delegated to each division and so a smooth-running division included opportunity-seeking. Perhaps the company had so much opportunity momentum (things in the pipeline) that smooth running would include the development of these opportunities. Perhaps the company had been so racked by problems in the past that problem-solving still needed to be the dominant idiom. It could be any of these explanations. Otherwise problem-solving without opportunity-seeking would lead to stagnation.

The great Nestlé corporation in Switzerland obtains about thirty per cent of its profits from one item: instant coffee. This is a very successful product and may long continue to be so, but it puts Nestlé in a very vulnerable position. A continued rise in coffee prices might change people's tastes in an irreversible manner. A newer technology might replace instant coffee. Problem-solving alone would not be sufficient for Nestlé. Opportunity-seeking is essential.

Three types of problem

Three different types of problem are shown in Figure 1. The first type is the 'block' type of problem. We know the road we want to take but there is a block in the way. The block may be the need for a metal with certain heat characteristics, it may be a labour relations upset, it may be a government regulation. The point is that we can locate, identify and focus upon the problem. We then attack the problem with our problem-solving kit and either remove the block or find our way around it.

In the second type of problem we 'run out of road'. In order to proceed we need more information. We may need more information about market resistance to a new vegetable protein product. We may need more information about the government's thinking on exhaust emission standards for cars. We may need more information about agencies in Nigeria that could handle our exports to that country. This information type of problem may not be easy to solve but at least we can try to solve it by getting the information.

The third type of problem is the most difficult to solve because it is the 'problem of no problem'. There is no block, the road is wide and open. There is nothing to react to or focus our problem-solving skills. We proceed down the open road and completely miss the opportunity turning. Later, if the main road peters out (market disappears), narrows (low profits), or is blocked (by government regulation) we may have to come back and search for the opportunity track.

It is common knowledge that when people are faced with a problem they often devise a solution that not only solves the problem but opens up an opportunity. The tragedy is that in many cases the opportunity could have been opened up long before the problem arose.

In 1975 the insurance companies in the USA reacted sharply to the increases in malpractice damages being awarded by the courts. Malpractice premiums payable by doctors rose by as much as 400 per cent. As a result doctors started their own insurance companies. They were in fact in a better position to assess the competence of their fellows and could also be harsher and more selective. By early 1977 some 60,000 doctors belonged to one of these groups. The groups proved profitable. It is true that the rise in rates might have made profitable what would have been unprofitable before. But since insurance companies are not philanthropic institutions it is reasonable to suppose that the advantages of a doctors' own insurance group would have applied before.

I was once involved in a discussion on the value of house journals as an advertising medium. The head of the sales force maintained that if the money was not spent on the house journal he could increase his sales force by five per cent. So I asked him

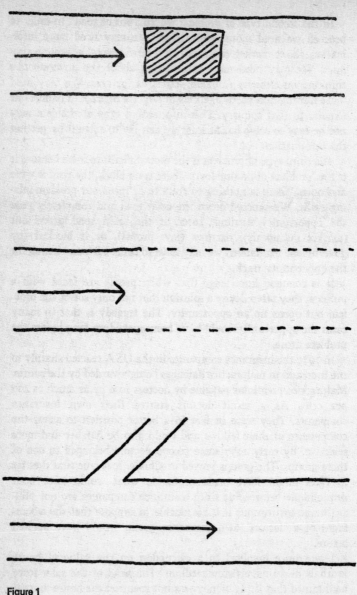

Figure 1

whether, in his opinion, this extra five per cent would earn their keep. He said he was sure that they would not only earn their keep but contribute substantially to the company profits. 'If that is the case,' I said, 'why don't you go ahead and employ them anyway?'

I was once having dinner at the high table at Trinity College, Cambridge, and fell into a discussion about the difficulty of getting computers to play chess. My neighbour happened to be the famous mathematician, Professor Littlewood, and we agreed that as a game chess achieved difficulty by being complex. We discussed whether it would be possible to design a game that was difficult to play and yet simple by nature. This created a problem or challenge and I set out to design such a game. The result was the 'L-game' in which each player has only *one* playing piece. The game can be played with a high degree of skill and in fact there are over 18,000 possible moves on the tiny four by four board. The game is now patented and marketed quite widely. And yet I could have set my mind to designing such a game at any time.

The American company Stuart Hall Co. found that with a fall in school enrolment its market in school supplies was disappearing. As a result the company re-designed its products to make them more fashionable and attractive – for example using such cartoon characters as the Pink Panther. Another change was to sell through chain drug and discount stores. As a result revenues increased from $14.1 million in 1975 to $18.8 million in 1976. But the opportunity for these changes had existed all along.

A problem is so powerful a stimulus to the development of an opportunity that we can actually mimic the process in searching for an opportunity. We can say to ourselves, 'What if the school market fell by half?' And then we see what ideas come up as we tackle that situation. This method, along with other provocative methods, will be described in the third part of the book.

The difference between problem-solving and opportunity-seeking is nicely illustrated by the attitude of a recruiting officer who receives a résumé from an executive who had been 'de-hired' by his previous employer. The problem-solver might say we have an unfilled post for someone like that or he may say that he is sorry but there is no vacancy. The opportunity-seeker will look carefully to see if the applicant has an unusual combination of abilities and experience that could be of value to the company. If so a job will be *created* for the applicant.

A classic example of opportunity-seeking or problem-finding is given by the development of Databank in New Zealand. This is a unique network that connects *all* banks and branches throughout the country to a unified computer system. New Zealand is therefore ahead of anywhere else in the world in terms of electronic banking, funds transfer and so on. This came about because Gordon Hogg did not wait for the individual banks to have 'problems' with their data processing but found the problem ahead of time, so creating an opportunity for Databank and for the banks themselves.

'An executive's style determines not what he is capable of but what he will allow himself to do.'

Executive styles

As far as I can see, in discussing styles there is no way of avoiding the too-easy caricature. It is not unlike characterization by means of the signs of the Zodiac: Taurus has these features and Virgo has those. In order to illustrate the key-points of difference one has to exaggerate them to the point of caricature. I shall therefore apologize in advance for doing precisely this.

What concerns me here is not so much an executive's style of management but his role with regard to the corporation that employs him. The style may be formed as much by the traditions of the company and the expectations of senior management as by the personality of an executive himself.

The train-driver

Trains have schedules. Trains have tracks. The train-driver sees his role as taking the train smoothly along the track to meet the schedules. Efficient performance with the established framework is the measure of achievement and success. The train-driver does not question the schedules or the tracks. He knows he cannot leave the tracks and therefore does not develop any inclination to do so.

The train-driver is the caretaker and operator of the established system. He must deal with all problems that arise to delay him or interfere with the ordained running of the system. When a problem with which he cannot cope arises he calls for help. If the decision-makers alter the schedule he operates the new schedule to the best of his ability.

In a large organization many executives are expected to be the train-drivers of the established system. This is certainly the case in the civil service or public service but it is almost as true in many large corporations (with the difference that performance is more easily monitored through such things as sales figures).

The train-driver may eventually get promoted to the position where he is making the scheduling and destination decisions. Suddenly he will be expected to acquire an ability to design systems rather than just operate them.

Those organizations that require their executives to operate as train-drivers do so for two reasons: either they assume that the system is so perfect that any alteration can only detract from that perfection, or they feel themselves unable to cope with the variety that would arise if executives were given decision and opportunity space.

The doctor

The doctor is a problem-solver. He deals in ill health. Unlike the train-driver the doctor does not operate the bodies with which he deals. The doctor realizes that bodies are independent and follow their own nature. So the doctor type of executive is content for each semi-autonomous part of his organization to go its own way – provided it keeps healthy.

This type of executive keeps a close eye on the information that is fed back to him in the areas of finance, sales, productivity, quality control, etc. As soon as he detects the beginning of ill health he moves in with his diagnostic kit and treatment recommendations.

So long as things are running smoothly – and by implication successfully – the doctor-type executive is happy.

'Don't tamper with success' is an old adage that can be used either to reward the strategy in successful companies or to condemn the strategy in unsuccessful ones. It depends what you mean by success. 'Smooth running' and 'lack of problems' is not the same as success. A company may quietly stagnate as the Addressograph-Multigraph Corporation did while its competitors made technological breakthroughs that eroded its duplicating equipment market (forty-five per cent of total sales).

As we have seen the problem-solver is not by nature inclined to search out opportunities – although he may use a lot of creative thinking in his problem-solving. After all the fire-fighter does not go around starting fires.

The farmer

There are expansion-minded farmers but here we are concerned with the farmer who is content to stay within his own patch. Within that patch he is open to innovation, change and a search for opportunities (new strains of crop, new breeding methods for pigs, new herbicides, cultivation without tilling, etc.).

The farmer is an operator, a problem-solver and an opportunist. We may note here that in 1977 US farmers could feed twice as many people as ten years before.

The executive 'farmer' is willing to search out opportunities but only in a defined direction. He would be disinclined to change direction or to diversify. If he was in the 'table-cloth' restaurant business he would be disinclined to get into the expanding fast-food market.

There is nothing wrong with the farmer style. It includes characteristics that are lacking in the doctor or train-driver styles.

The fisherman

The fisherman type is the risk-taker. He owns no farm. He cannot guarantee that when he ventures out he will return with a catch. He puts down his nets and hopes for the best. He is a pure opportunist.

Yet the fisherman is not the gambler he would seem to be. He has invested in skill, experience and equipment. Through such investment he reduces the uncertainty and increases the chance of substantial pay-offs: as witnessed by the success of the tuna fleets before they ran into dolphin troubles.

We can contrast the fisherman with the farmer. The farmer owns his farm and his effort is invested in it. He is unwilling to look for opportunities outside. Indeed, taken away from his farm he may no longer operate effectively. In the case of the fisherman, however, there is no farm so he invests in his own capability.

When we translate the comparison into management terms we find that the 'farmer' approach invests in a product line or a market. The 'fisherman' approach leads to an investment in management skills and techniques that can be transferred to any field or used to follow up opportunities wherever they arise. With the farmer the emphasis is on the field of operation; with the fisherman the emphasis is on the operator himself.

We can now summarize the four different attitudes:

Train-driver: Let me carry out to perfection the assigned tasks in the established system.

Doctor: Let me keep the system healthy and functioning well by detecting and solving any problems that arise.

Farmer: Let me get the maximum yield that I can out of this established area of operation.

Fisherman: Let me put myself in such a position that I can look for and follow up any opportunity wherever it appears.

'It is absurd to recruit intelligent men into an organization and then to blame them for acting intelligently.'

The opportunity-negative structure

Within certain organizations, like the civil service, the odds are loaded so heavily against change, innovation or the exercise of initiative that it would be quite illogical for an executive to look for opportunity. Let us look honestly at the downside risk of innovation in such an organization – and bear in mind that it is more the fault of the structure than the people operating it.

A civil servant must be relied upon to do what he is told – without the variations introduced by personal initiative.

A highly complex system cannot work unless all of its parts

work in a predictable fashion. An individual executive cannot be expected to have enough perspective to assess the far-ranging effects of his initiative.

A civil servant must be a team man. Otherwise he will arouse competitiveness and jealousy. Since there are no tangible criteria of skill, such as profits or sales, all enterprise is seen as self-promotion.

If someone deservedly earns the reputation of being an 'ideas man' because of the brilliance of his ideas he will simultaneously acquire the tag of being 'erratic' or 'unsound'. Those less brilliant than he will comfort themselves with the thought that if he is brilliant he cannot also be competent. 'Too clever by half' is another way of saying the same thing.

Some ideas work and some do not – that is the nature of all innovation. If a civil servant has an idea which works he will gain no special credit because it is part of his job and there is no sudden and obvious rise in sales or profits. If, however, an idea fails that failure hangs around the neck of the innovator for the rest of his career: 'he is the fellow who botched up . . .' or 'he is the fellow who thought up that crazy scheme for . . .'

In the commercial world an executive can offset mistakes by successes. In the United States no one is especially blamed for going bankrupt. Within a few months he can start off again – even with the same backers. So long as his track record contains successes then the occasional failure is overlooked. In the civil service there is no way of offsetting a failure.

The person who can be relied upon to do what he is told, to operate the system as it is set up and 'to drive the train on schedule' will get promoted into a position where in time he will promote people with similar abilities.

Virtually the only activity that falls within the opportunity space of a civil servant is that of report-writing.

Because any suggestion has to pass upwards through several layers of hierarchy there is little chance of its approval. It only requires one of these 'switches' to be in the off position for the idea to be killed.

Because when there is little else to do and no chance to be constructive, the mind falls into a critical mode where there are likely to be many more people against an idea than there are in favour. In the commercial world this problem can be overcome if someone senior enough fosters and protects the idea.

No one is to blame

The civil service is an extreme instance of an opportunity-negative structure and yet it is the fault of the structure more than the people running it. I have seen civil servants become opportunity-seeking and even entrepreneurial once they have left the service.

Few commercial organizations would be as opportunity-negative but it is worth looking at the characteristics listed above and noting which ones may apply to one's own organization.

'Just before it comes into existence every business is an opportunity that someone has seen.'

Obstacles to opportunity search

A difficulty is an obstacle unless there is a will to overcome it. On several occasions I have asked a roomful of chief executives to list the difficulties they saw in looking for opportunities. Below I have put together the main difficulties that were suggested. The list could be extended and with more time for consideration the executives could, no doubt, have improved the list. Nevertheless, the list gives a credible picture of the difficulties. Each difficulty was discussed with the group and the comments given below are related to that discussion.

Organizational

Urgent matters always have priority. The difference between what is urgent and what is important has been discussed in a previous section of this book.

Today much of our thinking has to deal with the urgency of labour problems. This is a variation on the first but it does suggest that a whole new area of concern is making it more difficult than ever before to escape from what is urgent.

No time to think. The complaint was that there was no definite time set aside for thinking as such. Executives were supposed to do their thinking on the golf course or in their baths.

The style of management: the boss knows everything. The feeling that there was no point in looking for opportunities in an autocratic company.

Communication is always downward from senior executives to lower levels. There was no willingness to listen to ideas or suggestions. There was no discussion or dialogue between the different levels.

Opportunity search is always delegated to too great a distance. It was felt that there was a tendency to delegate opportunity search to R & D departments, Corporate Strategy teams or other backroom analysts and then forget about it. It was felt that this act of delegation often seemed to satisfy the delegator as to his need to take any action over the matter.

Availability of resources. A general point which covers availability of people, risk capital, cash-flow, time and the people to hold the line whilst opportunities were being explored.

Shortage of expertise in implementing opportunities. This is an interesting comment because it suggests that certain executive skills might be necessary for opportunity development.

Shortage of imaginative thinkers. Lack of projective thinkers who could do more than just react.

Difficulty in obtaining information from which to generate opportunities and with which to evaluate them. This was related to the size of the company and was an especial problem with smaller companies. There are for instance 10,000 journals published in the field of chemistry alone.

Risk-taking related to small resources. The suggestion was that a large corporation had a certain availability of resources that could act as a cushion to absorb the risk of a new venture. With a small company a failed venture could have serious consequences.

Short-term profit problem. Accounts, financial managers, the balance sheet and the stock market all required short-term profits.

This made it difficult to develop opportunities that would initially give a negative cash-flow but were important in the long run.

Environmental

Union involvement and restrictions. Everything had to be cleared with the unions first. For example, it might be impossible to take the opportunity of introducing a new technology because the unions would not agree to a reduction in the work-force. Fear of hassles with the unions made executives reluctant even to look for opportunities.

Legal, government and quasi-government regulations. The complex bulk of standards, control, tariffs, licences, and other requirements were seen to stifle opportunity. For example – the FDA requirements for the launching of a new drug in the USA were seen seriously to retard the development of new treatments. In addition sudden changes in government requirements could wreck an investment in a new product line.

Bureaucratic constraints. This covered the time delays involved in getting such things as planning permission or product approval. It was not the regulations in themselves that were restrictive but the apparent inefficiency with which the regulations were administered. It was suggested that a sort of industrial ombudsman could be used to speed up the process.

Tax and price controls. It was stated quite forcibly that the biggest disincentive to opportunity development was that if a corporation were successful the government taxed away the rewards but if the corporation were unsuccessful it paid its own losses. This asymmetry between risk and reward was seen to discourage any venture attitude.

Ecological pressures. A company would fight shy of any venture which might just conceivably excite the wrath of environmentalists. It was felt that the time involved and the bad publicity made it unworthwhile. It was also seen that ecological issues usually offered a temptation to politicians to get involved.

The size of the domestic market. A small domestic market would make it impossible to look for those product or service gaps which were too small for the large corporations to concern themselves with. In a large domestic market like the USA even the most exotic product (like the pet rocks which were at one time selling at the rate of $100,000 worth a month) could be sold in sufficient volume. A large domestic market would also provide a base for exporting.

Lack of risk capital. Lack of risk capital in the money market. Lack of venture capital groups or true merchant banking. Complaints that the banks had an unenterprising policy and were only prepared to lend where little risk was involved. By definition opportunity development entailed risk.

Personal

A *tendency to follow trends elsewhere and to borrow ideas.* The basic second-in-the-field or me-too philosophy. Let someone else carry the risk and development cost and establish the market.

A *protectionist atmosphere breeds managers who are not competitive.* If local industry is protected or subsidized there is no incentive to look for opportunities.

Love of a quiet life. Opportunities create hassle and problems and risk. Why look for opportunities if things are ticking over satisfactorily?

Preference for reacting to situations rather than thinking about them in advance. The preference for reactive over-projective thinking that was discussed in a previous section.

Preference for action rather than thinking. Executives have chosen business rather than an academic life because they prefer action.

The preferred outcomes encouraged by management training. Management training emphasizes decision-making and problem-solving. Such training encourages coping, not opportunity speculation. Managers learn to play by the rules of the game and these rules do not contain an attitude to opportunities.

The difficulty of evaluating opportunities once they have been generated. It may be difficult to tell whether an opportunity is worthwhile. It may be difficult to tell which opportunity is the best from amongst several. If evaluation is so difficult, generating opportunities may simply be making work for oneself.

Traditional blinkers. We look at things in traditional ways and therefore have great difficulties in perceiving or appreciating anything new.

Lack of encouragement. There is poor motivation because opportunity-seeking attitudes are not encouraged in business.

Lack of financial motivation. Insufficient reward for innovative effort. The income tax structure that removes the bulk of any personal gain.

Lack of confidence. Many prople think that looking for opportunities is difficult and therefore do not try.

Lack of focus. Nowhere in the management structure is there a deliberate focus on opportunity search.

Lack of technique. Need for some methodology or systematization of opportunity search.

Comment

Many of the difficulties listed above would apply to any organization. Others apply to a greater or lesser degree depending on the size of the company and the country in which it is located. I do not propose to provide here instant solutions to all of the difficulties but I would like to make a few general comments.

While trying to increase its resources any organization must always work with what is available. It is possible to tailor one's opportunity search to the available resources. Another suggestion would be for a consortium of smaller companies to pool resources with regard to new ventures. If expertise is not available within the company it may be possible to hire it on a consultancy basis. In this way it is possible to use the expertise of a person it would not be possible to have on the payroll.

With regard to the environmental difficulties it must be admitted that these provide severe disincentives. There is a genuine feeling that almost every government, intentionally or otherwise, makes it more and more difficult for a business to expand. Where this is not already done it would clearly be in the interests of business to set up some powerful lobby to present the case for business and to work for the reduction of restrictions. Such a representative body should be able to take initiatives rather than just object to what the government proposes. It must also be said that a true opportunity takes the restrictions into account. An opportunity that would be an opportunity if there were no restrictions is not an opportunity at all but just wishful thinking. In some cases an opportunity may actually arise from a restriction. I remember being told by one entrepreneur that he loved the inefficiency of bureaucracy because once he, himself, had got through the tangle of red tape this then served as a 'barbed wire' barrier to keep out his would-be competitors!

The difficulties that arise from a particular management structure, for example downward communication, can be overcome by a conscious change in management structure. It becomes a matter of awareness followed by action.

'Our cultural attitude towards opportunity is more than tinged with envy. There are always more people who wished they had spotted the opportunity than those who have done so.'

Cultural attitude towards opportunity

The words 'opportunity' and 'opportunist' have bad connotations. They suggest a hovering vulture rather than a hovering eagle. They suggest someone who is hovering and waiting for an opportunity to emerge. Then that person swoops down and seizes the opportunity ahead of anyone else.

The negative attitude is partly based on jealousy ('why didn't I spot that opportunity?') but also on the feeling that an opportunity is only taken at someone else's expense. There is a feeling of expediency and short-term gains. Opportunity is equated with the activity of a speculative builder who builds and sells shoddy houses and then disappears from sight. There is a feeling of irresponsibility or even outright exploitation. The blackmarketeer and the wartime spiv were seen as arch opportunists. The fast-buck merchant and the fly-by-night operator are also opportunists.

Even the entrepreneur is contrasted negatively with the established businessman because there is a tinge of exploitation. Any gains are automatically regarded as being at someone else's expense. The go-getter and the go-go operator are also opportunists.

It cannot be denied that the irresponsible, selfish, exploiting, short-term profiteering opportunist does exist. But it must also be acknowledged that if it were not for people who saw and developed opportunities the standard of living would be very much lower. The United States was a land of opportunity. Henry Ford saw a way of making motor cars that would enable every family to buy a car. Corporations were sometimes slow to see the opportunities turned up by inventors but in the end the developments came about: radio and television, telephones, artificial fibres, air travel, anti-biotics.

The opposite of opportunity-seeking is not stability or conservatism, it is stagnation and atrophy. It is wrong to think of opportunity in terms only of new gadgets and expanded industrialization. It may equally be a matter of expanding food production, better methods of birth control, new sources of energy, redesigning jobs so that they are more enjoyable, increasing leisure time, improving education and so on.

We can seek opportunities in any direction we wish and for any purpose we wish. We may seek opportunities for the good of society as much as for the good of our corporation or ourselves. The trouble is that no one would believe such altruism. Society finds it difficult to believe that an organization like IBM can operate opportunities for its own benefit and at the same time serve society by developing and providing improved computers.

Society may well need to change its directions, goals and values but that does not necessarily imply an abandonment of the need to progress or improve. And that is what opportunity-seeking is about.

'Dealing with complacency is like trying to drill a hole in treacle: there is no resistance but at the end there is no impression left.'

Corporate attitude towards opportunity

Badly run companies tend to assume that all their troubles are external (market, inflation, wages rises, union troubles, government interference and regulations, etc.) and that there is nothing wrong with their thinking.

Successful companies feel that they are successful because of the competence of their thinking and they regard external problems as difficulties to be overcome.

In the heyday of management seminars it was noticeable that the more successful companies sent their executives along to the seminars. It would be unfair to suggest that the companies were successful because of the excellence of what was learned at the seminars. It would be easy to suggest that only successful companies had the spare cash to be able to send executives to expensive seminars. My own view is that sending executives to the seminars indicated the vital attitude of the successful companies: an attitude that implied that thinking was important; that there might always be something to learn; that their executives were worth developing. It is this attitude that probably made the companies as successful as they were. For example it was noticeable that British Leyland rarely, if ever, sent executives on seminars. No doubt they felt that it was a waste of time.

We can look now at some sound corporate attitudes towards opportunity-seeking.

Ride the cycle

Business has its ups and downs. There are boom times and recessions. There is nothing one can do to alter these or 'buck the trend'. In boom times you ride up the cycle and reap the profits. In times of recession you batten down the hatches and ride out the troubled weather. In recession times there is no point in looking for opportunities because the market is not there. In Australia (contrary to Keynesian theory) after-tax savings increased from 9.8 per cent of income in 1970 to 18.3 per cent in 1975 – which suggests that the consumers were just not consuming. The cycle-riders' theory is that in times of recession the poorly placed competitors may be forced out of business so leaving a wider share of the market to the survivors when good times came round again.

So the cycle-riders do not look for opportunities in times of recession. They are probably going through a cost-cutting exercise anyway (admittedly this is a form of opportunity search). In boom times everyone is so busy concentrating on sales and production in order to derive the maximum benefit from the boom that there is no spare effort, or motivation, available for opportunity search.

A contrary view is held by those companies that regard a recession as the ideal time to look for opportunities. Their reasoning is that no one else is doing that and when the boom does come round they will be ideally placed to benefit even more than before.

Survive the pressures

Here a corporation feels that all its thinking skill is required just to survive. Management feels that its main function is to find a survival strategy amongst all the pressures, problems and constraints. It is somewhat like a man defending himself against a hail of blows and not having time to think about buying new clothes.

Such corporations feel that management has now become a survival skill: dealing with financial and labour problems, dealing with the government. Some managements feel that this may only be a temporary phase and that when the pressure lessens there will be time to look for opportunities. Other managements suspect that the survival idiom will become permanent.

The survival attitude is one of permanent problem-solving – of permanent reaction to urgent situations that demand attention. There is always a fire somewhere that needs to be put out.

The distinction between what is urgent and what is important may need to apply here. A deliberate allocation of time and effort to opportunity development may serve to reduce the problems; for example, entry into a countercyclic field.

This is the passive approach. Something will turn up. It always has done before and will do so again. There is no need to look for opportunities because they will come along of their own accord.

There are different degrees of passivity. At one extreme is a corporation that will do nothing until a competitor, or a rapidly eroding market, forces action. At the other extreme is a corporation which will not develop opportunities itself but will undertake an active 'opportunity search' in terms of licensing ideas, borrowing them from abroad, imitating, being second in the field, and buying up small entrepreneurial outfits of the Boston route 128 variety.

There is no doubt that the 'me-too' philosophy can be successful – as in the case of *Penthouse* magazine which followed on the success of *Playboy*. The me-too philosophy is based on the consideration that the advantages of being first in the field are outweighed by the risks and that there is always a substantial market share available to late-comers who can build on the paid-for experience of the pioneers. It is easy to give contrary examples like the massive domination of their fields by IBM and Xerox. It may be best to hope that the first-in-the-field is an inefficient company with a poor product! Buying up smaller companies that have had the entrepreneurial drive to develop new opportunities may also be a cheaper way than running one's own R & D department. After all you only buy success and do not fund failure.

The truly passive approach is based on the expectation that when the time is 'ripe' an opportunity will present itself. If that were true then there would be no failed companies – ever. Furthermore, the ability to spot the opportunity depends on an opportunity-conscious attitude of mind and that has to be developed.

Complacency

It is almost impossible to distinguish between justified complacency and unjustified complacency.
'Our executives are all bright fellows, sensitive to market changes and with an eye open for opportunities.'

'We have a New Business division which is all the time sifting through the many opportunities that are put before it.'

'Our R & D department is very active and I can tell you that we have several new products in the pipeline.'

'Our problem is not to generate opportunities. We are inundated with them. Our problem is to choose the right one.' 'We have an entrepreneur as chief executive. If there is any opportunity around he is sure to spot it before anyone else.'

Now all these things may well be true but they bring to mind the fellow who said that he did not need to buy a book 'because he already had one at home'. Few companies are not doing something, somewhere that would qualify as opportunity search. But it may only be tokenism or a tiny part of what could be done.

It has been my experience that truly creative people (as demonstrated in their work) have been interested to read my books on creativity but the less creative have felt that they knew all there was to know. Complacency is not usually the characteristic of someone who is genuinely interested in a subject.

Complacency is a particularly dangerous attitude because it contains no possibility of change. A company that within its own perspective thinks it is doing a lot about opportunities may have a perspective that is very limited.

Technology-push fears

There is a justified fear that a technological development will create an opportunity that will in turn mop up so much of the available resources that the company fails. It happened to Rolls-Royce where the development of the RB 211 engine and the hyfil blades combined with a massive Lockheed order to destroy the company.

Certain types of opportunity do require a heavy investment in research, product development, product launch or plant. The cost of developing the Xerox process was $75 million. Polaroid is said to have spent $600 million on developing the SX camera. There is always the fear that a technological innovation may seem so impressive that the company is forced, willy nilly, to pursue its development. Companies run by scientists or engineers are particularly prone to this danger because such people are apt to look more closely at the elegance of a solution to a problem than at its market potential. A Californian company that successfully developed commercial uses for the laser eventually had to sack the chairman and founder because he could not resist developing a super surveying laser that would have been accurate to within millimetres over a twenty-mile distance. The companies that came together to form the UK General Electric Company had tended to be run by engineers and were technologically driven.

Faced with a technological breakthrough a company may be tempted to put all its 'opportunity' eggs in one basket and even with the most promising product this is a dangerous strategy.

Fear of an opportunity war

In service industries like banking and insurance and in some other industries the cost of innovation is not very high. But many corporations are restrained in their opportunity search by fear of setting off an opportunity war. If a service company offers some new service, its competitors will match this and perhaps go one better. As in a price war no one benefits in the end. The same sort of thing happened in the United States in the cosmetic industry. One company offered premiums as an inducement to customers. Competitors matched this and went further. In the end hitherto high profit margins were eroded and no one increased their market share. A company that is just breaking into a market can of course open up opportunities that an established company with the major share of the market cannot match. On the other hand an established company could, in theory, lower prices so as to drive the newcomer out of business. In the USA the anti-trust laws would be invoked if this were to happen.

Fear of an opportunity war also includes the situation where a company is unwilling to invest in the development of a new product because the lead time over possible competition is too short to recoup the development expenses.

Plain caution

The price of fertilizers rises. Entrepreneurs see an opportunity and build new plants. There is over-capacity in the industry and the prices fall again. The cycle repeats itself until the operators grow cautious. In certain industries, such as the production of polythene or plastic piping, production has to be on a large scale in order to bring down unit costs. So even when a genuine opportunity exists the response almost inevitably leads to over-capacity and the opportunity fails to materialize. The same thing can happen in paper and board mills and in the chemical industry.

A ship-owner reads his figures and interpets his trends and orders a new tanker. His competitors have read the signs in the same way as he has and they also order new ships. Eventually all the ships are built and there is a glut.

For reasons such as these there is a great deal of caution in following up the apparent opportunities offered by a rise in prices or poorly supplied demand.

Disinclination to expand

There was a time when the American attitude to business was a high volume one: expand sales and let the profit margins look after themselves. Those days are gone, possibly for ever. Too many businesses found that they were expanding sales with no real increase in profits. An airline might put on extra flights in order to cope with an increase – real or projected – in traffic. The increase in traffic did create more sales volume but many of the planes were flying with only partial loads and so profitability declined. An airline like Qantas with a loyal home market would, in contrast, restrict its flights even if this meant turning away some passengers. As a result it would operate with a much higher load factor and therefore higher profits.

In 1977 US industry was more interested in keeping prices high than in lowering them and increasing output. As a result much of industry continued to run at between seventy- and eighty-per-cent capacity. Volume for the sake of volume no longer made sense.

The idea that expansion for the sake of expansion does not necessarily make economic sense dampens enthusiasm for opportunity-seeking. But since return on capital is the name of the game there is still a good reason for looking for opportunities to expand in those directions in which the return on capital is higher.

Comment

The corporate attitudes listed here do not encourage opportunity search. And yet they are really only qualifying factors. They do not make an opportunity search unnecessary but they do emphasize the importance of the direction in which the search takes place and of the exact type of opportunity that is required.

'Unfortunately opportunity hunger arises from appetite and not from starvation."

Executive attitude towards opportunity

If it is difficult to generate a corporate opportunity hunger it is even more difficult to generate within an individual executive a feeling that there is a need to look for opportunities. Such a need seems to arise from personality, ambition, motivation, curiosity and that vital desire 'to make things happen'. Nevertheless, we can look honestly and objectively at all those things which make opportunity search so unattractive to executives. We can divide executive attitudes into: indifferent, reluctant, complacent and blocked. This leaves out the eager group. But apart from saying that executives eager to search out opportunities do exist, there is not much more to be said about such people – except that they seem rare.

Indifferent

It never occurs to many executives that they should concern themselves with opportunities. To be fair, there are executives who are not even opportunity-conscious as regards their own careers. Opportunity search is not seen as part of the ordinary executive role. That role is seen in 'train-driver' terms: running the organization as it is set up without seeking to alter things. Opportunity search is seen as being the concern of senior management, strategic planning groups, R & D, new business groups and the like. To some extent this is a matter of semantics. Opportunity is often seen as a large scale undertaking – like a tobacco company diversifying itself into the ice cream business. Such large scale decisions are seen to be outside the opportunity-space of an ordinary executive even though he may have views about the opportunity. Yet opportunities do not have to be large scale. There are opportunities in cost-saving, personnel relationships, procedures and innovations at all levels.

Another reason for executive indifference towards opportunities is that many executives feel that they are not expected by senior management to search for opportunities: they feel that they are just expected to get on with the job and leave the thinking to senior management. In many corporations it is undoubtedly true that independent thinking by middle management tends to draw frowns from their seniors. In the hierarchy of management it only needs one person to disapprove of opportunity thinking to kill that attitude. For its encouragement every person in the hierarchy needs to be seen to be in favour. In practice this is most often achieved by a dynamic chief executive who is interested in opportunity and feeds this attitude down the line.

Opportunity means hassle of one sort or another. Most executives are aware of this objective truth. What hassle really means will be discussed under the next heading.

An indifference to opportunity can arise from the energetic application of the 'train-driver' attitude or it can arise from sheer laziness. Paradoxically, laziness may, in certain circumstances, be a spur to innovation. This is in the area of innovation concerned with saving time, effort or money.

Basically indifference arises from only two causes: lack of understanding of opportunity and the executive role, and lack of motivation. In a survey of executives in the UK it was found that most of them wanted no-limit pay rises to be related to productivity. These executives went on to say that they felt they could increased company profits by six to ten per cent. Such an increase in productivity represents an extraordinary opportunity. The implication, however, is that the executives were unwilling to work towards this opportunity unless financially motivated. It may seem difficult to believe that a self-driven executive would deliberately turn down an opportunity because of lack of reward but over a period it seems likely that an executive does need some tangible indication that opportunity development is part of the game. High income tax rates in countries such as Sweden and the UK effectively remove the reward for extra risk, work or responsibility. Stock options can go some of the way towards providing an incentive but tend to be a little remote in a large corporation (since an individual executive cannot easily see that what he is doing is really going to affect the stock market valuation). I would favour 'project-pay' whereby the extra work involved in operating an opportunity project is directly rewarded. This would apply equally to the projects set up, as opportunities, by the executive himself as to those delegated by senior management. In countries with high taxation increased leisure or other perks might be the only rewards that mean anything.

Promotion-consciousness can also lead to indifference to opportunities. Opportunities have a longer time scale than direct executive coping and so the executive who relies on quick results may disregard them – trimming and cost-cutting opportunities are an exception. The risk of failure is also there. Failure of an opportunity project may be blamed on the executive who initiated the project even though failure is not his fault at all.

Reluctant

An executive who is indifferent towards opportunity pays the subject little or no attention. The reluctant executive is concerned with opportunity but reluctant to get involved because the downside risk is so out of proportion.

If you start looking for opportunities you create work for yourself both in the search and in what you have to do next when you have found what you think is an opportunity. This extra work involves thinking time and thinking effort. There are decisions to be made and uncertainties to be coped with. There are worries and anxieties that were not there before. There is a cost in time and money. My own feeling is that an executive who shies away from work and involvement of this sort should never be an executive but that is a harsh judgement. After all the attempt to make and keep simple one's life is intelligent behaviour.

Reluctance to get involved in an opportunity search also arises from the trio of dilution, distraction and dissatisfaction. An executive fears that his own efforts and those of his subordinates will be diluted by opportunity exploration. The fear is that the focused and single-minded effort required to solve a particular problem will be weakened by such dilution. The second fear is that of distraction. In the early stage of exploration an opportunity can be enticing, even exciting. The fear is that an executive will be tempted away from a routine task that needs to be done, in order to deploy his enthusiasm in an opportunity search. The third fear is that of dissatisfaction. There is a feeling that even to look for an opportunity implies dissatisfaction with the existing state of affairs. This 'divine' dissatisfaction, as it is called in the progress of science, is useful if it results in genuine improvement. But if it does not the dissatisfaction remains without the solace of an improvement. Some executives feel that it is better not to generate the dissatisfaction in the first place.

The need to achieve balance between operating the system as it is (the train-driver attitude) and seeking new opportunities (the fisherman attitude) creates difficulties. The human mind is not at ease with balance. We prefer to rest at one or other extreme. But over-indulgence in an opportunity search leads to a sort of butterfly behaviour with energy being directed at one thing after another and never settling on any particular thing long enough to get something done. It is hardly surprising that the opposite extreme is preferred: 'Don't waste time dabbling in what might be but get on with what is'.

There are many minds that find uncertainty uncomfortable. It is not that such minds are any less capable of coping with uncertainty than others but they just find dealing with uncertainty uncomfortable. They have the sort of feeling an accountant might have if a client told him that he was uncertain about some of the figures put forward. Since opportunity search involves uncertainty at least at two stages – the uncertainty of even finding an area of opportunity and the uncertainty that it will prove valuable – such minds are reluctant to get involved in an opportunity search.

An executive who knows that he is competent at his job may be reluctant to stick his neck out and risk making a mistake over an apparent opportunity. In many organizations the penalties for making a mistake are so much greater than the rewards for opening up an opportunity that this reluctance constitutes intelligent behaviour. In other situations it may just be a fear of having one's competence tested or over-extended. It is a sort of combination of Parkinson's Law and the Peter Principle: 'An executive will fill his working time with matters that fall within his competence'.

Quite apart from a reluctance to risk his own career or peace of mind, an executive may be reluctant to risk the well-being of the company. He may feel that the company is not in a fit state to chase after opportunities. He may feel that the resources are too slim to be stretched over several opportunity fields. He may feel that it is best if the company concentrates on what it knows how to do best.

Complacent

The complacent executive is not indifferent to opportunities, nor is he reluctant to get involved with them: he just feels that he is already doing all that needs to be done. He feels that he has a high degree of awareness and is sensitive to what is going on both inside his company and in the market place. He feels that as soon as an opportunity comes along he will be able to spot it and seize it. For him an opportunity search is not an active hunt that needs to be organized but a passive waiting. To use the fisherman analogy, he is a fisherman who puts down his nets and waits for the fish to come his way – instead of setting out to discover where the big shoals might be.

Opportunities do, of course, arise. But they are not always self-evident. An opportunity may only be spotted long after it has become possible. The specific and particular opportunities that arise within a particular company cannot be developed by copying what a different company is doing. In the disposable razor market Gillette cannot easily follow the behaviour of the Bic organization because Gillette would be competing against its own products whereas Bic is not.

The problem with complacency is that it can never be faulted in particular. In general we know that most complacency is totally misplaced but an individual may still feel that he has earned the right to be complacent. It is true to say that the people who have good reason to be complacent very rarely are, but again this is a general comment.

Perhaps the simplest test of complacency is to measure dissatisfaction. Instead of asking an executive why he thinks he is satisfied with his approach to opportunity-seeking, it may be more useful to ask in which areas the executive is dissatisfied. If there are no such areas of dissatisfaction the complacency is very likely to be misplaced. This is a valid test because complacency usually arises from a limited vision: an executive sees only a small world and feels he is doing all he can in that small world. An executive who sees a larger world will always be able to see some area in which he is dissatisfied. It is somewhat like a true craftsman rarely being complacent about his work.

Blocked

An executive may not be indifferent, reluctant or complacent in his approach to opportunities – he may simply be blocked. The structure of a corporation may be such that an executive is allowed so little initiative in his behaviour or his thinking that he never gets a chance to look for opportunities. Such restrictive structures do exist but even in their absence a passive corporate attitude may be just as blocking. An 'inertia block' is one where an idea just died for lack of interest or support. At some point every worthless idea should be expected to die but that death should follow some initial interest which explores the value of the idea.

A corporate block may be brought about by a single executive in charge of some division. He may create throughout that division a negative attitude towards opportunity because he does not want to cope with the extra work thrown up by opportunity-eager subordinates.

At a lower level there can be personality block when the opportunity-seeking of one executive is persistently blocked by a colleague with whom there exists a personality clash. In this case the blocking effect is not universal but applies only to that particular executive.

There is a common fallacy that a person who is good at spotting opportunities should also be capable of doing something about them. Yet this is not so. A person may be very perceptive at spotting opportunities for others but unable to follow them up himself. There are bank managers who expertly advise their clients on investment in the stock market, commodities or gold but keep their own money in low-yielding government stock – through timidity. A person may see a good opportunity but through caution or timidity be unable to follow it up. If an opportunity involves 'selling the idea' or persuading someone of its value, then one type of personality might be able to accomplish this whereas another type who sees the benefits of the opportunity even more clearly may be incapable. Caution, timidity, lack of drive, fear of failure can all interfere with the follow-through of an opportunity, yet the ability to spot an opportunity may be there. We tend to dismiss too easily those people who are unable to follow through the opportunities they have perceived. We tend to feel that the benefits cannot be so real if the originator cannot first sell the idea to himself. Yet we ought to remember that the designer of the Grand Prix racing car may not rate highly as a Grand Prix driver and may even be too nervous to try.

An executive may be unwilling to move abroad, change jobs or accept promotion because his wife will not let him. It may be unfair to castigate him as 'hen-pecked' for the same lady might have had an equivalent effect on many other executives with more compliant wives. An honest and objective assessment of blocks to performance is better than a blanket expectation that an executive should be able to overcome such blocks on his own.

A rather specific block to opportunity search occurs in the reaction of a listener to an opportunity idea that is proposed. There are many lukewarm and negative reactions. Perhaps the most dangerous of them all is the killer phrase: 'the same as ...' I have personally seen this simple phrase used time and again to kill the most valuable ideas. The listener sees some resemblance between what is proposed and something that is already being done or has been tried and failed. It is a way of saying: 'That is not worth doing because we are already doing it or because we have already tried it.' The reason the phrase is so dangerous is that it can be applied with all innocence. The receiver of the idea can genuinely see only the resemblance between the proposed idea and the old one. This is the only way he can understand the new idea. The receiver may be quite unable to see the crucial points of difference. It must also be said that if we make enough effort and are prepared to shift to a higher level of generality, most new ideas can be seen as being 'the same as' some other idea. It is not unlike the attitude of those people who claim there are only three basic types of joke and then proceed to focus on those features in a joke which will allow it to be forced into one of these categories. The simple antidote is to say: 'Let us focus on the points of difference.' This is a habit which every executive needs to develop for himself in order to counteract the natural dismissive tendency which he will find himself applying to most new ideas. A tiny point of difference may sometimes decide whether the new idea really is an opportunity or not; for example, the addition of an extra column of pegs made all the difference between success and failure for the best-selling game 'Mastermind'.

'An opportunity is a course of action that is possible and obviously worth pursuing.'

What is an opportunity?

To many executives an opportunity is a high-risk speculation. There are better ways of making profits than the pursuit of high-risk speculations. An opportunity does have to be a speculation because it is about the future. In that sense almost all our activities are speculations because we are trying to bring something about and believe that our actions will do this. But the 'high risk' feeling is erroneous. A true opportunity is not a high-risk area. A true opportunity should be obvious in its benefits. What is risked is the thinking time taken to consider an opportunity and to bring it to the stage where it is obviously worth pursuing further.

An executive may have to do a deal of thinking before he perceives that an opportunity is worth pursuing. It is this appreciation of benefits that motivates anyone to explore an opportunity. As an executive continues his thinking in pursuit of the opportunity the promise of the benefits may wax or wane or go through cycles of either. Further thinking may show the benefits to be illusory or smaller than initially supposed. Further thinking may show that the benefits are as imagined but that the cost and difficulty of achieving them diminish their value to the corporation. All this is thinking time and that is what is being risked.

The difference between an opportunity and wishful thinking is that an opportunity is possible. At the first sight an opportunity may not appear possible but with focused thinking the possibility should increase. If this does not happen then it is no opportunity. The possibility should increase both as regards the course of action that can be taken and also as regards the benefits that might arise from that course of action. In short an increasingly satisfactory answer to the two questions:

'What course of action could we take to bring this about?'

'What are the chances of the benefits being generated by our course of action?'

To turn an idea into a real opportunity requires thinking time and thinking effort. The first purpose of the thinking is to formulate the opportunity idea. The second is to assess the benefits. The third is to work out a course of action that is feasible. It must be self-evident that the better the thinking the less risky is an opportunity.

When an opportunity is defined as 'a course of action that is possible and obviously worth pursuing', it should not be supposed that the course of action that is worth pursuing refers only to undertaking the whole project. The course of action could just as well refer to getting more information; doing a market study; carrying out further research; or setting up a pilot project. It is the first step that may be obviously worth pursuing and depending on the result of that step the next step may be equally worth while. When looking at a large opportunity it is the executive's business to break that down into preliminary steps that are obviously worth pursuing. Even if the only step that is obviously worth pursuing is to ask an expert in the field, that is the step to be taken.

There is no short cut to opportunity search and development. Deliberate thinking time is required. The more of that we can risk the less we risk other resources. Nor should it be imagined that the thinking time is wasted if the opportunity is turned down. That thinking investment may prove useful in another situation later on.

Why us?

There are some opportunities that seem to be open to anyone who wants to get into the field. For example, the growth potential in the fast food area in the United States seems to be huge. There are other opportunities that are only opportunities for an organization that is already engaged in that area. The distinction between the two is not always clear. The consumption of polystyrene in Brazil is only 1½lb per head per year as compared to 22 lb in the USA. The consumption is likely to increase rapidly in Brazil's exploding economy. Is the opportunity there for anyone who wants to get into the field or only for someone who is already engaged in the plastics industry?

The classic curve of diminishing returns or marginal effectiveness is shown in Figure 2. Every executive is aware of the curve since his main aim in life is to stay on the steep initial part where an investment of money has the greatest effect. The curve crops up in all sorts of situations. More expenditure on advertising may produce relatively less return once a certain point has been passed. The same may apply to research, to price-cutting and to many other things. In order to understand the nature of an opportunity we can use the same curve – but reverse the axes. Instead of a cost-effectiveness curve we get an effect–cost curve. We are now interested in the situation where for a relatively small increase in cost we can get a large effect. In other words a particular company by using its established resources may be able to achieve and effect a lesser cost than would anyone else. That becomes an opportunity for that company – but not for everyone. As an illustration, when the Bic corporation decided to go into disposable razors it had the technical – and marketing – know-how for producing small plastic items in large quantities because it had already made a success with disposable ball-points and lighters.

The resources of a company may simply be financial. Flush with cash a company is in an expansionist mood. In the heady conglomerate days the resource was an attractive price earnings ratio on the stock market. The resource may be one of management strength which can be injected into an ailing company that has been taken over. The resource may be one of know-how in a particular field, such as plastics, glass or consumer goods. The re-

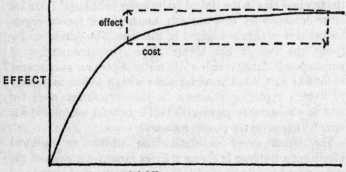

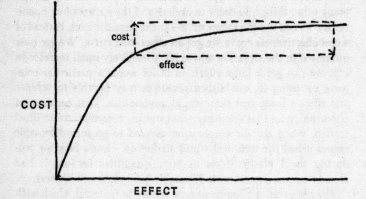

Figure 2

source may be a technical one, for example an enzyme that more effectively converts corn starch into high fructose sugar. The resource may be that of market muscle which involves warehousing, distributing networks and outlets plus a promotions budget. The resource may be one of market position or market recognition. When Volvo took over the Daf car company, Volvo was able to produce a small car with the market image of Volvo reliability and so charge a price few other manufacturers could have got away with.

The Santa Fe railroad started as a railroad. It has now been involved in real estate for one hundred years; in road transport for fifty years; in timber for thirty-nine years; in coal for eighty-nine years and in petroleum for seventy-eight years. It became involved in all these things because an opportunity to do so arose from its basic transport activity.

A distinction does have to be made, however, between new activities which are properly costed and are profitable in their own right and activities which simply mop up spare capacity. The latter are only profitable if the fixed costs involved in the main activity have to be incurred anyway. The danger is that activities which are started for this reason are then continued, unprofitably, when the spare capacity no longer exists because of a change in technology or increased production. In these matters the allocation of costs determines whether an activity is an opportunity or not.

Opportunities for expanding and opportunities for contracting

Figure 3 illustrates the two alternative types of opportunity. The top square suggests the existing activities or *status quo*. The middle square suggests an expansion in activities and the last square suggests a contraction. This contraction is not just a contraction in activities but may be a contraction in costs for doing the same things.

An expansion may involve an increase in plant capacity. For example Erol Beker of Beker Industries calculated that fertilizer would be in short supply so he increased capacity four-fold in three years. This resulted in serious over-capacity. The expansion

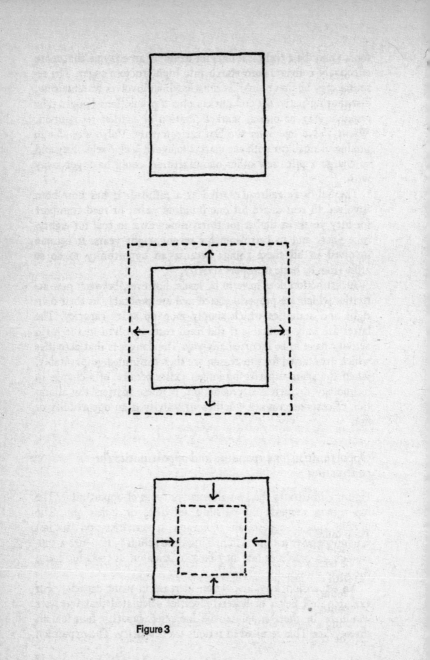

Figure 3

may be in terms of market penetration not only in depth but also in breadth. The brilliant position of Bacardi rum in the market allowed it to increase sales by 13.5 per cent in 1976 so giving it third place in the brand sales of spirits. Bacardi was marketed as a mixer, in particular with Coke, and even for making rum cake (70,000 cases of half pints for this purpose). The Dow corporation wants to expand down-stream towards consumer products because the margins are better. A Pan-Am pilot James F. Zockoll had to buy some drain-clearing equipment one week-end when no one would unblock his drains. From this he expanded into a profitable franchised drain-clearing service.

New products as an extension of existing lines or as new departures are obvious examples of the expansion type of opportunity (or, in many cases, replacement). Too often this type of opportunity is regarded as a luxury: 'We are doing quite nicely with our present product range'. But product obsolescence, pressure from competing products, shifts in the market all combine to make this type of opportunity an absolute necessity. Most executives find it difficult to decide how much expansion of this type is really essential replacement and how much is speculative luxury.

The contraction type of opportunity has much more appeal to most executives because the end results are so much more tangible and the risk is much less. Cost-cutting exercises of all sorts come into this bracket. If you can be seen to be carrying on the same activities at a lower cost then the increase in profitability is obvious. There is a multitude of well-established techniques of operations research (for example cost-cutting in distribution); value analysis; value engineering (cost-cutting in product design or production); work study; clerical work study and the like which are designed to increase productivity by cutting costs in this way. They are well worth considering as part of an opportunity search. The difficulty is that repeated application of these methods tends to yield less and less since there is less and less fat and inefficiency to be trimmed away. In other words there is a natural floor whereas with expansion there may not be.

Product-trimming is another part of the contracting type of opportunity. It may be a decision to get out of a certain field which is proving unprofitable (like RCA's $490 million decision to get out of the computer field). Or it may be a decision to trim product lines (like RCA's decision to cut down the number of products in its mobile radio division). Application of the traditional eighty/ twenty rule continues to be as valuable as ever: twenty per cent of our activities generate eighty per cent of our profits and eighty per cent of our activities only generate twenty per cent of our profits. There is a small danger here that some of the unprofitable activities might be essential for the success of the profitable: as in the case of a motor company that has built its reputation on its sports cars but gets most of its profits from family saloons. This effect needs considering but is sometimes exaggerated.

In catering it is estimated that the ingredients cost thirty-eight per cent of what is charged for a dish and labour charges contribute thirty to thirty-five per cent. Clearly there are opportunities in choosing ingredients, reducing wastage and pilfering, buying policy, reducing labour content and associated areas. A fast food chain that thought only in terms of expansionist opportunities (opening new sites) would soon get into trouble with a high sales volume but no profits.

Figure 4 shows in a visual way some approaches to opportunities:

We can look for a simpler and more direct way of achieving what we want.

We may find that by re-thinking what we want to achieve it becomes simpler to reach.

We can look to see whether with our resources and established direction there is something else we could achieve as well.

Direction, destination and means

You can look in a defined direction: north, south, upwards or downwards. Within that direction you may then see several destinations which you may want to reach. It is the same with opportunities. There may be broad directions in which a corporation wishes to look for opportunities or the direction itself may be an opportunity. For example an organization may wish to move from being production-oriented towards a market orientation. An organization may look in the direction of opening up new markets in the less developed countries. More specifically, looking in the direction of Nigeria as an expanding and rich market would also qualify as a direction.

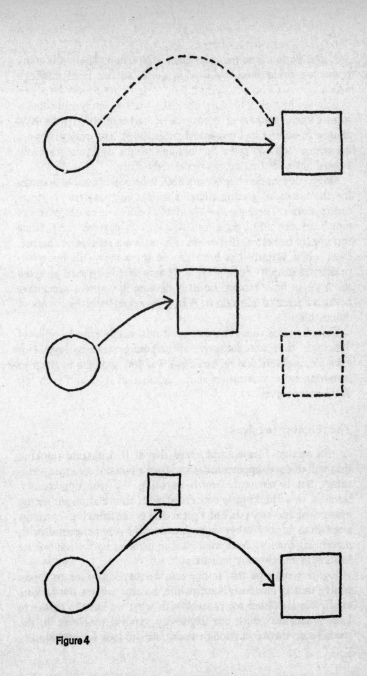

Figure 4

A destination is more exact than a direction. There are many towns we could reach by driving north but we need to decide which one is to be our destination. A destination may be a particular product or a product line (like Kodak's entry into the instant camera market) or it may be a market position (like Avis aiming to be first in Europe and succeeding). The only difference between a direction and a destination is that a direction is broadly defined but a destination can be defined tightly.

Once a destination has been defined it becomes possible to examine the means of getting there. This is a further area of opportunity search. There may be a variety of different routes, many of which are not all obvious until we have discovered them. Some routes may be better tried or less risky or more reliable or cheaper. Even when a route has been chosen there may still be opportunities to simplify or improve it. It may well be that an accepted route might have escaped scrutiny because the present users have never bothered to question it. A new user does have the chance of doing this.

Too often it is thought that opportunities only exist in terms of directions that are discussed at corporate strategy level (for example, a diversification strategy). Far less thought is given to searching for opportunities at the destination level and even less at the means level.

The thinking involved

In this section I have emphasized that it is deliberate thinking that will uncover opportunities and turn a fanciful idea into something that is obviously worth pursuing – a true opportunity. Some of this thinking is concerned with information-gathering, assessment and analysis. But a great deal of the thinking – perhaps more than in any other management field – is concerned with perceptual change. Perceptual change involves both what we are looking at and the way we look at it.

Figure 5 suggests that in one case we may fail to see an opportunity that is obviously worthwhile, because we are not looking at all. We are either too content with what we have to bother to look or too busy with our day-to-day survival problems. In the second case there is a strong commitment to look for opportunity

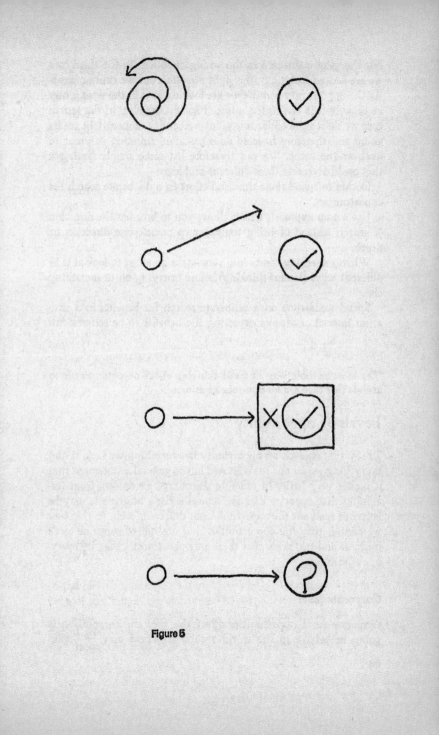

Figure 5

but the gaze is directed in the wrong direction. In the third case we are indeed looking in the right direction but we cannot identify the opportunity because we are looking at it in the wrong way or because it is lost in the midst of something else. In the fourth case we do see the opportunity but we cannot immediately see its value and therefore have to do some more thinking in order to uncover the value. We can therefore list some simple strategies that could overcome these different problems:

Decide to spend some time and effort in a deliberate search for opportunities.

Use a scan approach which allows you to broaden the direction of search instead of being too eager to pursue one direction in depth.

When something comes into view make an effort to look at it in different ways (lateral thinking) before hurrying on to something else.

Spend some time on a deliberate search for benefits in a situation instead of always expecting the benefits to be self-evident.

'The most sensible way to avoid thinking about opportunities is to assume that they are someone else's business.'

Levels of opportunity

To say that there is an opportunity in everything we look at and everything we set out to do is true, but so general a statement that it means very little. In order to discourage executives from imagining that opportunities are someone else's business it may be better to spell out the opportunities at different levels. In this way we can identify the opportunities that are indeed someone else's business and still show that there are opportunities that are everyone's business.

Corporate level

Corporate level opportunities affect the way the corporation is going to behave in the world around it. There may be opportunities for acquisitions, mergers, diversification and such like activities. A decision to drop trading stamps in a supermarket chain is a corporate decision to take advantage of the apparent cost-consciousness of the British housewife in 1977. An advertising campaign signalling price reductions instead of trading stamps was seen as an opportunity to increase market share at the expense of competitors. It was not so much a matter of price cuts but an opportunity to signal price cuts. An oil company sees an opportunity to move further into chemicals and also into coal and other energy sources. Direction decisions of this sort and opportunity search within these directions are taken at board level on the advice of corporate strategy teams. Someone outside these senior management levels may rightly feel that such opportunities are not his concern. With smaller organizations there would be less remoteness even for corporate level decisions.

The increasing emphasis on worker participation at board level, as in the Bullock report's suggestions in the UK, arises from a feeling that opportunity decisions taken at board level have a direct effect on workers and the availability of jobs. A suggestion that ICI should open a new chemical plant in Germany would be met by protests that jobs were being diverted from the UK. In this respect an involvement in opportunity decisions – even if not in opportunity search – may well spread downwards from board level in the future.

Management level

Figure 6 suggests the difference between corporate level and management level opportunities. Management level opportunities are concerned with the running of the organization. Such opportunities may include re-structuring, financial control and accountancy changes, leasing opportunities, personnel policy, cost-cutting exercises, setting up a deliberate opportunity audit structure and all other matters concerned with improving the performance of the organization. Some matters such as R & D operations and sales force organization do affect the outside world directly and here a distinction may need to be made between what is properly a corporate concern and the carrying out of this concern by management performance. I do not wish to suggest that there

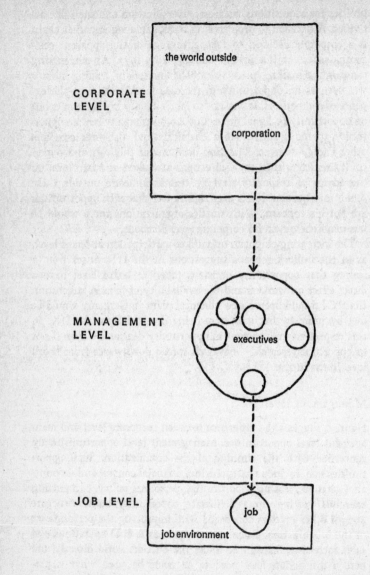

the world outside

CORPORATE LEVEL

corporation

MANAGEMENT LEVEL

executives

JOB LEVEL

job

job environment

Figure 6

be two absolutely separate areas of responsibility but that there should be an awareness of the need for consultation. Otherwise a corporate opportunity may be frustrated by a management opportunity. For example a division may trim its sales force just when a corporate decision has been taken to acquire a new company with a complementary product line but a weak sales organization.

Job level

Job level opportunities arise when a person looks around at the opportunity space created by his own job. It may be a matter of time management, of delegation, of consultation, of simplifying procedures, of changing habits, of developing new strategies, of learning, of putting aside time for opportunity search. A corporate strategist has two opportunity levels. His job level allows him to consider what opportunities there might be for improving his performance as a strategist, whilst at the corporate level he considers the opportunities for the corporation. The same thing applies at management level where an executive may be looking for management opportunities and also job level opportunities.

Personal level

Personal level opportunities are concerned with self-development, self-actualization (in Maslow's terms), promotion opportunities, mobility opportunities, status opportunities and all the various things which lead to the advancement of a person. I shall not be dealing with personal level opportunities in this book, but I must acknowledge that they are an important field and that in some cases they are directly to the benefit of the corporation whilst in others they might have the opposite effect, as in the case of an executive who makes a visible change not because the company needs it but because he wants some policy attached to his name.

'With a problem you search for the solution, with an opportunity you search for the benefit.'

Benefits and motivation

In the end all decisions are emotional. The purpose of thinking is so to place matters in our mind that our emotional reaction to them will in fact be the right decision. I do not believe that there is such a thing as an objective, unemotional decision. There are times when a businessman might like to keep on a friend but objective considerations suggest that the friend should be sacked because he is incompetent. The sacking of the friend is not an unemotional decision: it is simply that the emotion of self-preservation, the need to achieve and self-pride in one's business judgement have prevailed over the emotion of compassion.

There may be complex emotions involved in an opportunity search: the need to create; curiosity; the need to be different; self-importance; the need for recognition; greed and the like. Most of these favour opportunity search – though not on logical grounds. I am, however, more concerned with those people who are not naturally motivated to look for opportunities and will only do so if they can preceive real benefits. We need to consider three stages of benefits.

In the first stage there must be some tangible benefit in setting out to look for opportunities in the first place. Everyone might realize that in the long term it must be to the benefit of a corporation that someone looks for opportunities but this consideration has only a weak motivating effect in the face of the risks and hassles mentioned in a previous section. If opportunity search is expected of an executive, he is more likely to do it. If opportunity search is encouraged and is a visible corporate philosophy, an executive will seek to earn 'brownie points' by playing the game as the rules are written. If a deliberate opportunity audit exercise is made part of his executive function, an executive will carry out the exercise with his usual skill in performance. That is why it is so important to make opportunity search into a deliberate and focused procedure. If it is left to chance, motivation and good will, then little will happen because the immediate benefits of setting out on an opportunity search are simply not there.

Once a person has embarked on an opportunity search he needs to generate his own motivation by discovering the possible benefits of going further. As soon as an opportunity idea comes to mind he should concentrate on its possible benefits. If he succeeds in clarifying these benefits in his mind this will provide him with the motivation to take the next step. It is not unlike the story of a donkey carrying a harness which supports a carrot a few inches in front of the animal's nose. So the second stage benefits are those which the searcher spells out for himself through giving top priority to examining the possible benefits as soon as he thinks he spots an opportunity. There is, however, a grave technology-push danger here. An inventor working on an invention can see the benefits of carrying his invention through to the final working stage. This is his motivation. As far as the corporation goes this activity may be a huge waste of time and money. What is worse, the further the invention moves towards completion and the more effort that has gone into it, the more motivation there will be to market it. Many a corporation has taken this road to disaster. The best way to avoid the danger is first to look at benefits in terms of saleability and marketability. If these are not right there is no point in going further.

If the first stage of benefits is concerned with getting someone to start looking for opportunities and the second with the motivation for the development of an opportunity, the third stage is concerned with a decision on the opportunity itself. The third stage is concerned with the evaluation: 'We can clearly see the opportunity that has been spelled out for us. What we have to decide is whether the benefits are such that as a company we should get involved.' At this stage the benefits have been spelled out in the 'if' form. So most of the effort will be directed towards removing the risk, uncertainty and speculation. Once this has been done the next stage is to consider the problems and difficulties involved in taking up the opportunity. The final consideration is cost – 'Is it still worth it at this price?' When the benefits have been spelled out, the uncertainty reduced as much as possible and the cost (in time, effort and money) assessed, a decision can be made.

The three motivation levels can be summarized as follows:

Motivation to start looking in the first place.

Motivation to think through a particular opportunity.

Corporate motivation to take up the opportunity.

In all three cases the perceived benefits are the strongest motivating force. That is why so much effort needs to be directed towards perceiving the possible benefits. It is so obvious that it is surprising how rarely it is done.

Escape benefits and achievement benefits

A man may leave his wife because he wants to escape from her nagging. Another man may leave his wife because he wants to achieve happiness with another woman. A corporation may close down a troublesome and expensive part of its operation. Another may open up a new division because it wants to cater for the growing market in CB radios. Escape benefits have a more immediate effect but no growth potential. They may, however, release valuable resources for growth elsewhere.

Time course of search for benefits

How long should I go on looking for the benefits before abandoning an opportunity as being no real opportunity? The answer is difficult but no more difficult than the answer to the question: how long should I go on trying to find a solution to this problem? It depends on the importance of the situation. Figure 7 suggests that many opportunity scrutineers drop out too soon and so miss the potential of the situation. If it is a matter of thinking time then we can afford to go on thinking for quite a time – long beyond the stage of boredom or despair. If it is a matter of research and development time, a cut-off should be fixed beforehand. In both cases the cut-off will be influenced by the resources available and the alternative use of these resources.

Whichever way one looks at it, investment is always related to some general concept of benefit. There always has to be some such concept even if it is vague and later proves illusory. Someone who has the idea that good design and good promotion will create a market for luxury ball-point pens has the general concept of benefit that includes an unfilled market gap, margins that are high and are not price-sensitive, and possibly the establishment of a brand image that can later be extended to other products. Market

70

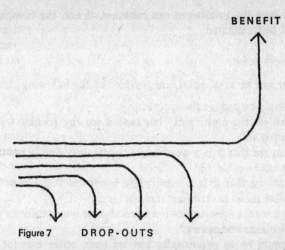

Figure 7   DROP-OUTS

research may subsequently show that people believe that all ball-points are the same inside no matter what the case looks like and that they are treated more as a commodity than as a branded product. Someone else invents a new board game which he tries on his friends who declare they find it fascinating. He sets out to produce and market it himself. His general concept is that the games market is vast and that with his fascinating game he will take some small share. In fact it turns out that the costs of promotion and distribution are so high that no one ever gets to hear about the fascinating game – even though they would have loved it if they had had the chance to try it.

The all black musical Wiz opened in New York to lukewarm reviews. It seemed almost certain to close within a short time. The promoters decided to gamble $125,000 on TV advertising. The result was that the musical broke all records in attracting non-theatre-goers. The general concept of benefit was that there existed a potential audience who would normally never hear about the show.

After a considerable investment of time and effort there does come a time when it is no longer worth trying to do the same thing better. In lateral thinking terms it is no longer worthwhile trying to dig the same hole deeper. A fresh approach is needed: a hole must be dug somewhere else. If such an approach can be found then the investment can continue. If not, the investment should be terminated.

Break-off point

Convenient break-off points are provided by the following phrases:

'I simply cannot see the opportunity.'

'I can see the opportunity but cannot see any possible way of evaluating it.'

'I can see that it is a worthwhile opportunity but I cannot see how it can be achieved.'

'I can see that it is a worthwhile opportunity and even how to achieve it but nevertheless it is not for us.'

'I can see the opportunity but I can also see huge problems with people, means and money.'

'It could be an opportunity but we have better uses for our resources and efforts.'

'It is indeed an opportunity but in my opinion the risks are too great and the rewards too small.'

All of the above are perfectly valid break-off phrases – if used at the proper time. The danger is that they are so easy to use that they can be used instead of thinking about opportunities. There is no way of telling whether they are escape phrases or conclusion phrases unless there is some evidence of exploratory thought preceding their use.

'We know that in general it is essential to look for opportunities but we also know that in particular it is very rarely sensible to do so.'

The opportunity dilemma

In this first part of the book I have tried to show why it is easy to pay lip-service to opportunity search and yet sensible to do nothing about it. In general, opportunity search is a wonderful thing vital to the development of our civilization. In particular, opportunity search is not very intelligent behaviour. That is the overall opportunity dilemma.

For a simple analogy we can look at investment in Broadway

productions. Four out of five productions lose money. But the one that makes money may make between 200 and 1,300 per cent. If we invest in a number of productions we shall probably do well in the long run. That is why opportunity search in general is a good thing. But four out of five productions are going to fail. With opportunities the failure rate may be even higher. If there is a four out of five chance of your failing it is not much consolation to know that somewhere, someone is going to succeed spectacularly. With the theatre investment the rewards of success can be spread to cover the lost investments but with an executive career or corporate survival that is not the case. The actual success of the musical *Wiz* does nothing to revive the musical *Rex* which cost $700,000 and played only six weeks.

Within this overall dilemma we can perceive several sub-dilemmas, two of which I had mentioned earlier but will repeat here.

Looking for opportunities involves risk, effort, hassle, distraction, dilution of effort and problem creation – but we cannot afford not to look for opportunities.

An individual executive can function very well without ever looking for opportunities and yet a corporation made up of such executives will stagnate to disaster.

It is always better that someone else looks for opportunities and no one is ever 'someone else'.

There is always something more urgent, more concrete and more certain in its pay-off than looking for opportunities.

We select executives for their intelligence and then hope that they will act unintelligently and look for opportunities.

We are very willing to reap the rewards of successful opportunities but unwilling to pay for the failures.

I have listed some of the obstacles in the way of opportunity search. I have summarized cultural attitudes, corporate attitudes and executive attitudes towards opportunities. If at times I have given the impression that such attitudes are only held by lesser men and are to be condemned, I apologize. I have tried to show that the difficulties are genuine, not imagined. I have tried to show that in particular it does not make sense to go looking for trouble even if that trouble is called opportunity. Some people do it, but in logical terms that is a defect in their good sense – for which the rest of the world is grateful. Because pioneers are stupid enough to take risks does not make stupidity a commendable characteristic.

Even if it did make sense to look for opportunities no one really has time for it. There are always more urgent things to do. The general running of the organization has to be carried out. There are urgent crises to attend to and problems to be solved. There is no spare thinking time.

Having written all this in an attempt to show why opportunity search does not make sense in any particular case I do have to repeat that in *general* it is something without which we cannot do.

The solution

We come now to the solution to the dilemma. Because opportunity search is not naturally a sensible thing to do we need to set up a formal requirement for it. We need to incorporate opportunity search in a deliberate and systematic manner into an executive's role. The executive needs to feel that this is expected of him. Because there never really is enough thinking time to look for opportunities we need to set aside a definite allocation of time to be used for this purpose. We cannot hope that opportunity search will be fitted into such time as may be left over from other activities.

In short, the solution is the deliberate allocation of time to a formal and systematic search for opportunities.

This approach defines opportunity search as an executive task to be performed even in the absence of inspiration or internal motivation. It also needs to be performed even in the absence of any great skill. In time such skill can develop. Even without a high degree of skill the habits and attitudes of mind used in the opportunity search exercise will be of value elsewhere.

By setting up this deliberate allocation of time and the systematic approach we create a situation in which it *does* make sense to look for opportunities. The executive is no longer wasting his time but is carrying out a defined task with a required output.

In the second part of this book I shall describe this systematic approach in terms of a structure or framework that can be applied within a company.

Part II: The Opportunity Audit and the Opportunity Team

This part of the book is concerned with a formal structure for systematic opportunity search. It may be helpful to repeat here the relationship between the three parts of the book.

Part I

This part of the book was concerned with looking at people, attitudes and opportunities. There was an examination of cultural, corporate and executive attitudes towards opportunities. The difficulties, dangers, disinclinations and doubts regarding opportunity search were described. The conclusion was in the form of a dilemma: in general opportunity search is essential but in particular it may not seem sensible. The proposed solution was the deliberate allocation of time to opportunity search and the use of a structure for systematic scanning of opportunities. It could be said that the first part of the book set up the 'need' for opportunity search on a deliberate basis.

Part II

In this part the formal structure for systematic opportunity search is described in handbook fashion. It is intended that this part of the book should provide a manual for the implementation of the structure proposed. The overall structure may be referred to as 'The Opportunity Search Exercise' which for ease of reference can be shortened to Opex. The exercise includes an Opportunity Audit to be carried out by individual executives and an Opportunity Team which has overall responsibility for opportunity management. The method of carrying out the Opportunity Audit is described. The different functions of the Opportunity Team (including the setting up of Task Forces) are listed.

Part III

This final part is concerned with the thinking that is required to fill in the 'envelope' of the structure set up in Part II. The methodology of thinking for opportunities is laid out. There is a check-list of different starting points including the three types of assets: intrinsic, operational and situation. Processes such as 'de-averaging' are considered. The distinction is made between 'moving-out' and 'moving-in' problems. There is a section on dealing with risk and uncertainty. And another section on evaluation. A new mapping process based on 'if-boxes' is introduced in order to clarify opportunity development.

The third part of the book must be used in conjunction with the second. The type of thinking described in the third part is required in order to give the output demanded by the structure set forth in the second part. An individual who is operating outside a corporate structure can move straight to the third part and use the methodology given there. He would, however, find it useful to read through this second part as well.

The logical sequence of the book is quite straightforward; examine the situation; isolate the dilemma; propose a solution; spell out the solution in practical terms; provide a methodology for carrying through the solution.

'In the opportunity search exercise an executive is active in setting up his own initiatives instead of always being the passive recipient of directives from above.'

Status of the opportunity search exercise

A positive attitude towards the opportunity search exercise is vital to its success. Without such an attitude, both on the part of the corporation and of individual executives, the exercise is not worth undertaking. The exercise is an area of achievement, an area in which executive skills can be developed and not a chore to be worked through.

Motivation will depend entirely on the status given to the exercise by the chief executive. Each year a letter from the chief executive should invite other executives to take part in the Opportunity Audit. It must be made clear that the corporation puts a high value on opportunity search. Any person works best when he is encouraged in what he is doing. There is a huge difference between, 'Don't bother me with your ideas but just get on with what you are doing,' and, 'In this exercise I am asking you to give me your ideas and to tell me what opportunities you can see.' We can take it for granted that without the specific focus of the opportunity search exercise the first attitude is always assumed. From early school days the brighter pupils learn to play the 'expectation game'. They find out the rules of the game, what the teacher expects, what the examination system expects, what society seems to expect. Later on as bright executives the same people may become very good at spotting opportunities once they discover that this is expected of them.

Skill area

An executive who wishes to flee challenges and avoid tasks is in the wrong job. Most of his fellows are there because they enjoy having something to tackle, some area in which they can put their skills to use. A tennis player is frustrated if he cannot get on to the court, a skier goes to a lot of trouble to get on to the slopes, an executive is delighted to have things to do – provided these things allow him to exercise his initiative. The opportunity search exercise should be regarded as just such an area in which an executive can demonstrate his effectiveness, his vision and his perception. An executive does not have many opportunities to demonstrate his skills. Coping with an allotted task may demonstrate competence but no more.

Entrepreneur

Within the context of Opex (the opportunity search exercise) every executive becomes an entrepreneur in his thinking. No matter how large the corporation may be, an executive is encouraged to use entrepreneurial thinking within his own opportunity space. It is important both for the individual and for the corporation that such an opportunity be given to entrepreneurial skills otherwise they will atrophy through disuse. Once the opportunity habit of mind is established through being given some practice, it can be applied as a positive ingredient in other situations. The purpose of Opex is 'to sanction initiative'.

Channel for upwards communication

In most organizations the channels for communication are directed downwards. A lot of lip service is often paid to upward communication. Many senior executives claim that they are prepared to listen to workers at lower levels but in practice their willingness is not matched by their availability. In any case, most junior executives are reluctant to communicate upwards unless they feel they have something very important to say. The opportunity search exercise provides a formal channel of upward communication which every executive is *asked* to use whether or not he has anything momentous to say. I once knew a student who said that he enjoyed taking examinations because that was the only occasion on which he could be certain that someone was going to read with great attention what he had written. A formal upward communication channel is very different from an informal one. In the opportunity search exercise every executive taking part knows that his Opportunity Audit is going to be read by someone senior.

Problems and opportunities

No one likes to admit that he has problems. An executive is reluctant to talk about his problems because it seems to imply that he cannot cope with the situation. He always feels that the listener's attitude is one of, 'why don't you get on and solve it?' There is a huge difference between an executive 'who is always having problems' and an executive 'who is always seeing opportunities'. Quite often a problem may be described and treated as an opportunity without playing semantic tricks. An executive who is reluctant to admit problems may be eager to list opportunities in the opportunity search exercise.

Surveillance

Without a positive attitude Opex may be seen as a form of Big Brother surveillance. The exercise could be seen as a means whereby senior management asked executives to report on their own capabilities. As such the exercise would be pointless because senior management should be able to assess an executive through his performance as an executive rather than as an opportunity-spotter. It is not essential that all executives should have a talent for spotting opportunities. But it is important that all executives be given an opportunity, through Opex, to signal the opportunities they can see. Throughout the exercise the emphasis must be on its purpose of sanctioning initiative.

Value

We can summarize the value of the opportunity search exercise as follows:

1. Executives are given a chance to stand back from daily chores in order to focus upon opportunities.
2. The exercise increases an executive's perception of his opportunity space and can enhance job interest.
3. A formal upward communication channel is provided.
4. The exercise encourages initiative by asking for it.

'Like the four legs of a table the four elements of the opportunity search exercise work together to give a stable and practical structure.'

Elements of the opportunity search exercise

It is assumed that everyone taking part in an Opex procedure will be supplied with a copy of this handbook. The common background saves a lot of misunderstanding and cross-purpose activity.

The four Opex elements are outlined here. Each of them will be described in full detail in subsequent sections of this handbook.

Opportunity Audit

The Opportunity Audit is similar to a financial audit. It is a survey, a review, a looking around and a stock-taking. Once a year each executive is asked to examine his own opportunity space and to see what opportunities he can find in it. He is asked to prepare a formal report that covers the following matters: description of how he sees his opportunity space; a list of four 'idea-sensitive areas' which are areas in which opportunities can be developed; a specific opportunity objective on which he would like to work, including benefits, plan of action and help needed; opportunities outside his own opportunity space – in other divisions or departments or on a corporate level.

The Opportunity Audit is then followed up at intervals of four months by reports which detail the progress that has been made towards the chosen opportunity objective.

Opportunity Manager

The Opportunity Manager is the central organizer of the opportunity search exercise. It is his responsibility to set up, coordinate and orchestrate the whole structure. His role is that of an organizer and liaison officer. He does not try to determine the direction of opportunity search but he sets up the framework within which executives can choose their own directions. He sets the Opportunity Audit in motion and collects the results. He acts as general communication channel, facilitator and ombudsman in the whole opportunity area. He creates communication channels with different departments, senior management, outside consultants and individual executives as required. He does not, however, choose the Opportunity Team nor chair its discussions.

Opportunity Team

The Opportunity Team is a permanent body though the membership may rotate. This team has ultimate responsibility for opportunity search, development and coordination within the corporation. The team is independent of such division as R & D or Strategic Planning though it may work closely with them from time to time. The Opportunity Team receives all the opportunity

Audits as input. It may also generate its own input from the outside world or from within the corporation. The Opportunity Team surveys, consolidates and evaluates the opportunity objectives put forward in the audits. The Opportunity Team allocates opportunity development resources from a specific budget or may recommend an opportunity to R & D, Marketing or any other department. The Opportunity Team may also provide information, liaison or organizational help as requested by an individual executive in his opportunity audit.

Where more than local help is required the Opportunity Team is responsible for putting together an Opportunity Task Force to tackle an opportunity.

Opportunity Task Force

This is no different from any other task force. It is project-oriented and comes into effect to tackle a specified opportunity. An Opportunity Task Force is set up by the Opportunity Team whenever it seems that a specific opportunity, generated by the audit, cannot be handled by the executive concerned even with additional help. The task force should, however, include the executive who has suggested the opportunity. The task force may consist of only one person or of a group of people from different departments. It may include outside consultants or the specific task may be delegated to an outside consultancy in the first place; for example, market research or a feasibility study. The task force may have an information-gathering role, a liaison or negotiating role, a project development role or a focused management role. For example, an Opportunity Task Force may have responsibility for a project that is being worked upon in the R & D division.

Purpose

The purpose of these four elements is to provide two things: focused attention on opportunities and channels of action. For those familiar with matrix management the elements have a staff rather than a line function. The Opportunity Team is, however, more than an advisory body. It must be able to take some action on its own. In a way it is the Opportunity Conscience of the organization.

'The purpose of formality is to avoid drift, distraction and confusion. The purpose of focus is to allow us to see things which are obvious once we are looking at them.'

The Opportunity Audit

The Opportunity Audit is a formal focusing procedure. The audit requires each executive to spend some time looking directly for opportunities instead of being distracted by more urgent problems. The search may prove unsuccessful but the effort is worthwhile. When we pay a fire insurance premium we do not hope to get our money back through having a fire. Similarly some time spent looking for opportunities is an insurance that if one is around it will be spotted. In addition the focusing exercise itself makes an executive more acutely aware of the opportunity space and what goes on within it.

Focus

An ordinary question is a language device for focusing our attention and demanding an answer. The Opportunity Audit takes place at a definite time. There are definite headings to be filled in. An output is demanded. All this may seem contrary to the spirit of free-ranging opportunity exploration by means of whim and inspiration. The truth, however, is that creativity does not suffer from being focused. The focusing structure merely creates the envelope which can then be filled by free-ranging thought. In the Opportunity Audit it is quite acceptable to say: 'I am looking in that direction because it seems important but at the moment I cannot see any opportunity there.' The purpose of the audit is to focus an executive's attention, not to force him to give answers.

Start of the exercise

At the start of the Opportunity Audit an executive receives two letters, this handbook and some prepared forms. One letter is from the chief executive officer inviting the executive to take part in the opportunity search exercise and indicating the value which the corporation puts on opportunity development. The second letter is from the Opportunity Manager who explains the mechanics of the exercise and the purpose. The Opportunity Manager will indicate that he is available for further discussion if an executive wishes to find out more about the exercise. The Opportunity Manager will indicate in his letter that the completed audit forms will be examined by the Opportunity Team. The completed forms as such will not be circulated to other executives although points extracted from them may be. In a small organization the Opportunity Manager may have a chance to discuss the audit individually, or in a group, with the executives beforehand. As mentioned above, it is important that the Opportunity Manager stresses the 'opportunity' nature of the audit: an opportunity for an executive to communicate upwards and to demonstrate his ability.

A copy of this handbook accompanies the invitation to take part in Opex. The Opportunity Manager can indicate in his letter that the most relevant parts of the book are Parts II and III.

Pre-printed audit forms are provided. The purpose of these forms is to focus attention and ensure brevity of reply. In exceptional circumstances the forms may be supplemented by appendices which develop particular points in more depth.

The letter from the Opportunity Manager will indicate the date by which the completed forms have to be returned to *him*.

Timing of the exercise

The Opportunity Audit takes place once a year. This does not exclude other communications with the Opportunity Manager in between audits. Nor does it exclude an executive making opportunity notes throughout the year and then inserting them in the audit.

In the northern hemisphere the audit forms would be delivered on the first Monday in June and would be returned by the first Monday in July. In the southern hemisphere the audit forms would be delivered on the first Monday in November and would be collected by the first Monday in December. This timing may be altered. The intention is that the forms be completed *before* the summer holiday season. This means that an executive will have been looking at opportunities just before the holiday break and his mind will continue to free-wheel in this area during his holiday. The fact that the forms are to be returned before the break also ensures that they get completed.

As indicated, about one month is allowed for completion of the forms. In fact about three hours' thinking time and two hours' consolidation time are all that is required.

All forms are to be returned to the Opportunity Manager as indicated in his initial letter. Special allowances and alterations in the timing are to be arranged with him directly.

Executives involved in the exercise

The decision as to who is to be invited to take part in Opex is to be made by the Opportunity Manager in consultation with senior management and division heads. Ideally *all executives* should be involved. There may, however, be a decision to restrict it to executives above a certain level or to certain high-fliers.

The Opportunity Manager collects the completed audit forms and passes them on to the Opportunity Team for examination. No more than 200 such forms should be given to an Opportunity Team. If more executives are to be involved then other Opportunity Teams should be set up on a divisional level in order to examine the audits. Such divisional Opportunity Teams would then pass on the most interesting ten per cent of the audit forms to the central Opportunity Team.

Under no circumstances should the completed audit forms be passed directly up the management hierarchy. In other words an executive's completed form should *never* be passed to his immediate superior. The forms should go to the Opportunity Manager and from him to the Opportunity Team. The names of current members of the Opportunity Team should be indicated to the executives completing the forms.

The output required in the exercise

On the Opportunity Audit forms space is allotted to each of the headings given below. Each one of these headings will be explained in full detail in a subsequent section in this part of the book.

Opportunity space. An executive is asked to say how he sees his own opportunity space. What changes is he allowed to make? What opportunites is he allowed to pursue? What decisions is he allowed to make? The simplest definition of opportunity space is to say that if an opportunity falls within an executive's opportunity space then he can act upon it. An executive may complain that he has very little opportunity space.

General opportunities. These may be no more than the identification of 'idea-sensitive areas' (an area where an idea can have a large pay-off). Within such areas an opportunity may be defined more exactly. Some opportunities may be developed in detail. It must be stressed that an opportunity must be more than just an intention to fulfil an executive task; for example the 'opportunity' of reaching the sales target is not an opportunity at all. By definition opportunity implies change or initiative. Problem-solving may be included here since in some cases an opportunity is defined as a problem; for example, an opportunity to improve the role of the supervisor. At least *three* separate entries are required in this section.

Specific opportunity objective. This may be one of the general opportunities or an additional one. The opportunity objective is something which the executive intends to tackle. The benefits arising from the opportunity should be spelled out. The course of action should be indicated and an opportunity map (see Part III for 'if-box' maps) provided. In this section the executive should indicate the type of help that he requires in order to reach the opportunity objective.

Opportunities elsewhere. This section allows an executive to indicate opportunities that fall *outside* his own opportunity space but which he can see. This section is not obligatory – it merely provides a chance for an executive to put forward his ideas. An executive should guard against over-filling this section at the expense of the section on opportunities within his own opportunity space. It is all too easy to spot other people's opportunities but not one's own. These other opportunities may lie in adjoining departments or in other divisions. They may also be corporate opportunities. In this respect this section serves as a sort of suggestion channel.

The thinking required in the exercise

In order to fill in the Opportunity Audit form the executive may have to do some thinking. The form only gives the output or end-product of that thinking. But what sort of thinking does the executive have to do in order to generate opportunities? The type of thinking required is described in detail in Part III. A large number of starting points are given together with a variety of thinking techniques such as including 'tailoring' provocation, the rapid switching from the general to the particular and back again, problem-solving approaches and the like.

Figure 8 indicates the thinking process that goes on before a selection of opportunities is put down in the Opportunity Audit.

Executives are urged to apply some of the deliberate thinking processes described in Part III rather than putting down the first thing that comes into their heads in order to complete the form. The quality of a thought-through opportunity is easily distinguishable from pious waffle which might seem to satisfy the requirements of the exercise.

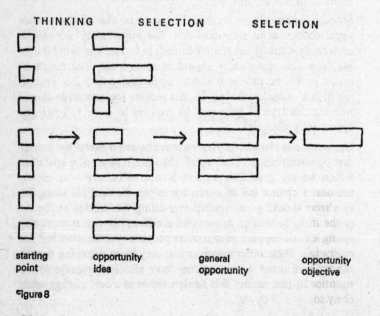

Figure 8

The main purpose of the exercise is not to fill in the forms but to encourage deliberate attention to opportunities and the development of the type of thinking needed to uncover opportunities. The Opportunity Audit is only a tangible end-product of that thinking. It is the applied thinking that matters. In this respect executives should not be complacent in their belief that their normal analytical skills will suffice to spot any opportunity that is around. There should be some effort to go beyond what seems safe and adequate.

Where possible the description of the thinking methods in Part III can be supplemented by specific seminars designed to train executives in this type of 'opportunity thinking'. I have given several such seminars and there is no doubt that the habits can be learned and applied.

'Opportunity space is defined by all the worthwhile things we have it in our power to do – if only we could think of them.'

Opportunity space

Lately, in my seminars, I have taken to picking up a raw egg and offering to throw it to any executive who is prepared to catch it. Someone always volunteers and so far there have been no nasty accidents. My biggest worry was when someone right at the back of the group offered to catch it. I did not doubt his catching ability, but rather my ability to throw it directly to him. In the event he caught it beautifully and later revealed that he was an excellent cricketer. The moral of the egg-throwing operation is that it is not much use tossing out ideas if no one is willing or able to catch them. Similarly, it is not much use dreaming up opportunities if no one is willing or able to do anything about them. The 'receivability' of an idea, or an opportunity, matters as much as the idea itself. That is why the Opportunity Audit starts by asking executives to define their opportunity space. If an opportunity falls within a person's opportunity space then that person can act on the opportunity. So if an executive starts by paying attention to his ability to 'receive' an opportunity he is more likely to think of opportunities upon which he can act.

There is not much point in generating wonderful opportunities and then regretting that one cannot act upon them. The danger is lessened by this prior attention to opportunity space.

Definition of opportunity space

'If an opportunity is within our opportunity space then we can act upon it.' That is the simplest and best definition – but it is not much use for describing our opportunity spaces. The opportunity space includes all the changes, decisions and choices that we can make. It includes the assets we are using and the actions we can take:

'I can makes changes in these areas.'
'These are the decisions I can make.'
'These choices are up to me.'
'I can take action of this sort.'
'I have the use of these assets.'

Opportunity space defines both our freedom of action and also the assets we have (for a distinction between intrinsic, operating and situation assets see Part III). Such assets may include time, know-how and contacts.

Even within a large tightly knit organization where every executive's role is laid down there still exists an individual's opportunity space. Even if the only freedom an executive has is to express himself in a telephone call, a report or a memorandum, that is part of his opportunity space. Similarly his reaction to those around him is part of his opportunity space.

For an example we can have a look at the opportunity space of a man who owns a hot dog stall. He has a certain amount of freedom of choice as to where he places his stall. He must take account of police regulations and competitors but within those constraints he is free. He will need a licence to operate and he will have to conform to standards of hygiene and food care but he is free to choose his menu, sauces and mode of cooking (within limits). He is free to develop his personality, decoration and promotions. Bearing in mind the price at which he purchases his raw materials, he is free to set his own price – unless there is a hot dog price cartel. He is free to take a day off or operate at whatever hours he likes.

He is free to employ assistants provided he conforms to the minimum wage and other employment requirements. So we see that there are many constraints and regulations by which he must abide but that his opportunity space is quite extensive.

For a different example we can look at the opportunity space of a ward sister in a large hospital. Here there is much less independence because there are many hospital regulations, standards and traditions to be maintained. The ward sister has some choice in rostering and organizing her nurses. She sets the standard in the ward and gives encouragement or criticism. She has a lot of freedom in her relationship both with her staff and with the patients. She can decide how to deal with visitors within visiting hours and what policy to adopt with inquiries. She can make recommendations to the medical staff and in many cases make decisions. She has a strong influence on how long a patient stays in hospital. In practice there is a marked difference between wards run by different ward sisters. That must arise from their activities within their opportunity spaces even though all sisters work within the same overall regulations.

Examination of opportunity space

In carrying out an examination of his own opportunity space an executive should pay attention to the areas listed below.

Areas of activity: List the different areas of activity and consider the available freedom of action, choice and decision within each of them. Even when there are overall regulations or targets to be reached, consider what flexibility there is within these constraints. Do not take it for granted that the existence of a regulation destroys all freedom of action. After all most tables have four legs but furniture designers exhibit a high degree of choice in making them.

Types of operation: Go through the different types of activity or operation that occur within the job description. How much opportunity space is there in the carrying out of these operations? Are the operations defined by the end-product or by the actual method of getting there? Does one take the stereotyped approach for granted? Has the rigidity of an approach ever been challenged? If so has it been challenged in an abstract way or in comparison with a suggested improvement? There are many ways of driving a car even if the destination and the route are the same.

Reaction patterns: Examine the reactions that are expected in different situations. If someone swears at you it is within your opportunity space to swear back, shrug or smile. Attaching importance or assessing priorities usually lies within an individual's opportunity space. So does the sequence within which things are done (provided they all get done in the end.)

Example of opportunity space

A person whose work involves giving seminars to executives might describe his opportunity space as follows:

'Opportunity to alter the presentation and to try out new methods. Opportunity to collect new examples and stories for future use as illustration. Opportunity to study the thinking of those attending the seminar. Opportunity to carry out simple experiments of a psychological nature. Opportunity to test the reaction to new concepts. Opportunity to clarify one's own ideas as they are explained or defended. Opportunity to have one's own ideas changed or improved. Opportunity to make contacts. Opportunity to make friends. Opportunity to arrange further work of a consultancy or in-house nature. Opportunity to learn about different types of industry. Opportunity to learn about the business climate in different industries. Opportunity to put people in touch with one another or to provide contacts. Opportunity to recommend or praise a colleague. Opportunity to find out which type of promotion was most effective in bringing participants to the seminar.'

The above description defines, in broad terms, the opportunity space. Within this space specific opportunities could then be developed in depth and detail.

The same opportunity space could be described in an alternative way:

'I can alter what I say and see the reaction. I can carry out experiments. I can note down new examples and stories. I can listen to disagreements and pick out the valid points. I can approach and talk to different participants. I can ask them questions and listen to what they have to say. I can build up contacts. I can ask the participants how they came to hear of the seminar. In short I can talk and be listened to or I can ask questions and listen. I have a captive audience who are more or less friendly. I have an audience of experienced and skilled executives.'

In this second description the words 'I can' are equivalent to 'opportunity to' in the first description. Potential and opportunity are closely related.

Description of opportunity space

The degree of detail used in the description of the opportunity space is important. Generalities should be avoided because, although they do cover what is implied by them, they do not serve to direct attention. The opportunity space provided in the seminar situation could be described as: 'A teaching situation in which the pupils are experienced executives'. Such a description does cover most of the aspects listed above but it does not direct attention to such aspects as the opportunity to find out which communication method was the most effective in bringing people to the seminar. Somewhere between minute detail and an all-embracing generality there is a degree of detail that lists aspects of the situation in such a way that they can become a focus of attention. To say that someone is a friend may logically imply that the person is willing to help you out of trouble but it is more useful to spell out such willingness when describing the person.

In describing his opportunity space an executive may find that he has very little of it. He may wish to take advantage of the Opportunity Audit to signal to senior management that he would like more room for initiative. The description of the space should, however, be as objective as possible and not deliberately slanted so as to make a point of political protest.

Purpose of opportunity space description

The first purpose is to increase an awareness of those areas in which there is freedom of action. From an effort to describe the opportunity space can come a consciousness of opportunities. In some instances the description of the space will almost be a list of opportunities.

The second purpose is to define, in advance, the type of opportunity that is 'receivable' so that when one sets out to develop opportunities these can be treated in such a manner as to make them fall within the opportunity space.

Job description and opportunity space

It may at first seem as though opportunity space is the same as a job description. The distinction between the two is, however, important. Opportunity space describes the space in which changes can be effected. A job description describes the expected role of the executive. A careful look at a job description may lead to some awareness of the opportunity space that exists in the job. A description of a child does not itself indicate the potential for growth or change. To say that an executive is expected to make buying decisions is to describe his job; to say that he has flexibility in negotiating the price, arranging the payment terms, choosing the seller and choosing what is to be bought is to describe his opportunity space. Opportunity space is space for change and initiative.

'If a situation seems likely to be affected by an idea then we may call that situation an idea-sensitive area.'

Idea-sensitive areas and general opportunities

In this section of the Opportunity Audit an executive is asked to put forward general opportunities or idea-sensitive areas. An idea-sensitive area is an area which seems fertile for the development of an opportunity. It is an area in which further thinking may uncover a definite opportunity. It is an opportunity-rich area. The benefits arising from an idea in that area are obvious – all that is required is the idea. A general opportunity is a trend or direction which seems to offer benefits. An idea-sensitive area is an area to look at in order to find an opportunity. A general opportunity is a direction within which a more specific opportunity may be formulated.

Idea-sensitive areas (i.s.a.)

I once did some work with a mining company which was concerned with cutting costs. A lot of time was to be spent studying the mining and production processes. It soon became obvious, however, that these processes had been studied and improved so often that at most only a two per cent change in costs would be possible. On the marketing side, in contrast, it was quite easy to see how a fifteen per cent saving could be made. The marketing arrangements were indeed an idea-sensitive area whereas the production process was not.

In a car there is said to be sensitive steering when the car responds to the lightest touch on the wheel. A sensitive skin is one which burns easily on even slight exposure to sunlight. A sensitive person is one who can detect nuances of mood and who may get upset very easily. In general the word 'sensitive' suggests that the response or reaction is considerable even when the input is slight. So an idea-sensitive area (i.s.a.) is an area where an idea will make a considerable difference. In other words, it is an area where it is worthwhile to try to generate ideas.

The concept of an i.s.a. seems simple enough to understand yet in explaining the concept during my seminars there seems to be some difficulty in distinguishing an i.s.a. from an 'important' area. All idea-sensitive areas are important but not all important areas are sensitive to ideas. It may be suggested for instance that the food or bathroom arrangements are i.s.a.s in the running of a seminar. In fact they are important areas just as is the quality of the presentation but ideas in these areas are not going to make that much difference. A true i.s.a. in this context is the high cost of letting executives know about the seminar. The costs of direct mail and advertising tend to be very high. The result is that those who come to the seminar are paying for this high cost of communicating with those who do not come. A new idea concerning communication would make a big difference to costs and profitability.

It is said that the use of UPC (Universal Product Code) on supermarket items would considerably reduce the cost of labelling and would therefore increase the profit margins several-fold. Each product bears on its label an identifying strip of special bar-code which is then read by a device at the check-out counter. Through a small computer the current price for that item is then passed to the cash register and added into the shopper's total. Changes in prices can be fed directly into the computer without having to re-label all items. There is, however, considerable consumer resistance because shoppers cannot see the price of what they are buying. Apparently labelling of the shelves is not sufficient as items get replaced on the wrong shelves. This customer resistance is obviously an area which is highly sensitive to ideas. As soon as a customer sees, and believes, that UPC is in her interest then the resistance would cease. For example the suggestion that unlabelled items would be cheaper than the ordinarily labelled items beside them on the shelves – so the labelled items would be left behind and would thus indicate the price.

'I feel sure that there is an opportunity here, if only we could see it.'

'This is a fertile area because the potential is so great if only we can get it right.'

'Let us concentrate on this area because an idea here could make a big difference to us.'

Being able to put one's finger on one or more i.s.a.s is useful because it provides that focusing effort which is so essential to opportunity search. Under the general heading of idea-sensitive areas we can identify different types of i.s.a.

High-cost area (h.c.a.): The traditional area that absorbs much of the costs in a process: the bottleneck. The high cost may be in terms of: money; time; people involvement; unreliability; fault density; friction on a personnel basis; boredom; risk; or responsibility. All these are forms of payment parallel to money as such. We can identify h.c.a.s, focus upon them and then search for opportunities of reducing the high cost. For example in many organizations the public relations area is an h.c.a. in terms of the time and involvement of a very senior executive. In a survey in the USA the chief executives reckoned they spent as much as forty per cent of their time on public relations exercises.

Specific-problem area (s.p.a.): An identified problem that requires a solution.

Further-development area (f.d.a.): Here the opportunity lies in the further development of an on-going process. This covers improvement of any sort (in style, design, production costs, reliability and price). An f.d.a. may include extending a line of products or capitalizing on an asset that is at present under-utilized. The distribution channels for a particular publication would constitute an idea-sensitive area of this type: 'What ideas can we generate for further development of the distribution of this publication?'

Emotional-target area (e.t.a.): We might as well acknowledge that much opportunity search is on an emotional basis when we allow this to include hunch and whim. There may be no overt logical reason for focusing on an area but an executive may have an emotional feeling that it is important. A bank manager may feel that his personal contact with customers is an area worthy of attention. He may acknowledge that this is purely an emotional feeling. The point is that an emotionally driven opportunity search is worth pursuing because the motivation is so much higher.

For the purpose of the Opportunity Audit an idea-sensitive area should be sharply defined. Unless the definition is sharp there is no point in claiming it as an i.s.a. The benefits arising from a 'successful' idea in this area should also be clearly described. In addition the executive should indicate why he thinks the area could respond to an idea.

General opportunities

The type of thinking required to generate opportunities will be described in Part III of this book. Some thinking of that sort will be required before this part of the Opportunity Audit can be completed.

In this part of the Audit an executive is required to put forward *a minimum of three suggestions.* The suggestions may take the form of i.s.a.s or general opportunities. There may be any mix of these.

Philosophically the distinction between an i.s.a. and a general opportunity would be hard to sustain. In practice, however, the distinction is useful. An executive may be able to focus upon an area where the benefits arising from an idea would be considerable. He has set out to look for an i.s.a. Another executive may prefer to think in terms of general opportunities: by examining assets, circumstances, traditional ideas and attitudes. For example an executive may decide to focus on the actual seating in a cinema. This could not be said to be an i.s.a. Nevertheless as he thinks about the seating the executive may develop ideas regarding pockets for sale literature, as in airlines, or movable seats that can be grouped for parties or private room viewing. Each of these ideas could be put forward as a 'general opportunity'. In an hotel the marketing of the restaurant would certainly be an i.s.a. Without the right idea the restaurant could be a cost burden on the hotel. With the right idea the restaurant could be a significant contributor to profits. But a general opportunity in the same area might arise from considering the traveller as fitting into a number of different categories: the business traveller who wants an overnight bed; the conference attender; the business traveller who wants a temporary office; the holiday traveller who wants a base; the holiday traveller who wants a temporary home; the holiday traveller who wants to obtain much of his pleasure without leaving the hotel. Perhaps there might emerge a general opportunity of offering unserviced rooms for those who want them or for including hotel-use vouchers for entertainment and meals in the hotel restaurant.

With an i.s.a. we identify a worthwhile area. With a general opportunity we start thinking about an area and see if this thinking leads to a general opportunity.

Separate ideas

The minimum of three suggestions required in this part of the Opportunity Audit should include ideas that are as separate as possible. But how separate is separate? It is probably enough if the executive thinks of them as being distinct ideas. The same idea expressed in three different ways does not qualify.

The part set aside for listing these three ideas (general opportunities or i.s.a.s) can be supplied by appendices which give further information. Such appendices could also include additional ideas. The appendices, if any, should be as succinct as the main part of the Audit. Further information can always be requested. But the ideas should not be so general that they include everything and indicate nothing.

Opportunity space

Both the idea-sensitive areas and the general opportunities put forward in this part of the Opportunity Audit must fall *within the executive's own opportunity space*. There is provision later in the Audit form for opportunities that fall outside his space.

'If the purpose of the Opportunity Audit is to sanction initiative, that initiative must be put forward somewhere in a form concrete enough to be sanctioned.'

The specific opportunity objective

It is somewhat easier to spot opportunities for other people than to spot those that you are going to have to do something about. But the Opportunity Audit is itself an opportunity for an executive to put forward something which he regards as an opportunity and about which he wishes to do something. This is his initiative and the Audit provides a formal channel through which he can obtain sanction for this initiative.

The specific opportunity objective may be one which arises during the 'opportunity thinking' that an executive goes through for the purposes of the opportunity search exercise. It may also be an opportunity which he has seen for a long time and which he now puts forward in this part of the Audit.

The specific opportunity needs to be set up as a task or an objective. It is no longer enough to write in general terms leaving out the details of implementation. The following headings should be covered:

Summary of the opportunity

A succinct description of the opportunity. This must be brief but must not be so general that it says nothing. About 100 words should be sufficient. As few as possible of these words should be taken up with setting the scene, explaining the background or general explanation. That can come into the benefits section. There should be enough in this summary to excite interest.

Benefits

This is the most important section. The benefits must be spelled out in some detail. The executive must give his reasons why he thinks the benefits will follow the action that he proposes. If the benefits take the form of savings the executive should show some knowledge of the extent of the savings; after all, the opportunity is within his own opportunity space. It is in order for an executive to state that he wishes to explore the possible benefits. In that case he must state why he thinks this would be worthwhile. In considering the benefits the following points – which are repeated in Part III – should be covered.

Where from? Where are the benefits ultimately coming from? Is the consumer paying indirectly, or the government (as in tax avoidance), or is a saving being made in production costs?

How? How are the benefits actually going to be obtained? What is the mechanism? Is it direct or indirect? The benefits of improved working conditions are obtained in one way and the benefits of a higher sales commission in another.

Scale? What is the scale of the benefits? Quite often the benefits from an apparent opportunity are real enough but so small that the effort is not worthwhile.

Depending on what? Are the benefits contingent on something happening? We can set out to educate supermarket shoppers about the benefits of UPC but the benefits will not be there unless the education process works. Sometimes benefits are contingent upon an expected change – such as in raw material prices or government legislation. Such contingency must be spelled out.

Dangers? What could happen to cut off the benefits? A competitor may already have a better product nearing launching. The drug licensing authorities may condemn a whole class of products, as happened with cyclamates. There might be a sudden price change, as happens quite often with sugar or coffee.

Fall short? In what way might the actual benefits fall short of the expected benefits? The obvious instance is where test market enthusiasm is not matched by consumer preference. Another instance is where a scaled-down prototype has a lesser performance when scaled up to the real thing. The novelty effect of changes in working conditions can also wear off.

Problems? What problems are likely to be encountered when trying to enjoy the benefits? Union disagreement or lack of co-operation is one example. A price-cutting war is another. Technical production problems and delays also come in here.

Assumptions? What assumptions are being made? There is no harm in working on assumptions – business would be impossible otherwise. It is as well, however, to spell out the assumptions that underlie the expectation of benefit from taking up the opportunity. For example, there might be an assumption about the continuing expansion of the charter travel market or a continuing increase in the price of oil.

An opportunity is defined by the expected benefits rather than the means for putting it into effect. That is why the benefits have to be considered first. Such consideration must be honest or objective if it is to be credible. Glossing over a weak point only weakens the opportunity. Ignorance is acceptable provided it is defined as a need for further information.

Description of the opportunity

The nature of the specific opportunity can be described here. An opportunity map or 'if-box' map should be used if possible. This is a technique for visualizing an opportunity and it is described in Part III. The if-box map separates the areas of uncertainty – risk, problems to be solved, people to be persuaded – from the action channels which are there to be used as soon as a decision has been made to use them. The person reading the description in the Opportunity Audit should have the unambiguous impression that the executive putting forward the opportunity has a clear idea of what he is about.

Plan of action

This includes the stages of achievement or the sub-objectives. It may be that the first opportunity objective is an exploration, testing, or feasibility study. This then becomes the specific opportunity objective. The final objective should also be mentioned but the focus should be on the objective that is to be reached. As mentioned before, an opportunity 'is a course of action that is possible and obviously worth pursuing'. If at the moment all that is obviously worth pursuing is the feasibility study, that is the true opportunity. What turns up in the feasibility study may make the next stage 'obviously worth pursuing' but that cannot be ascertained at the moment.

The time stages and overall planning of the whole opportunity can be presented but the detailed presentation need only cover the part up to the specific opportunity objective.

The executive does not have to wait until next year's Opportunity Audit in order to set forth the next stage of objective. That can be done as soon as the first one has been achieved. This will be done through communication and liaison with the Opportunity Team. The Audit is only an initiating process. Once an opportunity is under way its own timetable is not tied in any way to the timing of the Audit.

An opportunity may start within an executive's opportunity space but may then extend outside as the opportunity grows. By definition, an executive should put forth in this section a specific opportunity that does fall within his own opportunity space – at least up to the point of definite benefit. He must be able to see the opportunity through. The opportunity may then be extended or copied elsewhere. There is provision in the audit form for putting forward opportunities that do not lie within one's own opportunity space.

Resources

The executive should specify the resources that will be needed to carry through the opportunity. Full details need not be given. Some indication is, however, required of the amount of time, money, and people that will be involved. The executive should indicate what can be achieved from within his own resources or budget and what may have to be supplemented from outside – this also comes into the 'help' section. Basically, under this heading the executive demonstrates why he considers the opportunity to fall within his own opportunity space.

Help

This is the formal opportunity for the executive to ask for help in pursuing his initiative. The help requested may take the form of an allocation of time or a relief from some other duties. It may involve an assistant or secondment to a project team. The help may take the form of contracts or information or other liaison services. The help needed may be of a technical or statistical nature. The help may consist of the advice or expertise of an outside consultant. There may be a request for help in testing an idea. Help may be needed from the marketing department or from R & D. Help in the form of a budgetary allocation may be asked for.

It is very important to distinguish between help and passing over the opportunity to someone else. As mentioned, the specific opportunity objective must fall within the executive's own opportunities space – it cannot be a matter of thinking up an idea and then asking the marketing people to take it over.

The final decision as to whether the opportunity really does lie with the executive's opportunity space will lie with the Opportunity Team who scrutinize the output of the Audit.

Sticking-points

A sticking-point is not necessarily a problem. It is a point that is recognized as likely to offer uncertainty, delay, difficulty, friction or a need for a new direction. Sometimes a sticking-point is only a sticky-point. You may know for example that you will have to get agreement from a particular executive before you can go ahead. You know that in the end you will get this agreement. You also know that there will be a lot of hassle before then. A sticking-point holds things up. There need be no uncertainty, risk or problem to be solved. Alternatively there may be all of these. An awareness of the major, foreseeable, sticking-points is what is required for the Audit at this point. Such an awareness gives credibility to the opportunity objective and also invites help.

Time course

An opportunity that is always about to be taken, sometime, is of less use than one which has a specified time for implementation. An indication of the time course needs to be given with the specific opportunity objective. This time course can be tied into the progress report which is due four months after the Opportunity Audit.

'Progress is assessed by looking forward to see how much of the task is yet to be done rather than by looking backwards to see what has already been achieved.'

Progress reports

Three types of opportunity may emerge from the Opportunity Audit.

Self-starter: In this type of opportunity the executive can begin at once to take action. The matter falls within his opportunity space and he is able to get on with it without needing permission or help. A progress report at four-monthly intervals, requested by the Opportunity Manager, records what has been achieved and what remains to be done.

Self-starter plus help: In this type of opportunity the executive has requested help from the Opportunity Team. This request may be accepted or rejected. If it is accepted, the executive proceeds with the opportunity and turns in a progress report four months after the Opportunity Audit (not after the request has been accepted). If the request for help is turned down the executive may then continue to communicate with the Opportunity Manager and the Opportunity Team with regard to a modification of the original idea or a new opportunity.

Task force: In this section an Opportunity Task Force will have been set up by the Opportunity Team to tackle a particular opportunity. This task force should also report at four-monthly intervals.

Four-monthly intervals

The progress reports are always at four-monthly intervals from the end of the Opportunity Audit – that is, when the Audit forms are collected. Initially this four months will be eaten into by the deliberations of the Opportunity Team. For each specific opportunity objective the reports continue at four-monthly intervals even after another Opportunity Audit has taken place. The opportunity objectives acquire a life of their own independent of the Audit.

The reports are requested by the Opportunity Manager who keeps a file on all the specific opportunity objectives that are being pursued. It is his responsibility to obtain the reports which are then passed on to the Opportunity Team.

Content of the progress report

The progress report should focus on how much of the task there is yet to accomplish before the specific opportunity objective is reached. If this has already been reached the report may put forward a new specific opportunity objective, i.e. the next stage in the overall opportunity development.

The report should list what has been done but it must be remembered that a great deal of work does not by itself mean that the objective is near achievement. Inefficiency or unforeseen circumstances may leave the objective as far off as before. One is not as interested in how much a high-jumper has practised as in how high he jumps on the day. Effort merits reward but is not the same as achievement.

The progress report should mention the sticking-points that have emerged and the ones that seem very likely to emerge. Solutions to problems should not be given in detail unless the solutions are thought to carry lessons that are of general use.

The progress report should list any changes in the thinking that have occurred. There may have been changes in the original plan of action – forced by circumstances or the degree of help available. There might be new thinking about the potential benefits arising from the opportunity (either increase or decrease). There might be changes in the concept itself.

If a specific opportunity objective has had to be abandoned the reasons for this should be indicated as clearly as possible. Often the only thing of value that can be obtained from a failure is information – so this should be comprehensive.

'Most of us have many more ideas than we can act upon.'

Opportunities in other areas

In this handbook I have tried to emphasize opportunities which an executive is able to act upon himself – opportunities that fall within his own opportunity space. Indeed, this is the reason for defining opportunity space in the first place. It is only too easy to think of opportunities in an abstract fashion: 'Wouldn't it be a good idea to ...' and 'Wouldn't it be a good idea for someone to ...' On being asked to look for opportunities the temptation is to suggest this type of opportunity since there is the fun of having the idea without the responsibility to do anything about it.

If, however, an executive has already defined his opportunity space and then picked out both general opportunities and a specific opportunity objective there is no reason why he should not put forward opportunity suggestions that fall outside his opportunity space. The suggestions can be put forward under this heading in the Opportunity Audit.

Other departments

A salesman who is involved in selling mini-computers to the small-scale business user may put forward various opportunity suggestions: financial arrangement for the buyer; a leasing system; purchase of the buyer's existing equipment and sale of it to a second-hand dealer; joint purchase schemes for the very small user; setting up a bureau; offering insurance; contracting out service attention. All these ideas affect his own working but do not fall within his own opportunity space since he would not himself see them through.

An executive in a marketing department may see an opportunity for synergistic distribution with a non-competitive product that sells in small quantities to the same outlets. The suggestion properly fits in the transport and distribution department.

A personnel manager may see many opportunities in different departments – for changing working conditions or switching jobs. It is within his opportunity space to recommend such changes but not within his power to carry them out.

A designer may suggest that instead of producing a wide range of tuned mobile radios it would make better sense to produce basic untuned units and then to add the tuning according to the order. This would mean much less capital tied up in stock and much less warehousing. It is within his opportunity space to make the suggestion but unless it is a design project which he has been assigned it is not within his opportunity space to put it into effect.

Corporate opportunities

As suggested earlier, this part of the Opportunity Audit acts as a formalized suggestion channel. It can happen that an apparently trivial idea in the mind of an executive can trigger off a large opportunity for the corporation. It may be something that the executive has read about, or overheard or come into contact with on his travels. If each executive is acting as part of the sensing system of a corporation its ability to sense what is happening outside is going to be that much greater.

A friend of mind in Sydney happened to read in a newspaper

that two partners were looking for an investor to share in their construction of a pleasure steamer for the Lane Cove park. The idea was casually mentioned to a businessman who looked into the matter, invested in it and now is part of a very successful venture.

The executive need do no more than hint at or suggest the opportunity. He is unlikely to be in a position to assess the benefits, the cost or even the feasibility. The idea is put forward as a trigger or stimulus.

Once such a formal channel exists executives might make more effort to think about corporate opportunities. Without such a channel communication is so complicated that most people do not bother unless they are convinced that they have a tremendous idea.

'The role of the Opportunity Manager is to manage the opportunity search exercise and generally to coordinate opportunity development within a corporation.'

The Opportunity Manager

The Opportunity Manager is the organizer, manager and liaison officer for the whole opportunity search exercise. This extends from setting up the Opportunity Audit to running the Opportunity Team and coordinating opportunity development through task forces and individual effort.

The Opportunity Manager does not have to be a creative person himself. In fact it may be an advantage if he is not for he will not then feel competitive. But he does have to be able to understand an idea and to communicate it effectively. He needs to be enthusiastic and energetic. He should have enough status to operate at all levels in the corporation including the highest. This authority should be achieved by means of his personality rather than his seniority. He should get on well with people, not be timid about bothering and badgering them, and be able to get things done. To some extent these are the characteristics of an 'internal' salesman rather than a technical man. Energy and the ability to get on with people are the prime considerations. I have seen people communicate effectively an idea which they did not understand at all. Some of the tasks of the Opportunity Manager are listed below.

1. *To organize the mechanics of the opportunity search exercise:* The Opportunity Manager sees that the Opportunity Audit forms and a copy of the handbook get to the right people at the right time. He is responsible for the initial briefing or a letter explaining the purpose and nature of the exercise. He is responsible for setting the date and the completed Audit forms should be returned to him. He is responsible for the progress reports and for organizing the Opportunity Team. He sees to it that the Opportunity Team examine the completed Audit forms and that the results of this examination are fed back to the executives concerned. He is responsible for any other administrative matters concerned with Opex.

2. *To act in a general liaison capacity with regard to opportunities:* The Opportunity Manager may have to put people in touch with each other, to find things out, to convey information and to open doors. All these functions are part of a general liaison role. It must be recognized that in the area of opportunities the Opportunity Manager provides an automatic communication channel. He may even be the only person in the corporation whose specific function includes that of internal communication in all directions.

3. *To provide a communication by-pass:* In an earlier section we saw how an idea could easily be killed if it had to pass upwards through each of the stages of the normal management hierarchy. It is only necessary for one level of management to be unenthusiastic for the idea to die. Research has shown that most successful innovation occurs when a senior manager has taken a direct interest in the idea and its development. Such interest fosters the idea and tides it over bleak patches. The Opportunity Manager acts as a communication by-pass to take an idea from its point of origin to a more senior level without the idea having to follow communication channels. He must be sure that the idea really does lie in the area of opportunity and that he is not just used as a more convenient communication channel for other matters.

4. *To give help and advice:* An executive may need help in filling out his Opportunity Audit form or in deciding how to proceed with his specific opportunity objective. The Opportunity Manager provides such help and advice. Even outside the Opportunity Audit the Opportunity Manager is expected to give advice and help in the general area of opportunity. For example, he will often be called upon by irate executives who have had their request for help turned down by the Opportunity Team. He will have to explain the reasons for rejection.

5. *To provide a listening post and to be an ombudsman:* It should generally be known that the Opportunity Manager is willing to listen to ideas and suggestions in the area of opportunity. He provides a formal listening post. In a similar way he can act as an ombudsman in this area by taking up matters and communicating them as required to more senior levels. He should, however, try to avoid getting involved in matters which are not in the opportunity area otherwise he will spend much of his time sorting out other matters.

6. *To provide a 'fixit' service:* When there is a hitch, a hold-up or a hiccup in the development of an opportunity he should endeavour to provide a 'fixit' service to overcome the problem. He may be able to do this himself or he may be able to call in the right person to do it. He is the plumber who is called when something goes wrong.

7. *To set up and run the Opportunity Team:* The Opportunity Team is a central element in Opex. Setting up the team, organizing it and overseeing its smooth running is the duty of the Opportunity Manager. In consultation with the chief executive he may be responsible for selecting the members of the team. The Opportunity Manager does not chair the team or direct its efforts. He acts more as the general secretary of the team – ensuring its effective functioning. Communication to the team and from the team is handled by him. He also arranges the meetings and their agenda.

8. *To organize and coordinate the Opportunity Task Forces:* In a particular case a Task Force may be set up to develop an opportunity. It may not be possible for the Opportunity Manager to be

an effective member of each task force but he is *ex officio* an automatic member. He helps the team with liaison and problem-solving. He also chivvies them for progress reports and acts as a communication channel with the Opportunity Team.

9. *To bring together people to discuss opportunities:* Quite apart from the Opportunity Team and Opportunity Task Forces, the Opportunity Manager can bring together people both to discover opportunities and also to consider them. This is part of his general function in the opportunity area. The groups may come together on an *ad hoc* basis or on a periodic basis. A group may also be brought together with a specific problem-solving brief.

10. *To focus attention upon specific problems:* The Opportunity Manager can single out for attention specific problems or idea-sensitive areas. These problems can then be circulated in a formal manner to executives for their attention. There is a big difference between being able to think about a problem and specifically being asked to think about it – with an expected outcome.

11. *To act as a liaison officer with outside consultants:* Outside consultants may be used at various stages in the opportunity search exercise. Consultants may be used for feasibility studies or for task force management. They may be called in by the Opportunity Team to consider and evaluate the opportunity suggestions put forward in the audit. Consultants may be involved in the task forces, and indeed a task force might consist entirely of outside consultants. Finally, they may provide help to an individual executive when carrying out his specific opportunity objective.

12. *To report on and represent the opportunity function:* At planning and other meetings the Opportunity Manager will represent the opportunity function in the organization. He will not necessarily have a decision role in this area but he will be called upon to supply information and to give an overview of all that is going on in different departments, calling in the appropriate department head if necessary. The Opportunity Manager will also have the duty of compiling an annual report which will give both the outcome of the Opportunity Audit and also a review of all the opportunity activities that have been going on in the organization.

One difficulty that may arise if the Opportunity Manager is effective is the loading on to him of all types of problems that may have little to do with his opportunity function. The philosophical borderline between a problem and an opportunity may be quite narrow. It will be difficult for the Opportunity Manager to accept one problem and then turn down another. He may find himself becoming a general trouble-shooter for the organization. This would not be a bad thing if the organization does not have such a person. If the Opportunity Manager seems to be burdened with genuine work, that work needs doing. In that case he should delegate part of it or recruit an assistant to help him. In a large organization the opportunity role may be shared by a small team, but the temptation to form a large static department should be avoided.

In the beginning, while he is still shaping his role, the Opportunity Manager may take on too much work for fear that not enough will turn upon its own. This is a common fault with any new position. The temptation should be resisted, for by creating work the Opportunity Manager may overload his capacity to deal with the genuine work that is slow to emerge. It will take some time for executives to get used to the idea of an Opportunity Manager as a communication channel. Or to the notion of opportunity search at all!

'The role of the Opportunity Team is to act as the opportunity nerve-centre of an organization.'

The Opportunity Team

The Opportunity Team is a group of executives with the specific function of receiving, evaluating and acting upon opportunity input. As one of its inputs the Opportunity Team receives the Opportunity Audit forms that have been completed by executives. As part of its output the team may sanction individual initiative, allocate help, call in outside consultants or set up specific task forces to develop opportunities. The value of having a definite opportunity team is that the emphasis is directly, and primarily, upon opportunities as such. Any other department has a vested interest in a certain area: the R & D department often has a technological-success orientation; the financial department is concerned with financial control; the planning department is concerned with caution; the new business department is concerned with new activities as such. Opportunities can and do arise in each of these departments but they are secondary to the main purpose. Furthermore, there is no coordination of the opportunities except through the chief executive who has to adjudicate between the claims put forward by each separate department. The Opportunity Team provides a body with the specific task of looking for and looking at opportunities across the organization.

The mechanics of the Opportunity Team

There are seven members in all. The Opportunity Manager is automatically a member and so is the chief executive officer. In addition there are five other members. At least two of these should be at top executive level, otherwise the Opportunity Team will be regarded as a minor body with only research status. If possible, the head of the marketing department should be one of these two senior executives. The Opportunity Team should not, however, simply be a meeting of the heads of all different departments because they would then defend their own departments and the opportunity focus would be totally lost. The members of the team should be chosen for their ability to work hard because the task is an activity one and not just representative. The members should be chosen for their positive and constructive approach and for their ability to get things done. Cost consciousness and financial judgement should be included somewhere on the team or it could be coopted on a consultancy basis. It is important to point out there that the team has a generative function and must be able to open up and develop opportunities. The function of the team is not to act only in judgement: screening out ideas and applying cost judgements. Initiation and support is as much part of the team function as evaluation. That is why quite young executives can be tried out as members of the Opportunity Team.

The members are part of the team in addition to their other

roles in the organization. If the opportunity load is great, one or two of the executives can be released to devote themselves full time to this activity. In this case they would act as assistants to the Opportunity Manager as well as playing their part in the team.

As described in a previous section, the Opportunity Manager is the leg-man or secretary of the team. It is his function to organize its meetings, its inputs and its outputs. He is the leader of the team in an organizing, but not in a decision sense. The chief executive officer is the decision leader of the team.

The members of the team may rotate on a yearly basis provided they do not all change at once. If a member of the team is unable, through lack of interest or pressure of work, to fulfil his function on the team he should be replaced as soon as possible after consultation between the Opportunity Manager and the chief executive officer.

The team may call in other people to help them in their deliberations on an occasional or semi-permanent basis. These other people might include outside consultants. I, myself, would find it useful to sit with the Opportunity Team in an idea-generating capacity rather than being given formal problems to be solved at a later stage. Consultative help from the finance or R & D departments could also be called in.

The frequency of the meetings of the team would vary with the work-load, with the competence of the Opportunity Manager, and with the ability of the team members to work on their own and then come to the meetings to coordinate their thinking. For example, each team member might work separately on a batch of the Opportunity Audit returns. The Opportunity Manager can also consult on an individual basis with team members. A half-day meeting once a month or a full day once every two months would be about right for physical meetings. I must emphasize that most of the teamwork will be done outside these meetings. Membership of the Opportunity Team is not just an honorary title requiring only an occasional attendance at decision meetings – it is a working role.

Input to the Opportunity Team

The Opportunity Team will receive the Opportunity Audit forms. It is the business of the Opportunity Manager to organize this. Batches of such forms will be given to each member of the team except the chief executive officer (unless he so requests it). There should be no attempt to sort out the audit returns so that they go to a team member who has expertise in a particular area. The team members examine the batch of forms they have been given and sort these as they wish. Their comments may either be written or tape-recorded. The Opportunity Manager may wish to contact each team member separately and discuss the audit forms he has received. Finally the team meet and discuss the Opportunity Audit forms.

Quite apart from the opportunity suggestions, the Personnel Director and the chief executive officer may wish to look at the opportunity space definitions since the audit provides an opportunity for an executive to state how he sees his own job. He may for example complain that he has too little opportunity space and hence no room for initiative or decision.

In addition to the major input from the Opportunity Audit the team is at the receiving end of other suggestions that are channelled to it through the Opportunity Manager in his role as 'listening post'. Once he has established credibility as a 'suggestions' channel the Opportunity Manager will be able to feed ideas to the team. He may act on his own initiative with many of these ideas but should then report his activity to the team.

The Opportunity Team may itself commission feasibility studies, consultancy work and opportunity search workshops. These will provide further input.

Since the function of the team is to coordinate and over-view the whole opportunity development in the organization, there will be opportunity reports from different departments, such as R & D. Such departments will retain control of their own activities but the team will need to know what is going on.

Progress reports from individual executives or task forces will provide further input.

Opportunity search activity by individual members of the team may also provide input but it must be pointed out that this is not the prime function of the team. Indeed it could be harmful since if a team member spent too much time developing his own opportunity ideas he would be less effective as a team member for coordinating and evaluating opportunities across the board.

Evaluation

One of the prime tasks of the Opportunity Team must be to evaluate the different opportunity suggestions that come to them either from the audit or from other sources. The thinking involved in evaluation is described fully in Part III and will not be anticipated here. It is suggested that all members of the team familiarize themselves with the section even if they do not wish to examine the opportunity-generating techniques also described in Part III.

Evaluation must always start with an assessment of benefits. If these are not obvious, some attempt must be made, by the team or by the suggester of the opportunity, to make them obvious. If potential benefits cannot be seen it is not worth spending further thinking time on the matter. Caution must be used when the benefits are claimed in general terms such as:

'We are the leaders in the field and must be seen to be in front.'
'It is a prestige project and our general image will benefit.'
'Lots of more profitable things will spin off in the future.'
'We will be buying experience.'
'If we don't do it someone else will get there first.'

Caution is needed because some of these arguments may indeed be valid. It is not always possible at first sight to see what may develop. Many large American corporations that were built up on small innovations are in fact choking off the supply by wanting to see, at once, a full market potential. Nevertheless the phrases listed above are dangerous because they could be used to justify any innovation at all – and clearly that is ridiculous since some must be worthless. A project may be followed for prestige purposes provided it can be shown that in this area it will offer benefits. (Perhaps the project should be news – and attention – worthy.)

Where, through the medium of the audit, the team is asked to sanction an executive's opportunity initiative or to provide some help, the team may take into account whether the opportunity is only of local benefit within his department or whether the results might become generalizable to other departments. In other words, whether his activity will provide a pilot scheme for something of general value.

Where an executive simply outlines an idea-sensitive area (i.s.a.) in his audit return, the team may encourage him to do his own thinking in this area or may set up a group or workshop through the Opportunity Manager to help with the thinking. An executive may be able to point to a crucial area but unable to develop any ideas himself within that area. The team should accept such an area identification as a valid and important input.

The sort of general framework which the team may use in evaluating opportunity suggestions should be condensed to check-list questions such as the following:

Is it worth it for us to do it?
Are we able to do it?
At what cost?
How do we set about doing it?
What is the competitive position?
What are the problems and uncertainties?

Each such question covers many areas – The first question covers the benefits, the potential market, the assets of the company and the other activities which might be excluded if the suggested activity goes ahead.

In all instances of evaluation it must be emphasized – as it is elsewhere in this book – that evaluation is not simply a matter of applying screening criteria to fixed suggestions. It is much more a matter of being clear as to the type of idea that is acceptable and then working on the suggestion to see if it can be developed towards the ideal. The two processes are very different. Many a good idea is rejected because in its raw form it deserves rejection. Thinking time, thinking effort and some thinking skill may be required to convert a feeble idea into a wonderful one – without any change in the principle of the idea. The Opportunity Team should be capable of providing such thinking or buying it in if they cannot. There are few things more sad than an excellent idea that has been rejected at first sight because no one was prepared to think it through to its true value.

Evaluation ends with a decision. Every Opportunity Team

should construct its own decision output categories. The ones suggested below will indicate what is required:

Rejection: Not worth spending more time or effort on the idea.

Held in abeyance: Awaiting further thinking and evaluation effort, perhaps requiring outside help.

Filed for future reference: Added to the opportunity stock for consulting and perhaps re-activating in the future.

To await right moment: An approved opportunity which is readied for action when the circumstances are more favourable or are just right. (This is a dangerous category, for too many ideas may be held up awaiting better trading conditions.)

Low gear action: The opportunity is to be acted upon but in low gear.

High gear action: Allocation of priority and resources. This may be towards a pilot stage or investigatory procedure and not necessarily towards full implementation of the suggestion. It means that whatever the action is, it should proceed with full backing.

Reaction of the Opportunity Team
to opportunity suggestions

For most of the time the team will be reacting to opportunity suggestions that reach it through the audit returns or from other directions. This reaction will take one of several possible forms.

Feedback: Something that is fed back to the suggester of the opportunity. The evaluation decision will have to be fed back. The whole opportunity search programme will collapse at once if there is just silence. Enough emphasis cannot be put on this need for an answer. Rejection decisions will be difficult to handle until the exercise has established a reputation for honesty and objectivity. In the beginning a rejection decision will be interpreted as meaning that the organization is not really interested in suggestions no matter what it says. The opportunity search exercise will be seen as a propaganda exercise. It is therefore the business of the Opportunity Manager to spell out with full objectivity the reasons for rejection. It may be that the cost of change was estimated as being too high; it may be that the idea had already been tried elsewhere and had failed; it may be that the benefits seemed too small. What is vital is that the person offering the opportunity feels that his effort has been appreciated and that the idea has been seriously considered. If the Opportunity Manager can praise some aspect of the idea and yet show why it has been rejected he will have done his job well. A lengthy to and fro argument between the originator and the team over a rejected idea should be avoided. Nevertheless there must be some opportunity for the originator to show why he thinks he has been misinterpreted.

Elaboration: The team asks for further details. The idea seems promising but the team asks for further thinking on the part of the proposer of the opportunity. He may be asked to build upon the idea, to make it more practical, to spell out the benefits in more detail, to comment on the risks or even to incorporate the principle in some different idea. This 'treatment' of an idea is described in more detail in Part III. The proposer may be asked for his further comments in writing or in consultation with either the Opportunity Manager or a member of the team. In exceptional cases the proposer may be interviewed by the whole board. This request for elaboration should not be used as a cosmetic device to soften the blow of rejection. That only adds unnecessary work. Such a request for elaboration could include the following questions:

'What action can you take?'
'What help do you want from others?'
'What are the difficulties and uncertainties?'

Where an opportunity map (see Part III) has been provided, alterations in this may be suggested by the team. Where it has not been provided the team may ask for one.

Sanction and encouragement: This implies approval of the opportunity idea. When an executive suggests, in his audit return, a specific opportunity objective that falls within his own opportunity space, the team then sanctions his initiative in going ahead with the suggestion. When an executive focuses on a particular idea-sensitive area the team may agree with his focus and encourage him to develop some ideas in this area. In neither case is any help required from the team. Nevertheless the team's awareness of what is going on serves several purposes: it encourages the executive and gives authority to his activities; it allows the coordination of effort, for example several people might focus on the same i.s.a. and could therefore be brought together in a working group; it may allow the team to offer information and other help.

Allocation of help: Provision by the team if specific aid is requested. As we saw in a previous section, one of the purposes of the Opportunity Audit was to provide a formal channel whereby executives could request aid for initiatives within their own opportunity area. Such aid may take the form of money, people or equipment. The team may wish to impose certain constraints such as time-scale and a cut-off point but as far as possible the aid should be without strings. Progress reports will be available as part of the Opportunity Audit procedure described in an earlier section. It must be obvious to an executive that his efficient use of such aid reflects on his executive ability.

Thinking help: The focusing of attention on an idea-sensitive area proposed in the audit. This may be done directly by the Opportunity Manager without passing through the team. An executive proposes an i.s.a. in his audit return. The team itself may provide thinking help in this area or it may suggest someone who can (including outside consultants). The Opportunity Manager may organize a group workshop to think about the i.s.a. or he may focus attention on it by circulating it for comments to other executives and then collecting their output. Whereas with ordinary aid the executive suggesting the opportunity feels able to get on with it, with thinking help the request is for combined attention to an important i.s.a.

Task forces: When an opportunity seems worth pursuing, either in an investigatory or an implementation manner, the Opportunity Team has to decide whether the proposer of the opportunity is in a position to do enough about it himself or whether a task force should be set up. A task force is a small group of people who treat the opportunity development as a project. They work with the proposing executive and also with relevant departments such as R & D or marketing. The purpose of the task force is to provide more opportunity development muscle than could the individual. The rather difficult relationship between the proposer of the opportunity and the task force will be considered in the next section.

Coordination of opportunity search and development

In the Opportunity Audit there is provision for the executive to put forward opportunity suggestions that affect departments other than his own and even the whole corporation. The Opportunity Team is there to bring such suggestions to the attention of the people concerned and to ask them for a reaction to the idea. In order to avoid a blanket rejection of any suggestion that comes in from outside, the usual approach to opportunities can be reversed here. The usual approach is that the person suggesting the opportunity has the duty to spell out its benefits. In the situation described now the department that rejects a suggestion from outside should be required to state its reasons for this rejection. Otherwise it is too easy to tell outsiders 'to mind their own business since they know nothing of the work of the department'.

Quite apart from the Opportunity Audit there will be a certain amount of what might be called opportunity work going on elsewhere in the company. The Opportunity Team should be aware of what is going on and should coordinate it. Whether the team is given overall responsibility for all opportunity development depends on the nature of the company, the chief executive officer and the strength of the team. For example the team should be aware of the new products that are being developed but whether the team has overall responsibility for new product development will depend on the nature of the company. If this is desired the first Opportunity Team should automatically include the head of the new product division (and similarly with R & D).

If outside consultants are brought in either as a task force or to generate opportunity ideas, their efforts are coordinated through the Opportunity Team who provide the briefing. The day-to-day liaison with the consultants is, however, carried out by the Opportunity Manager.

Taking the initiative

It may be that the Opportunity Team will be overwhelmed by suggestions. There may, however, be times when the volume or quality of suggestions slackens. The team should then create its own initiatives. Seminars on opportunity search can be organized in order to get the executives thinking in an opportunity mode. Formal cost-cutting exercises can also be initiated. Specific i.s.a.s and problem areas can be put forward by the team for executive thinking and comment. In short, the team can provoke ideas when it feels the flow is insufficient. Nevertheless there is a danger, mentioned earlier, that if the team becomes too preoccupied with its own opportunity suggestions it will be too busy to react properly to the suggestions coming in from other quarters. This would be fatal since the team is not an opportunity department but a coordinating nerve-centre which receives and processes opportunity suggestions from all parts of the organization.

The calling in of individual outside consultants as idea-provokers would also be part of the team's initiatives. I have often taken part in such sessions, which usually last a day. In that short time quite a large number of new ideas or approaches can be suggested. After all, a brilliant idea may take only a matter of seconds. The important part is, however, the follow-up. Otherwise there is the danger of everyone enjoying themselves at such a session but nothing tangible emerging. The most promising ideas to emerge from the session should be developed by individuals to the point where they can be assessed as serious opportunity proposals. An idea-provoking session would normally consist of the idea-provoking consultant, the Opportunity Manager, some members of the Opportunity Team and other parties invited by the Opportunity Manager. The number of people present should be between five and ten. The proceedings are tape-recorded. Such sessions may also be set up by the Opportunity Manager on his own initiative and working with people in a particular department.

Review and report

In addition to maintaining an effective filing system, the Opportunity Team should produce a report once a year. This report will be a review of the on-going opportunity activity within the company. The report will not list all the inputs of the audit but may take those outstanding and may group the rest in order to indicate the type of opportunity that is being suggested. The report should include progress notes on specific opportunity objectives. The report should not go into great detail but treat each project in a paragraph or so. The previous year's report should accompany the Opportunity Audit forms for the current year.

The description of failures in the report is a difficult matter. Yet it is important that they be mentioned. Other people may learn from the mistakes or may be able to avoid them when carrying out similar projects. On the other hand an executive would not like to be publicly associated with a failure. The safest procedure might be to ask the executive concerned to say why he thought the project had failed and to use this description (though it does carry the risk of all the blame being put on senior management).

The report should also include a file index which refers to the material on file at 'opportunity HQ'. This will allow an individual to go and consult material that he feels may be of interest to him. The report may also list some of the more important i.s.a.s in order to encourage thought about them. Creative people are often grateful for having their thinking directed towards matters that are deemed to be of importance to the organization for they then know that their output will be treated seriously.

Budget

The size of the budget allocated to the Opportunity Team is of importance and will vary with the nature of the company and the priority given to opportunity search. The budget should not be so large that the team becomes a closed-in department of its own because it will then lose its value as a nerve-centre. Nor should it be so small that the team can take no initiatives beyond asking other people for things. The team should certainly be able to set up their own seminars and idea-provoking sessions and even to engage outside consultants.

The budget can be regarded as falling into two parts. The first part is the house-keeping or secretarial budget which pays for the administrative expenses, salaries (not of the team members who have other roles in the company) and consultancy. The second part is the 'aid' budget from which help can be given to executives for them to take initiatives within their own opportunity areas. This aid budget should be large enough for something to be started on the say-so of the team. This is the crucial point. The opportunity search exercise will not work if the team can do no more than recommend matters to other departments. The team must be in a position to say that something has been started and that it seems very promising. At that stage the matter can be handed over. In other words there must be some concrete stage – however small – between an opportunity suggestion and selling it to the department concerned. 'If you think it is so wonderful then try it,' is the sort of remark which the opportunity team ought to be able to respond to.

In estimating the size of the budget it is important to bear in mind that the opportunity search exercise is a sort of insurance premium designed to keep everyone in a state of readiness to perceive and act upon opportunities when they arise. It is not like the cost of operating an advertising budget which at any moment has a tangible output. Where substantial savings have been made as a result of a seized opportunity a note should be made of these savings. Naturally there will be a tendency to say, on the one hand, that all improvements have been due to the opportunity search programme, and, on the other, that all of them would have happened anyway.

Difficulty

Opportunity suggestions are fragile and so is the mood in which they are put forward. Quite apart from the exercise of ruthless, no-nonsense decisions, the team must bear in mind that it is not only dealing with the current crop of suggestions but that it is trying to build up a climate for future, and perhaps better, suggestions. In a pile of one hundred suggestions each is only worth one per cent of attention and yet to the person putting forward that suggestion it was one hundred per cent of his output. The opportunity search exercise is a long-term attitude as well as an immediate output.

'*The value of a task force is that it cuts across lines of allegiance or interest in order to focus on the task in hand.*'

Opportunity Task Force

Whereas in an organization an executive is described by the division to which he belongs, in a task force the belonging is created only by the task.

The Opportunity Team can set up a task force to tackle any opportunity which is felt to be worthwhile and which would not be developed properly otherwise. For example, a specific opportunity might fall between two departments and hence be neglected by both. A task force with members from each department would be required. By definition, in the Opportunity Audit an executive puts forward a specific opportunity objective that falls within his own opportunity space – he should therefore be able to act upon it directly. The team may feel, however, that the opportunity is so important that a task force should be set up even though the executive could have made a start on his own. Where several executives make the same opportunity suggestion they can be brought together as a task force to develop the opportunity. Where an opportunity that has been started by an executive within his own opportunity space grows too big for his lone efforts a task force may be set up. For such things as feasibility studies a task force of outside consultants could be brought in. The same thing may be done with cost-cutting exercises, although in this case the force would consist both of company people and outside consultants.

Members of the task force

The executive suggesting the opportunity should automatically be a member. He may not, however, have the ability, personality or status to lead the task force. This may create some resentment since he will feel that his idea is being taken out of his hands. Whether or not he leads the force he must remain a key figure. In turn he must recognize that because he had the idea in the first place does not mean that he is necessarily the best person to develop it. The Opportunity Manager is automatically a member of the task force but if there are many task forces his role may remain that of liaison rather than active contribution. The head of the division would also be an automatic member, otherwise resentment and friction are bound to arise. Here again his role may be passive – provided he is kept informed of what is going on. A person with special knowledge in the area should be made a member of the task force, for example the personnel director where relevant. Where a task force is going to need help from another division someone in that division (not the head) should be included, someone from R & D or the Operations Research department. In all a task force should consist of three active working members with others who are there because lines of communication are much easier if they are within the force rather than outside it. For the three active working members (including the original proposer) ability is more important than status.

Whether the task force members are seconded, full-time, to the force or whether in addition to their other jobs will depend on the perceived importance and pay-off from the opportunity.

Briefing of the task force

The task force is briefed by the Opportunity Team – not by the proposer of the opportunity. The task force may later seek to change the objectives but this must be done by consultation with the team, which has a better overall view of how the opportunity fits in with the activities of the company. The briefing is in terms of objectives and parameters not in terms of means. The objective may be information: 'Find out whether this would be feasible,' or 'Find out whether this would have any advantages for us.' In the labour relations area the task may be exploratory: 'Find out how this would go down,' or 'Try to ascertain the union attitude to this.' The task may also involve setting up a test-bed for some idea or undertaking a pilot study. The end-product of the activity of the task force would usually take the form that the proposal was possible and that the benefits were considerable. The negative end-product would be just as useful: 'It is not worth pursuing this further.'

The briefing should include specific objectives and also specific cut-offs in terms of time or cost. Report-back procedures should also be built into the briefing. Where an opportunity map is used a specific report on each 'if-box' (see Part III) may be required.

Authority of the task force

What authority will the task force have to cut across other lines of authority and to interfere with the workings of other departments? All task forces have the general authority of the Opportunity Manager which has to be defined at an early stage as a staff function. In addition, a properly constituted task force should include anyone whose authority is likely to be infringed. In the final analysis the authority and status of the task force will depend on the priority given to its task by the chief executive officer. The task force should, however, work in a manner that does not lead to confrontation over authority.

Projects

The opportunity development being handled by the task force may eventually grow into a full-sized project. By then the role of the task force will have ended and a specific project management team will have been set up. It should be made clear to the task force that their role is to develop the opportunity to the point where the next stage of development, such as a project, is obviously worth pursuing. The project team can, of course, include members of the original task force, although some of these may have too many responsibilities elsewhere.

Report back

At the end of its project (as defined by the briefing) the task force reports back to the team. This report or de-briefing should include the final conclusion which is always in the form of whether or not it is worth taking the matter further. The reasons for this conclusion should be spelled out: unexpected difficulties; predictions not borne out; expected benefits proving too small; uncertainties turning into negative certainties; unfavourable cost estimations; high cost of change; unfavourable reception by those concerned.

In addition to the final conclusion the task force can also comment on the methods they used and on their experiences. It is likely that such experiences could prove of use to others. The conclusion and the detail should be kept separate.

In exceptional circumstances where the opportunity still seems to offer real benefits, the task force may be asked to try again using different methods.

Part III: Thinking for opportunities

This third part deals with the methodology of thinking that is required for discovering opportunities. It answers the questions:

'How do I set about looking for opportunities?'

'Where do I start to look for opportunities?'

An executive could, if he wished, ignore the first two parts of this book and turn straight to this third part and use it entirely on its own. As we have seen, the first part deals with the background and perspective of opportunity search; and the second deals specifically with the opportunity search exercise (Opex) which is a specific structure within which opportunity search can be carried out. The thinking required by each executive as he takes part in the opportunity search exercise is described in this third part. For that reason each executive taking part in the opportunity search exercise should have a copy of this book.

An individual who is not taking part in an opportunity search exercise and may not even be an executive may equally use this third part. He may, for example, be a lone or would-be entrepreneur looking for opportunities.

The general attitudes and processes of thinking described here apply to any type of opportunity search. At times a particular technique may seem to be more applicable to opportunity search on a corporate level, but the principle of the process can as easily be applied on the level of simplifying a humble procedure. For example, a reference to 'intrinsic assets' may apply to a huge rolling mill or to a single skilled worker on a particular job.

Contents

The fundamental thinking processes will be described briefly. The difference between 'moving-out' and 'moving-in' will be explained. Much of management thinking is limited to the 'moving-in' or problem-solving mode. A check-list of twenty starting points will be provided. Each of these starting points or attention areas serves to initiate opportunity thinking. The starting points include: me-too, trends, variable value, de-averaging, synergy, intrinsic assets, operating assets, situation assets, 'left-behind' and challenge. In contrast to these starting points there is a list of end-points in which the end-product of the thinking is known in advance but the route to that end-product has yet to be discovered. The end-points include: problem-solving, quality improvement, need identification, gap-filling and the 'something' method.

The treatment of ideas is an important section, for very often potentially valuable ideas are killed off before their value can be made apparent. There is also a section on risk and uncertainty. The 'if-box' notation is introduced for the creation of opportunity maps. Finally, guidelines are suggested for the assessment of benefits and for the evaluation of opportunities.

'Thinking is the operating skill whereby intelligence acts upon experience.'

Review of fundamental thinking processes

In this section I intend to review the fundamental thinking processes. Most people regard thinking as a fairly straightforward process: 'Give me the facts and I will give you the logical conclusion.' This is a very limited view of thinking and completely excludes the sort of creative exploration that is essential for opportunity search. I have been involved in running what is the largest programme in the world for teaching thinking as a skill in schools and in the course of our development work we have looked at thinking across a wide range of ages (five to adult) and IQs (70 to 140). I have also had the opportunity of studying the thinking of thousands of senior executives, scientists, engineers, computer analysts and artists. I would not hesitate to say that thinking is the most neglected of our skills. In school, apart from mathematics, we teach only description and knowledge sorting.

We can define thinking as 'the purposeful exploration of our experience maps'. The excellence of our minds arises from the function of the brain as a pattern-making system that allows incoming information to form itself into patterns that can be stored and used. This pattern-making function is described fully elsewhere.* For the sake of simplicity we can regard the complex of patterns in our memory rather like the street map of a town. Some of the routes are familiar. Sometimes a familiar route makes it impossible for us to explore and find a shorter cut. Sometimes we know the destination but have to find our way there by putting together sub-routes which we know. Sometimes an obvious route only becomes obvious after we have found it – and we wonder why we did not spot it in the first place.

We can start by considering some of the basic operations that we carry out when thinking. These familiar operations are really 'intentions' – they are operations which we intend to carry out. In carrying them out we may use a whole range of mental activities.

Focus

This is the most important and the most difficult thinking operation. It is difficult precisely because it seems so simple and so obvious. There are few people who can choose to focus their attention on something and keep it there. That is why 'check-lists' of attention areas are so useful as a help to thinking. If an executive is asked to focus on the short-term benefits of an opportunity, he will find no difficulty in doing so, but left to his own devices he might have only considered benefits in a general, rather vague, way. Our language device of the 'question' is there in order to get us to focus. Asking the right question of others and also of ourselves is a key part of thinking. We can also direct our attention by having a defined area in which to look. If an executive is asked to look at the 'operating assets' of an organization that is not the same as being asked to look at the 'assets'. In this third part of the book distinctions will be made in order to allow a more precise

* See *The Mechanism of Mind*.

focusing of attention. It is necessary to follow these distinctions rather than lump things together. If a doctor asks a student to observe the way the patient looks to the left this is more precise than asking the student to 'look at the patient's eyes'.

Analysis

This is the operation with which most executives will be at ease. Our education system pays a good deal of attention to analysis and so does management training. In order to cope with the world we have to treat it in 'chunks'. We look at a bicycle, or cash-flow, or sales figures. Each of these chunks contains a large number of ingredients: sales figures for each week or for each district or for each salesman; sales figures for the different products, etc. In short, in analysis we look beneath the 'chunk' in order to see the components. In science we look beneath the effect in order to see the interacting causes.

Abstraction

In this operation – also familiar but a good deal more difficult than analysis – we seek to extract the general principles or mechanisms that seem to be operating in a situation. We seek to separate the principle from the particular situation. I prefer to call the operation 'function extraction'. The ability to extract and deal with functions is very important for creative thinking. The difficulty arises because many people can only see things in concrete terms and feel uncomfortable dealing with abstractions which seem theoretical. There is an even greater difficulty in knowing the most useful level of abstraction. For example we might say of a bicycle:

'A transport device.'
'A one-person transport device.'
'A one-person transport device which uses no outside fuel.'
'A one-person transport device with two wheels that is driven by turning a crank with the legs.'
Words like 'device', 'thing', 'mechanism', 'process' allow one to describe the function without spelling out the details. There is considerable skill involved in making the most fertile abstractions.

Alternatives (lateral thinking)

A computer services company was having trouble with its training course. At the end of the course sixty per cent of the entrants left. The company was worried because it had set up the course to train the people it needed. I was asked for suggestions as to how the course could be improved. The analytical thinking had led to the conclusion that the trainees were 'dissatisfied'. This seems logical enough. But if we deliberately look for alternatives to 'dissatisfaction' we quickly find 'satisfaction'. It turned out the trainees were so satisfied with the course that people who never had any intention of working for the company availed themselves of the excellent education offered by the trainee course. The Nigerian government had the same problem. When they removed the commercial accounting segment from the first year of their public service training programme the number of entrants dropped sharply. The trouble is that there is no *logical* reason for looking for alternatives unless we are dissatisfied with what we have. And yet in creativity it is vital to be looking for alternatives no matter how satisfied we may be. There therefore has to be a deliberate intention or exercise of will to seek alternatives. The challenge process comes in here. As we shall see later, it is often necessary to challenge something that seems perfectly adequate in order to explore alternatives. If we understand creativity such a challenge is indeed logical, but if we do not understand, it seems absurd to challenge something which is satisfactory. In looking for alternatives we could look for alternative ways of carrying out the same function (for example, different designs for a screw-driver) or for alternative functions to serve the same purpose (for example the use of nails or glue). Curiously we do not have a verb to describe the need to look for alternatives. That is why it was necessary to create the term 'lateral thinking'.

Alternatives may also be found for the way something is viewed. The classic example is the glass which is seen as half empty by one person and as half full by another. All of us need to internalize the phrase: 'There may be another way of looking at this.'

Synthesis

The opposite of analysis. We put together different ingredients or pieces of information to arrive at a whole. The pieces may themselves have been obtained from analysis. Planning, problem-solving and prediction all make use of synthesis. We construct scenarios of the future from past experience and an analysis of present trends and influences. Models of things whch do not exist – and the future never exists at the moment – must all be created by synthesis. At the final point all creation is synthesis but this leads to a very dangerous attitude of mind. The attitude is that creation needs nothing beyond synthesis. As a result an executive will assemble all the factors and information and hope to synthesize these into something new. It does often work but there are two limitations. The first is that we cannot know what is needed until after we have found the final idea – therefore important things may be left out. The second is that the creative effort may require us to look at things in a different way or to look for alternatives rather than an assembly of traditional concepts. Creativity often requires the sort of provocation that is described later in this section.

Search, judgement and matching

Another very familiar process. We scan our experience to find something that matches what we have in mind. We might have a mental image of the executive we need for some particular role and then we scan through all the executives to see which one matches the requirements. With judgement the situation presents itself and we see whether it matches the requirements or criteria we wish to apply. Matching itself is the operation of putting two things side by side in our minds and commenting upon the points of similarity or difference. It may also consist of constructing something to match a pre-chosen set of requirements. For example, we might set out to construct an opportunity that matches pre-chosen characteristics of cash-flow, time scale, capital needs and so on.

As we shall see later, the judgement process is invaluable but there are dangers. The biggest killer of any new idea is the phrase 'the same as'. The new, and perhaps crucial, aspects are ignored and the familiar aspects are focused upon with the result that the idea is dismissed.

Modification

Although this is really a composite of many of the operations described above, we ought to treat it separately. It involves judgement, analysis, synthesis, abstraction and alternative search but it deserves an entry of its own because as an 'intention' it does not arise from these other intentions. With modification we take something as it is, for example an idea, and proceed to change it by a process of forced evolution. This process may involve removing faults or improving general characteristics such as simplicity or it may involve moulding the idea towards some desired shape. In later sections we shall deal with the process of 'tailoring' in which an idea is tailored towards an acceptable form. This is instead of simply judging an idea as it is and throwing it out at once if it is not suitable.

Provocation

This operation is important for creativity. It is a definite part of lateral thinking and as such is described more fully elsewhere. We can summarize the process by the statement: 'There may not be a reason for saying something until after it has been said.' All our traditional thinking is based on the logical reaction to information. The conclusions or statements we derive are soundly based on this information. With provocation this is not so. A provocative statement need have no logical connection with the existing state of affairs. It is used precisely in order to provoke new ideas. The importance of a provocative statement is 'where it gets us' not 'where it has come from'. In our analogy of the town street map it is like saying: 'I wonder what would happen if I went via the post-office', when the post-office is not obviously on the route. But in exploring that provocation a new route might be discovered. A provocation is a mental experiment – in order to see what happens.

A deliberate provocation is usually preceded by the word 'po' (which stands for 'provocation operation' and is derived from hypothesis, suppose, poetry) in order to signal its provocative nature. An advertising agency seeking a new advertising medium made the provocation: 'Po we should bring back the town crier.' In itself this is a ridiculous suggestion because of the noise of modern cities but it led to the notion of a medium which you had to listen to because, unlike many others, it could not be turned off. This led to the idea of public telephones which were free because every twenty seconds a 'commercial break' message was injected into the conversation.

Repertoire of operations

In practice all thinking consists of movement from one idea to another. This movement is obtained in two ways. The first way is when we simply run through our experience. We might call this the 'carry-on' method. If we are discussing taxis someone might remark that in Istanbul they have a variety of taxi which picks up many passengers with different destinations – operating like a mini-bus except that the passengers choose the destination as for a normal taxi. Someone else might recount how in Mexico City there are normal taxis and then special taxis which ply defined routes but can be stopped by additional passengers anywhere along these routes. Another person might recount an experience he had when he badly needed a taxi and could not get one at all. The people taking part in the discussion would have a certain common experience of the organization and operation of taxis. From consideration of experience of all sorts new opportunity ideas may emerge – for example for a type of multi-taxi.

The second way of obtaining movement may be called the 'catch-up' method. The distinction between 'carry-on' and 'catch-up' is shown in Figure 9. In the 'catch-up' method we move to the plane of operations and decide either what we are going to do or where we want to be. For example we decide that we want to end up with an analysis of the taxi business. Or we may decide that we want to focus on the fares, extract the function of the fare, and see if we can suggest alternatives. In our analysis we might consider the taxi itself, the driver, operating costs, market size, competition, legislation and regulation. In our search for opportunity we might consider cutting costs or cutting out unprofitable parts of the operation. We might consider raising fares but this would require the approval of local government (and might well reduce the market size). We might try to increase the profitability per journey by taking more passengers (also requiring approval) or offering other services. Through better scheduling we might try and match supply and demand more exactly. All this is straightforward and involves the application of standard management thinking strategies on the plane of operations.

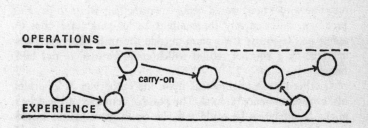

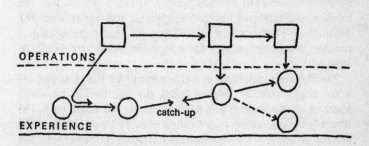

Figure 9

Alternatively we might focus on just one aspect such as 'demand'. We might then extract the function of a taxi and describe it as: 'a means of getting someone to the place he wants to go when he wants to go – with exactness'. We might then focus on 'want' and consider some alternatives: desperate want, ordinary want, casual want, impulse want, tempted want. At once we can see that someone who desperately needs a taxi to get to the airport or to a hospital does not have the same want as someone who would take a taxi instead of a bus if it were more convenient and not much more expensive. So the idea might emerge of a 'premium taxi' which charged double normal fares and was consequently little used. On the other hand such taxis would be available for someone whose need would make it worth their while to pay the premium. Alternatively there might be 'off-peak' taxi rates to tempt people to use taxis more outside the rush hours (perhaps operated by a voucher refund which could be used to pay taxi fares).

Another person might focus upon the taxi-driver as he drives his 'captive audience' around. The possible activities of the driver might be analysed: he could talk, he could listen. There would then be a dive back into experience: 'In what situations would talking or listening be profitable?' The thinker would have set himself this target to 'catch-up' with. Selling insurance or acting as preliminary contact for car sales and other goods might be one suggestion. Doing market research or carrying out opinion polls might be another. Getting financial tips might be a third (by direct question rather than eavesdropping!). Using a provocation the thinker might reverse this last suggestion and might want the driver to give out financial tips. This might lead to an up-to-date cassette 'newsletter' service for which the passengers would be charged.

The thinker would then run the scenario for the ideas and see what might actually happen (need for government approval, abuse of system, lack of profitability, market too small, etc.). The idea might be modified to get round some of these problems. Or else the principle of the idea could be extracted and then re-clothed in a more practical manner, for example, handing out or selling newsletters rather than playing a cassette.

Another thinker might focus on the methods of financing a

taxi-fleet. He might consider whether there was any alternative to driver-owned or company-owned. Such alternatives as company-owned and driver-leased, for a month at a time, might emerge. Or a joint ownership between the driver and the company. Or even a system in whch two drivers own a single cab and a second cab is owned by the company.

As a provocation we might even suggest that the person who drives the cab need not be a driver. The person might simply be a caretaker who collected fares, saw that the cab was not stolen (perhaps a secret alarm or turn-off switch) and ensured it was returned to a taxi rank. The passenger would then drive himself.

The important thing is that once we acquire the skill of 'movement' in thinking then the number of possibilities is virtually unlimited. We may of course choose to confine our thinking to an i.s.a. (idea-sensitive area, as described in Part II) because we have already defined that area as one in which a new idea would be profitable – and hence a worthwhile opportunity.

'Sometimes we set out to reach destinations but at other times we set out on a voyage of exploration.'

'Moving-in' and 'moving-out' as modes of thinking

It is possible to convert everything into a 'problem'. If there is a desired state that we wish to achieve we can call getting there 'problem-solving'. But the type of thinking required in open-ended problems is very different from that required in closed-ended problems and this difference is ignored if we treat everything as problem-solving. There is a considerable danger in this because managers are taught to be problem-solvers: define your objective, define your problem, see what has to be taken into account, then solve your problem. The sort of thinking required in opportunity search is quite different. Only part of the time can we define the objective or end-point. It is true that we want to end up with a profitable idea or a worthwhile opportunity but that is too general to serve as the end-point in the usual type of problem-solving. It is as vague as an inventor setting out 'to invent something new' or a new product manager setting out 'to find a new product'.

If we know exactly where we are going then we are unlikely to arrive at an unexpected destination. Where an opportunity is obvious, ordinary closed-ended problem-solving may be required to solve the problems that prevent us from using that opportunity. But that is different from setting out to find opportunities that will only become obvious *after* they have been found.

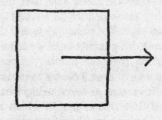

MOVING-OUT

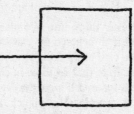

MOVING-IN

Figure 10

The difference between 'moving-out' and 'moving-in' is illustrated with standardized symbols in Figure 10. In the moving-out mode we have a starting point. We then move out from that starting point. We do have a general idea that we are looking for situations that could be beneficial but this is only a flavour at this state. We move along from idea to idea until something begins to look promising. We then try to crystallize this idea. When we have a definite idea we see if we can tailor or transform it so that it becomes worthwhile. At this stage we do have to become conscious of the type of idea we are looking for, of the constraints and requirements. But instead of applying these as a judgement screen to the idea to see whether or not the idea satisfies the criteria, we attempt to modify the idea to see if we can pitch it into the acceptability area. The steps in the process are suggested in Figure 11: there is a starting point, next there is a period of movement as the mind moves out and starts developing ideas, finally there is an embryo idea, which is then transformed in a series of steps to see whether it can be made to land in the acceptability area which is defined by the requirements.

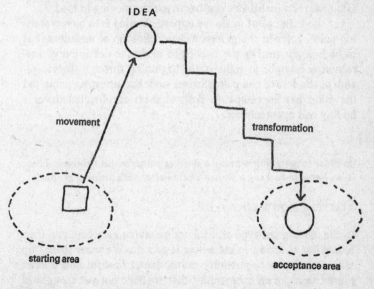

IDEA

movement

transformation

starting area

acceptance area

Figure 11

In the moving-out mode there is a great deal of exploration and experimentation. We may find ourselves considering ideas we have never thought of before. Each idea we have acts as a sort of provocation towards another idea, just as each mountain scaled enables us to see the route to the next one.

In the moving-in mode we know where we want to end up and we know what we have to deal with. This is more like ordinary problem-solving. We react to information and analyse it to produce the best answer that is consistent with that information. This is standard management behaviour. In opportunity search, however, we may only know the 'type' of situation we wish to reach without knowing the exact situation.

These two modes of thinking are quite distinct and it is important to appreciate the distinction. In the moving-in mode a line of thought which does not lead towards the desired end-point will not be taken but in the moving-out mode it will be. Yet the two modes are complementary. In the course of solving a closed problem one may have to use some creative speculation in order to open up a new approach. In the course of tailoring a speculative idea towards a useful idea one has to use the moving-in mode.

For the moving-out mode the important thing is to have a starting point. Later in the process a clear definition of usefulness has to be brought in. For the moving-in mode the definition of usefulness is brought in right at the beginning through the acceptance of the desired end-point. So one mode has a starting point and the other has an end-point. Both of them are directed towards finding real opportunities.

'In order to get going we need a starting point for our thinking. There is no harm in making a formal check-list of such starting points.'

Starting point check-list

In the moving-out type of thinking we start somewhere and then follow our thinking to see where it gets us. We want to end up with a profitable opportunity rather than a fanciful idea but we cannot think of an opportunity that we have not yet thought of unless we start somewhere. The check-list of starting points set out in this section is not exhaustive nor is it meant to be novel. Some of the starting points are more appropriate to certain businesses and certain individuals.

Intrinsic assets

The national airlines of countries with small populations have a hard time competing for passengers. Aer Lingus has only a small native population to draw upon and must also compete on the overcrowded transatlantic route. Yet Eire is a very pleasant, under-populated country with charming people and strong traditions in medicine and nursing. These are intrinsic assets. The average cost of a hospital stay in the United States in 1977 is between $1,500 and $2,000. A transatlantic charter seat on an aircraft could be had for about $200. There is therefore an opportunity for Aer Lingus, in conjunction with others, to set up hospital services in Eire and to ferry over cold medical and surgical cases for diagnosis and treatment.

Montague Burton is the name of a chain of well-known high street tailors and outfitters in the UK. When consumer spending falls tailors are apt to suffer since the purchase of a new suit can always be delayed. The intrinsic assets of the organization include a large number of excellently placed high street shops. Obviously these could be sold off for their real estate value. Alternatively there is an opportunity of using these shops to expand the range of menswear that is sold – for example selling shirts, sportswear or leisure wear.

Intrinsic assets can include cash, land, capital equipment and plant of any sort, people, a strong brand image, distribution channels and distribution outlets, market position, patents and licences, know-how, experience, technology, existing services and products, etc. As an illustration, the intrinsic assets of a brand image like Kelloggs can be used to launch other food products. A number-two market position is also an asset because it may allow activities which the market leader could not contemplate – it could also be used directly as an asset as Avis did with their famous slogan, 'We try harder.' Failure in an area can also be an intrinsic asset because the experience built up in the course of that failure may have a value if applied elsewhere. Market muscle and

141

know-how are assets which can be applied to products which others have failed to launch. The question, 'Where do our strengths lie?' will uncover many intrinsic assets but by no means all, for an important asset may not be regarded as a strength until an opportunity has been built around it.

Know-how and people are important intrinsic assets even though they are not permanently owned by a corporation. One of the most important medical drugs of all time, digitalis, was discovered because Dr Withering had fallen in love with a lady who liked painting flowers. In order to woo her he also became interested in flowers and when he heard of a folk remedy that cured the oedema of heart failure (dropsy, as it was called) he soon identified the foxglove as the active ingredient and from it came digitalis which serves to increase the efficiency of a failing heart. His botanical know-how had proved to be a useful asset.

A careful appraisal of obvious intrinsic assets would include the questions:

'Are we using these assets fully?'

'Are there any other ways we could put these assets to use?'

In addition time should be spent looking for those intrinsic assets which are not at all obvious. This may be because they are so taken for granted by people within the organization that an outside view is required. It may be that they have never been regarded as assets because they have been the spin-off from another activity. For example, the holes in the ground and the millions of tons of sand and gravel accumulated by the English China Clay company in its extraction of china clay, are unquestionably assets even though they are also environmental liabilities.

Operating assets

An operating asset arises from the way something is carried out – it is an operating asset of a travel agency that the money is paid in advance and therefore constitutes a float. This is even more true of insurance companies whose main source of income may be the investment of the premiums until such time as they are paid out in claims. There is often overlap between intrinsic assets and operating assets but it is useful to keep the distinction as a help towards focusing on the particular way in which something is done. A car and a driving licence are both intrinsic assets but the fact that you drive past a certain place each morning is an operating asset.

It is a useful exercise to consider the operating assets of a cigarette-smoker. He has an excuse for making a social contact because he can ask for a cigarette or a light or offer either. He has an additional means of advertising his taste, self-image or status by means of his choice of brand. He may have an additional means of indicating his mood by the manner in which he smokes. He has a useful 'pause' mechanism which allows him to pause before making a reply (this is even more marked with pipe-smoking as illustrated by Sir Harold Wilson when he was UK Prime Minister). Finally there is some activity to occupy the hands.

Steel service centres only exist because of their operating assets. They can stock and deliver special steels within twenty-four hours compared to a ninety-day delay if the same steel is ordered from the steel-makers. They can also stock steel on behalf of regular customers, so acting as bankers and warehouse facilities. The service centres can buy specialized machines which individual customers could not keep fully utilized.

Operating assets in terms of convenience, choice, point of complaint, window-shopping are the justification for shops. The operating assets of a taxi-driver have been mentioned in an earlier section. There are 250,000 life insurance salesmen in the USA. They could be regarded either as an operating asset or an intrinsic asset of the insurance industry. Is there something else they could be selling?

In a seminar I once offered $20 to whoever could put up the best idea for using that $20 as an opportunity there and then. The ideas that came back were mainly to do with gambling or organizing a lottery. Using the operating assets of the situation (my giving a seminar) I then asked the participants to write cheques on the basis that the cheques were not returnable and the highest value cheque would win the $20 plus seventy per cent of all contributions. I had no idea what would happen. To my surprise the exercise produced $730 from the thirty participants. What was of value to me was not the actual profit, but the psychological experiment which showed a fascinating variety of approaches to the situation.

143

The best way to consider operating assets is to list the activities and then to break each down into steps, each of which is described in a separate stark sentence. If we looked at the simple activity of a customer buying goods in a shop we might reach the sentence: 'The assistant gives the customer her change.' Are there any operating assets there which could provide an opportunity? Obviously something could be given back with the change. Or perhaps we could have vouchers which would have double their face value if used for purchases in the same store. These could be stamped and issued by a machine, so saving time. Change machines, credit sales, exact change channels, charity boxes and possibly even miniature fruit machines might be other ideas. In another context one entrepreneur hit on the idea of providing executive packs of small change for use in foreign countries.

Situation assets

A situation asset is an asset that depends on the current 'situation' or circumstances. Usually it arises from a change in circumstances. Often the change is legislative. The sale of mopeds boomed in the USA in 1977 when many states decided to treat them like bicycles rather than motor vehicles, provided they proceeded at less than 17 m.p.h. Playboy Enterprises Inc. set out to build a casino in Atlantic City NJ as soon as legislation was passed that permitted casino activities. Part of their intrinsic assets in this situation was the experience acquired in operating casinos in the UK. The London property millionaires of the 1950s all seized on the opportunity offered by a change in legislation which permitted office development in a city starved of such development.

A change in price can also offer a situation asset. The sharp rise in the price of sugar (cane sugar) made it worthwhile to develop high fructose corn syrup as a sugar substitute for industrial sweeteners. The sharp rise in coffee prices in 1976 and 1977 expanded the tea market. At the same time the rise in price might seem to offer an opportunity for new growers to get in on the act. Up to a point this is a valid opportunity but what tends to happen is that too many new people get involved, with the result that when all the planting comes to harvest there is a glut and prices fall. It is usually dangerous to regard a rise in prices as an opportunity for expanding into that area.

The bad winter of 1976 is estimated to have caused something like $467 million in damages to roads and bridges in Pennsylvania alone. Obviously an opportunity for anyone involved in these activities. A marked increase in executive redundancy during the recession created a situation in which 'outplacement' or 'de-hiring' firms flourished. They took over the task of terminating employment and finding the sacked executive a new position. From all accounts they were reasonably efficient.

Sometimes it is difficult to distinguish a new situation from a trend (towards something new or away from something established). Trends, however, have their own entry in the check-list of starting points. Trends can usually be arrived at by analysing data. New situations have to be noticed or perceived. Sometimes the change may be obvious to everyone – at other times the person who is able to spot the opportunity arising from the change is out in front on his own.

In looking for opportunities arising from situation assets the trick is to go further than saying, 'How does that change affect us?' It is more a matter of saying, 'What new situation has arisen? Does this new situation offer any opportunities? Are these opportunities of interest to us?' The difficulty is to be able to recognize when a change in the old situation has given rise to a completely new situation. On the whole, imagined shifts in consumer tastes in response to a new situation (like the fuel crisis) tend to be mistaken. Shifts in taste are trends and trends can be analysed but not anticipated. There is a world of difference between an actual change in a situation and the imagined consequence of this change. Opportunities should be based on the actual change not the imagined consequences.

'Left behind'

As we get better and better at doing something we tend to 'leave behind' areas which could develop as new opportunities. A supermarket has to be comprehensive for a shopper rightly expects to find all his food requirements in a single store. To be comprehensive the supermarket must be large. Supermarkets tend to be out of town (in the USA) because of the need to provide parking places since in general public transport is so poor. This development of the supermarket concept to a high pitch of efficiency means that the convenient satisfaction of urgent needs has been 'left behind'. The man who needs a packet of cigarettes or a pack of beer is not going to drive out to a supermarket and stand in the check-out queue – even if the supermarket remained open late. It is calculated that in the USA convenience stores, such as the 7-Eleven stores of the Southland Corporation, have eight per cent of the retail market. This type of operation is growing by fifteen per cent a year. The convenience store does not have to be comprehensive, it can choose to stock items which are fast-moving and known to be in demand. A customer does not expect the convenience store to have everything he wants. Customers are also willing to pay a premium price (of up to fifteen per cent) for the convenience of popping into the convenience store when they want and coming out with what they need.

A boy at school may show some skill in mathematics. He is encouraged to specialize in mathematics. He does well at it and eventually ends up with a university teaching post as a mathematician. What has happened is that his excellence in development along this one line has in fact restricted his development elsewhere. Given a chance he might have developed as a business executive but this path was blocked because of his rapid progress in another direction. In the USA medicine gets ever more specialized because specialists earn high fees and ultimately a patient wants to be treated by a specialist. What is left behind by this development is the 'general practitioner' who knows the patient as a person and who can direct the patient to the appropriate specialist. An advertising agency gets well known for its creative flair. This line is pursued with skill. Eventually the sort of advertising that actually tells the consumer about the product is left behind.

It is almost inevitable that sheer excellence in one direction will open up opportunities in its wake. For example, the development of newer and faster mainframe computers opens up huge opportunities in the selling of second-hand displaced computers to those who like the lower cost and do not need the superior technology of the new model.

In focusing on this area of what has been 'left behind' it is important to be honest about what is being done well and about the direction that is being taken. Once this has been defined the next step is to see what has been left behind. The third step is to see whether any opportunities can emerge from what has been left behind. The fourth step is to ascertain the size and profitability of the opportunity.

Synergy

Synergy occurs when two or more assets are combined to give a benefit which is greater than the sum of the separate parts. In practice the opportunity-seeker may look around for complementary activities such as the combination of petrol stations and supermarkets. Or he may 'provoke' some ideas by putting together in his mind two arbitrary businesses in order to see what emerges – for example, putting together a hospital and hotel (leading to the idea that for diagnostic purposes it is usually much cheaper to stay in a luxury hotel than in an ordinary hospital).

In the conglomerate days it was often pretended that the new acquisitions were synergistic with the existing activities. In general this was not so except that an agile mind can make out a case for any two activities being synergistic – the real benefits were related to stock market valuations. Supposed synergism can be a danger. When the British fibre maker Courtaulds decided that its production facilities were synergistic with fashion and design operations the call went out for vertical integration through acquisition of small garment houses. The results were less than satisfactory because the individual flair and operating methods of the garment houses could no longer operate inside a large corporation.

Synergy is not the same as simplification. If two parts of an organization are collecting information it may make sense to combine the two collecting functions – this is simplification. There is, however, a synergy between selling and doing market research.

Variable value

I once sold for £5 a car which today would be worth about £3,000. It was a Railton Straight Eight but as a student I could not afford the cost of maintaining it and it was not reliable enough for general student runabout use. I was almost paying someone to take it off my hands. The classic instance of variable value is when one person's waste becomes another's source of profits.

An English-speaking person in England has little chance of using his ability to speak English as a source of income. But if he were to go to Brazil he might find that he could make a living just by giving private lessons in English to business executives. Moving something from one place to another – from abundance to scarcity – is an obvious example of variable value. Making the movement not through space but through time is just as effective. An example is the rise in value of old models of motor cars that are in good condition (an individuality rather than an historic value).

It is said that Jaguar cars offer very good value when bought second-hand. This is because the price (in the UK) often seems very low for the quality of engineering. One explanation is that Jaguar-buyers are not the sort of people who buy second-hand cars and hence there is no real market. Another explanation is that repairs are expensive but this would apply to other cars such as BMW.

Variable value means that the value resides not in the thing itself but in the value to the person who is selling it and the value to the person who is receiving it. The opportunities are vast both for genuine entrepreneurial activities and also for exploitation. In Britain in the hot summer of 1976 street vendors of orange juice were charging 45p for a paper cupful.

Another area of variable value is when things in isolation have no value but when aggregated together do have a value. For example, small savings might not have much value on their own but aggregated by such means as unit trusts (mutual funds) they acquire a higher operating value. The very concept of insurance is based on aggregated value of this sort.

A milk carton can advertise milk but that is rather superfluous. The space could be sold at a much higher value for the advertising of other products. This is as true for cereal packets as for the backs of airline tickets. One entrepreneur has even set up a scheme for renting the side of private automobiles to advertise products – as a sort of mobile poster.

The concept of variable value is one of the most fundamental in opportunity search because in the end all business is based on the concept that the value to the buyer is rather higher than the value to the maker and it is this added value that has to provide return on investment.

A slight increase in the cost of a product, for example by offering a choice of colours, might add greatly to the value. Conversely diminishing the value slightly, such as by omitting one function from a pocket-knife, might lead to a considerable reduction in cost.

When using variable value as a starting point it may be best to focus on three areas of value: value as perceived by the buyer, high-value areas as perceived by the supplier, low-value (waste) areas as perceived by the supplier. These values are then mentally manipulated to see in what circumstances they might be different. Although there is an overlap, this consideration of variable value is not the same as value analysis. Value analysis considers the true value within a fixed context: variable value consideration alters the context to see if the value alters.

Challenge

'Challenge' is a basic mental process which is used to challenge complacency and the taking for granted of existing operations. By applying the challenge process we can make a starting point out of anything. In our minds we say: 'If we challenge the way this is now done might we come up with a different way which will cut costs, increase profits or expand the market?'

Although it sounds easy, the challenge process can be difficult to apply because we very soon find ourselves criticizing that which we challenge. We do this in order to find something that 'needs' changing. The danger is that we then only challenge things that can be criticized and as soon as that happens the whole point of the challenge is lost. Ordinary criticism has its use but it is different from challenge. The reason we need to challenge things which are beyond criticism is that there can be considerable potential in this area. Consider an area so full of potential that almost any idea or method of proceeding is adequate. Thereafter this method of proceeding is never challenged because it always seems adequate. So the huge potential in the area is never tapped because the first idea that came up was adequate and has therefore blocked all further exploration. The process is suggested in Figure 12.

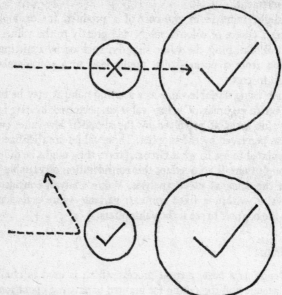

Figure 12

There are five possible reasons why something may be done the way it is done at the moment.

Tethering: Here a variety of constraints, regulations, considerations, and influences combine to keep things as they are. In many cases this produces a fatalistic attitude: 'There is nothing we can do to change this and we have given up thinking about it.' Fear of union reaction is common in this type of situation.

Particular reason: There may be a single reason which is itself open to challenge. Sometimes the reason applied in the past but no longer does so. – Qantas airlines have more stewards than hostesses because the original flights were luxury clipper flights and it was felt that the better class of restaurant had waiters and not waitresses.

Continuity: Here there is no particular reason and no obvious benefit. There has never seemed to be any need to challenge the matter and as a result it has never been challenged. For example, the custom of producing house journals as advertising media for pharmaceutical companies.

Arbitrary choice: Something has to be done and one way seems as good as any other.

Up-to-date review: Here there has been a review of procedures and the item has survived the review because the original reasons are still valid or because no better alternative has emerged. It may also happen that there is a better alternative but the cost, in cash and disruption, of changing to the alternative is too high in relation to the benefits.

I was once asked for some ideas for increasing the productivity of service engineers in a city. I challenged the need for them to drive motor cars. When they were put on motor cycles their productivity increased because there was less hold-up in city traffic.

We expect the mail service to deliver letters to our home address. We could challenge this destination and suggest instead our place of work. This would cut down the number of delivery points by a considerable factor. We might have a two-tier addressing system. The postage for an 'A' address (place of work or other accumulation of people) would be less than for a 'B' address (the current home address). There would of course be problems, such as holidays, but these could be surmounted if the reduction in costs made it worthwhile.

In the work situation itself challenge is one of the most fertile starting points, which is why the process has been incorporated in so many formal procedures such as value-engineering and cost-cutting exercises. In the opportunity search exercise the approach is somewhat different because we do not start from high cost areas or areas of production difficulty but from any point at all. As we move out from the starting point we look around for possible benefits that might arise from the alternatives we are suggesting.

I was once working with a group of children in Sweden and one of the problems given to the group was that of a chemical plant which had difficulty in persuading workers to work the week-end shift. The children suggested a separate work-force of week-end workers. There were several times as many applicants for these jobs as for the ordinary jobs.

'De-averaging'

This is an ugly expression but a useful one. The process of market segmentation is well known. Instead of treating a market as a whole an attempt is made to break it down into different segments which have different needs and tastes and then to cater for each of these. The 'de-averaging' process is very similar. We tend to think of things as wholes or averages or ideals. This is a matter of convenience. We might talk of 'shoppers'. But the idea of a shopper can be broken down into two distinct groups. There are the chore shoppers who just want to get it done. They are quite happy to drive out in their cars to shopping centres once a week and to load up the car with what they need. They want simplicity and efficiency and low prices. Town planners who assumed that this was what all shoppers wanted found that they were mistaken. There is another group of shoppers: the social shoppers. For many women going shopping is the only escape from the home, the only 'adventure' or activity of the day, the only opportunity for social contact with friends or even just the shop assistants. The social shopper did not want everything simplified and anaesthetized.

From de-averaging shoppers in this way we could develop two opportunity concepts. The first is that of the professional shopper who would, for a commission, do the chore shopping for a group of families. This professional would be able to shop around, get the best buys, get bulk discounts, take telephone orders and deliver to his customers. Something of the sort has already happened in some countries on an individual basis. The second idea would build on the social aspects of shopping not just with coffee centres in stores but with group activities.

We could de-average patients into those who wanted someone to listen to their problems and give them support and those who wanted an efficient diagnosis and prescribed treatment almost like a car service station. Alternatively we could de-average patients into those requiring acute treatment, those requiring maintenance (diabetics, hypertensive), and those requiring a periodic overview. There are several ways of de-averaging something depending on what we choose to look at. At the end of the process we want to end up with some broad groups, not an analysis into tiny groups. We would also like to see how this de-averaging suggests new opportunities. For example de-averaging taxi-users into those who urgently needed a taxi and those who could afford to wait would lead to the idea of the premium fare taxis suggested earlier.

Perhaps the most fertile area for de-averaging is in dealing with different people in the work situation: the job-motivated, the group-motivated, the habit-motivated and so on.

The Laker Sky-train concept is yet another attempt to de-average transatlantic airline passengers into those who need to get there on time and in comfort and those who want to get there in the cheapest possible way and do not mind about comfort or schedules.

In practical terms the de-averaging concept can be applied to customers, processes, people at work, products or anything else. The question to ask is: 'What are we dealing with here? Is there an average concept which could be broken down?'

Significant point

It is a very useful exercise when reading a newspaper or a magazine to try to pick out the significant point in the piece that is being read. This significant point is in the general context of opportunities. For example, a short piece about IBM's system 32 and a particular software package mentioned that this package had proved especially useful to a retail fashion house in following stock movement and maximizing stock control. The manager of the fashion house pointed out the problems that arose from over- or under-ordering as fashion was so ephemeral. Although the piece was about computers the significant point was this problem of stocking by fashion houses. From the significant point arose the concept of 'Second Sell Ltd' as an organization that would buy up unsold stock from the fashion houses that had to be right up-to-date and sell it at low prices to those who felt no need to be so up-to-date. This is not unlike the success of the 'Reject' shops which are understood to sell slightly damaged goods at reduced prices. The customer feels that he is getting a bargain because the slight damage does not matter at all to him but the low price does. In themselves both these are examples of 'de-averaging'. An article which mentions that fifty-three per cent of married women in England go out to work might have as its significant point the forty-seven per cent who do not go out to work. Is this because they do not need to or do not want to or cannot? This might lead to ideas of developing work which can be done at home or even the Avon lady type of home sales force.

Almost any point can be seen as significant if a context is already prepared for its reception. That context might arise from experience, from the nature of one's business or from an opportunity attitude. It is a useful exercise to practise picking out significant points and constructing an opportunity context around them. Even if there is not much success at first the opportunity habit of mind that may be developed in this way will prove useful elsewhere. As always, the opportunity search must look towards potential benefits as soon as possible.

Disadvantage into advantage

Almost everyone knows the story of the salmon-canners whose product no one wanted to buy because it was much paler than customers expected salmon to be. But sales picked up as soon as the product was advertised as 'the only pale salmon'. This classic tale of turning disadvantage into advantage illustrates a starting point that can be used for opportunity search. The example of the watch-dog that would not bark has been mentioned earlier.

In New Zealand the government seeks to restrict the import of cars by imposing quotas and high tariffs. From time to time the restrictions are made even more severe by an insistence that the full price of a car must be paid in cash at the time of purchase. This disadvantage, from the car-dealer's point of view, might be turned into an advantage through the development of joint purchase schemes. Some legal and financial framework might be provided to enable two families to join together to make the purchase. A market might even develop in part-ownerships. When the restrictions were lifted this approach would be found to have expanded the market because those who could buy solo cars would do so and those who could not would still be able to buy part cars (or second family cars).

In the insurance world a disaster like the jumbo jet collision on the runway in the Canary islands is almost welcomed because it is followed by an increase in insurance premiums which had otherwise lagged behind the inflationary increase in costs.

'Under what circumstances . . .'

This is a variation of the preceding starting point. It need not, however, apply only to a disadvantage. It could apply to any characteristic or feature or activity. Under what circumstances would that charactistic become a distinct advantage or open up an opportunity? We have seen earlier how the 'reject' selling concept arose from goods which were slightly damaged. Such damage actually created an opportunity because it gave credibility to a low price claim. Similarly the 'clearing-out sale' label is often used to give credibility to low prices.

A real estate agent once told me that he had a problem in persuading one of his assistants to install a radio telephone in his car. I suggested that he install a second-hand telephone. This was acceptable. The original reluctance had been due to the assistant not wanting to be available at all times. The second-hand equipment provided the usable excuse that the equipment was not working properly at times when the assistant did not want to be available. Even if this excuse was never used it was there if necessary.

Under what circumstances would a burglary be an asset? As an excuse to get rid of papers and records which should normally be available. Under what circumstances would a burglar alarm be an asset? Through linking it with an insurance policy. Under what circumstances would the sale of an insurance policy be an asset? Perhaps by selling a group policy to adjoining households and hence giving them an interest in protecting each other's property.

Like extracting the significant point the 'under what circumstances' exercise is useful opportunity practice. The actual starting point is of course some feature or activity which is then considered through the framework of altered circumstances.

Under what circumstances is a recession an advantage? If you have enough cash to buy up bankrupt companies at below their true cost.

'What business are we in?'

This is a fairly traditional approach. The answer to the question provides the starting point for opportunity thinking. The difficulty is to pitch the answer at a level of generality that is fertile. A newspaper executive might ask himself the question and then say 'survival' or 'making profits'. This sort of reply would be too general to be useful. At the other extreme a reply like 'to fill the equivalent of six pages of advertising and five of editorial matter' would be too detailed. In between there might be replies like 'selling advertising space' or 'off-line communication' or 'increasing the value of our advertising space through increasing circulation'. In carrying out this procedure it is important to accept that people's expectations are real. It may be true that with television and radio no one actually needs to read news in a paper. But people do expect to read news in a newspaper.

As with many other opportunity search processes there is no one right answer that can be reached by analysis. There are many alternative answers, some of which might well be inadequate. The purpose of these answers is to set off a train of thought (through provision of a starting point). Once an opportunity idea has gelled it is judged in its own right. For example, the suggestion that newspapers should use surplus advertising space to sell goods in which they have a direct commercial interest would be judged on its merits.

Sometimes the answer to the question may be very simple. Many organizations are in the business of selling 'convenience'. Although convenience is a somewhat vague concept which has no absolute definition it is usable. What can be done to make things more convenient? What is the effect on convenience of this idea? The convenience of margarine as compared to butter was mentioned earlier. The convenience of a no-booking shuttle service on a regular air route was also mentioned. In modern society trouble, hassle, uncertainty, complexity and frustration have replaced the primitive fears of animal existence. Anything which serves to reduce them has a market value under the heading 'convenience'.

The question 'what business are we in?' can be transformed to 'what are we trying to do?' when it is the work situation itself that is under scrutiny.

Me-too

The 'me-too' concept is the most obvious and perhaps the safest source of opportunities even though it may not be very satisfying intellectually. The entry of Kodak into the instant photography market in competition with Polaroid was a delayed example of me-too. The success of *Penthouse* magazine was a me-too as regards the concept established by *Playboy*, although here – as with many me-too situations – there was an updating of the product.

The pharmaceutical industry is full of me-too products wherever this is not prevented by patents. Several companies have their own version of the beta-blocker therapy that is used in hypertension because hypertension is such a huge market since the patient has to take the therapy every day for years and often for the rest of his life. One has only to open a copy of a business journal like *Fortune* to see what a huge range of copiers are on offer. In a sense all of them are me-too products riding on the success of the Xerox copier. It is hard to believe that initially the Xerox process was only thought of as an aid to printing.

As soon as a film on exorcism or witchcraft is a success there is a spate of me-too films on the same subject. Sometimes the films come from the same production company in the 'son of Lassie' phenomenon but usually other companies are offering their versions of the theme as well.

The logic of the me-too situation is sound. Someone else has shown that a market exists. Someone else has developed the market and spent money doing so. Someone else has made the mistakes and learned from them. It makes sense to move in with a parallel product and reap the benefits of the experience of others – no matter how unfair it may seem.

In matters like films or publishing assessing the public taste is difficult. It is a hit and miss matter. So if someone is fortunate enough to have a hit then everyone is grateful for this disclosure of public interest – and cashes in.

The me-too temptations are not without danger. The market may not be big enough for two major suppliers. The result is a price or promotion war which reduces the profitability of the opportunity. An established leader in the field may have sufficient muscle and money to lower prices to the point where the new entrant cannot compete. After all, the market leader may have already written off his development costs. With pocket calculators the prices started at over $150 and came down to less than $10 as more me-too people moved into the field. With the 'mood-ring' that changed colour according to the skin temperature of the finger (so reflecting mood) the original producer and inventor sold his product at $150. Within a month there were forty different suppliers in the field and the price was down to $5.

In considering any opportunity the negative side of me-too must be taken into account. How long will it take competitors to enter the field and what protection can there be? The establishment of a brand name may be powerful – as it was with Pentel, the originators of the fibre-tip pen. Ironically, a brand name may become so powerfully established that it loses its brand value and becomes a general term for the process: as happened with 'xerox' for copying and 'hoover' for vacuum cleaning.

The ideal me-too situation is where a small company has opened up the market but is clearly unable to supply the demand. A licence may be obtained, a take-over may be attempted or a me-too parallel product developed. The important thing to remember is that if the me-too situation looks good to you it will also look good to other peple and a market that is under-supplied at the moment may well be over-supplied by the time all the me-too opportunists enter the field. There has to be some special advantage that a company possesses in the field before a me-too suggestion becomes a me-too opportunity. Up-dating or alteration of the original product or a technical improvement could provide such a reason.

Brought in from abroad

Whatever happens in the USA very quickly travels to Europe. The CB radio boom in the USA moved to Europe within two years. Handic sales in Sweden in 1976 approached $12 million and it claims twenty per cent of the European CB market. Two young entrepreneurs in Australia discovered in the USA a good insect repellent that was not yet marketed in Australia and built up a business on its introduction to that market.

The reverse route, from abroad to the USA, is very much slower. There are many successful products outside the USA which have not yet been marketed in the USA. The reason is that the USA tends to be a more adventurous market and hence feels that there is little to be found elsewhere.

Bringing something in from abroad is a sort of 'me-too' operation except that it is usually done by agreement or licensing. In the UK Wilkinson Sword were successful in bringing in and marketing the Foster Grant line of sunglasses from the USA. In fact they were so successful that they have started buying additional lines from other sources like France.

Obviously it does not follow that a product which has been a success in one country will repeat that success elsewhere. Each market has different characteristics. The very successful game 'Mastermind' which was a big seller in Europe made little initial impact in the USA. In such cases it is important to distinguish whether it is the product itself that is inappropriate to the market or the marketing method used. In the UK the 'Mastermind' game was helped to a considerable extent by the low price – since it was marketed by the plastics company Invicta – and the association of the name with a well known TV programme. In the USA the game lacked the individual attention it required in order to penetrate the market.

A periodic eyes-open trip around the world should be part of the opportunity search process. The large trade fairs help in this respect but do not make unnecessary a visit to the actual marketplace of the shops and stores. Publishers usually have scouts who can signal back to headquarters anything promising in the field. Manufacturers could do likewise.

Bringing in something from abroad applies to ideas and processes as much as to products. There may be new approaches in motivation and job satisfaction. The temptation is to dismiss such approaches as being irrelevant to the local scene on the basis that the background regulations and behaviour of people differ from country to country. This should be brought in as a consideration after looking at the idea rather than as a blanket excuse for not looking at any idea from abroad.

Market size

It is said that any business that had one quarter of one per cent of the aspirin market would be doing very well. The chewing gum market in the USA is worth $370 million a year. The chewing tobacco market is supposedly worth $100 million. The tennis market about $400 million. In 1975 the cough medicine market in the UK was worth £11.5 million. The UK beer consumption is about 40,650,000 barrels a year – a quarter of it in lager.

It is usually the growth of a market, in terms of a trend, that is more appealing than the actual size. Size itself is more often used as a reason for not entering a market – on the basis that it is not large enough. Nevertheless where a market is huge there is a temptation to get in there and get a piece of the action. As with so many other opportunity temptations, the reasons why a particular newcomer expects to prosper in the field need to be spelled out. Such reasons might include established distribution channels, low production costs, related know-how or the established public image value of a name (as with the Mary Quant entry into cosmetics).

Paradoxically there are opportunities to be found in a declining market. The major producers may be getting out of the market so fast that there is an unfilled need.

Buying one's way into a market is usually more successful than entering it as a newcomer because no matter how sensational one's new product may be, it takes a long time for the wonder of it to become known to intermediate buyers. The ultimate consumer may be aware of the benefits because he is a user but the stockist is not a user and will therefore stick to the established products and only slowly react to customer feedback. A stockist's reaction to selling his entire stock of a new product might be: 'It was a risk buying it, thank goodness I have managed to move it,' rather than 'That new product has moved quite fast, I must order some more.' Most stockists will only hold a new product from a new entrant into the field if there is a promise of a substantial promotion campaign.

Is a market with many small operators more accessible than one with only a few large ones? It all depends. If each of the small operators has been there a long time it is probably because they have demonstrated some advantage – in supply, reliability or product differentiation – and such advantages are not easy to establish rapidly. Alternatively, small operators cannot easily match the promotional muscle of a large competitor. A market with a few large competitors can respond by a price-cutting or a promotional war. Equally, a new entrant, provided there is sufficient financial muscle, can adopt strategies which are not available to the established supplier. For example, as mentioned earlier, the Bic company entry into the disposable razor market forced Gillette into the same field. But whereas Bic could compare the disposable razor favourably with established razors Gillette could not afford to do so because it would mean downgrading its major source of income.

It is well worth looking at market sizes from time to time. It is amazing how ignorant executives may be about market sizes other than those in which they are directly involved.

Trends

Another traditional source of opportunities: trends in leisure behaviour, trends in market growth and so on. In France it is estimated that the growth in the mini-computer market will be about forty per cent as compared with fifteen-per-cent growth in the mainframe market. Percentage rises must of course be related to the established base. In Spain the 1977 tourist figures showed a ten- to twelve-per-cent increase over 1976 but an increase by itself is not yet a trend. In the USA the average growth rate of fast-food chains has been twenty per cent a year. Already 27 cents of every food dollar goes on meals taken away from home. It is estimated that if the trend continues by 1980 about forty per cent of all meals will be taken away from home. In 1977 in the USA there seemed to be a trend back to club-type discos as a source of entertainment.

Spotting a trend and getting in early with a good product has always been the classic recipe for opportunity We sometimes think of trends as natural phenomena due to the confluence of a variety of influences. But trends may be artificially created. A lot of publicity interest in a particular subject may set off a trend which then becomes self-sustaining just as a book may not merit its place on the best-seller list but once placed there generates enough interest to provide the required sales to keep it there. The mistake is to suppose that trends can be created by deliberate promotional effort. They cannot – unless the effort is of the more subtle public relations type.

It is important to distinguish between fads, fashions, switches and growth. A fad is something with immediate appeal and hence rapid market penetration. The mystery is why some fads, like the Frisbee, develop into semi-permanent markets whereas others, like the Hula-Hoop which was marketed by the same company, seem to fade away. Fads have an explosive intensity and the psychology is that of an appeal-hunger. Fashions are more complex because there are many layers. To some extent a fashion only works if there is a group who receive the fashion ahead of others. On the other hand a fad must have real appeal substance whereas a fashion may have no substance at all. A switch is the most powerful form of trend because it implies permanence. It means that one way of doing things is being substituted by another. For example the switch from records to cassettes is a genuine – if only partial – substitution. The switch from saloon cars to hatchbacks is also a genuine trend. A growth trend, as with the fast-food market, means that more people are willing or able to be consumers in a particular market. As people become more affluent there will be a trend towards two-car families or two-TV-set families. The most useful sort of growth is where a price or ability threshold is crossed. For instance, it may be the decline in family size which allows parents to leave home in the evening – or gives them more disposable income with which to do so. Increased holiday time brought about by union pressure means a growth in the holiday industry. The distinction between fad, fashion and growth is an important one but it is not always easy to make. Was the trend towards bicycles a fashion or genuine growth in this market? Is the trend towards smaller cars a fashion set off by a temporary concern with energy or a genuine growth – in this case the distinction may not matter because if all the manufacturers only make smaller cars that will be all there is to buy. In general an enabling factor gives rise to growth (such as the relaxation of regulations controlling mopeds in the USA) whereas transient concern may only give rise to a fashion. The linkage of smoking to lung cancer caused a negative fashion in cigarette-smoking but not a true trend. Sales dipped and then recovered.

Looking for the ancillary activity on the fringe of the trend can be profitable. It is rather like making a fortune not out of oil-drilling but out of supplying the oil rigs in the North Sea. If the mini-computer market is expanding will there be a need for more software? The answer is not always obvious. For example it may be that mini-computer users (unlike mainframe users) have such standardized requirements that they can all use a few basic software packages. Riding on the tails of a trend can be profitable because the trend creates a fierce demand market.

Separating a trend from the result of a successful marketing effort may not be easy. A marketing innovation may lead to an increase in sales but this new level of sales may remain static or even drop off unless a succession of marketing innovations follow. A genuine trend involves a rise of sales where no special innovation has been tried. But the growth of fast-food chains in the USA may be because the decor and standard have improved so much – rather than a genuine change in eating habits. It could be argued that this improvement in standards has actually opened up a new market (the adult as distinct from the teenager or traveller). Discount trends may be particularly risky. At times of recession people may be much more price conscious than at others.

A trend away from something becomes, in practice, a trend towards something else. A trend away from identical mass production in cars may become a trend towards individualized cars or replicas of famous marques of the past. It can be useful to identify trends as being away from something because the opportunity-seeker may then put in his own destination, such as car livery designed by famous artists.

Focus on areas of weakness and areas of strength

In the course of focusing on the different sorts of assets described earlier in this section there may have been attention paid to areas of strength. There is no harm in doing this again but in a more general sense: 'What are the areas of strength in the organization?' We can list those areas and then look at each in turn to see whether there are any opportunities that arise from them. If management services are a strength, there may be an opportunity to take over companies that are less well run. If R & D is a strength it may be focused on a market trend or gap defined by outside marketing consultants. If distribution channels are the strength new me-too products or products from abroad may be fed through the channels. If cash-flow is the strength there is an opportunity to look at those business areas which require a short sharp injection of capital to get them going or to rescue them.

In the same way it is possible to list the areas of weakness and to generate opportunities from these. An ailing part of an organization may be sold off to someone else to whom it may be more useful (variable value). A multiplicity of unprofitable products can be simplified. Undifferentiated (commodity-type) products can be differentiated. Packaging can be changed. An area of weakness should not be regarded as an area for 'patching-up' but as a high opportunity area that merits focused thinking attention. It is seldom that success in one area can compensate for failure elsewhere. Excellence in product design cannot compensate for poor sales effort. Excellence in financial management cannot compensate for low productivity. Excellence in problem analysis cannot compensate for poor planning. Excellence in decision-making cannot compensate for a deficiency in idea generation.

Idea-sensitive areas

The concept of the i.s.a. (idea-sensitive area) was introduced in Part II. In the course of the Opportunity Audit executives were asked to pick out areas in which a change in idea could have a marked effect. These were areas that could respond to an idea – hence they were idea-sensitive areas. Such an area might be a high-cost area or a bottleneck or a problem area or a high-pay-off opportunity area. Obviously an i.s.a. provides an ideal starting point for opportunity search, which is why it is reintroduced at this point. As with many other starting points in this formal check-list there is a considerable degree of overlap – an area of weakness may itself constitute an i.s.a.

'If only we could come up with an idea in this area . . .' is the verbalization of an i.s.a. In itself that remark constitutes a rather vague starting point. The next step is to create some idea. It may be a matter of suggesting an ideal 'wishful thinking' solution. It may be a challenge to an existing procedure and a suggested alternative. It may be a provocative remark as suggested later in this section. What is important is that some start is made.

Suppose a credit card company identified as an i.s.a. the need to indicate rapidly to retailers the fact that a card had been stolen. A starting idea might be a card-reader with a memory. This could be a telephone-linked mini-computer which would have fed into it overnight the numbers of missing cards. The operator would then punch in the number of the presented card and a red light or buzzer would tell if the card had been stolen. This would also have a deterrent effect. From that idea could come another one of a computer-linked telephone so that the retailer would dial a number and then continue to dial in the card number – a buzz would indicate a faulty card. Another idea would be to put the onus on the customer by having card-clearance centres which would validate (for a small fee) the card for that day. All these ideas arise from the starting idea and can follow in a matter of seconds.

It may be argued that an i.s.a. would fit more appropriately in the end-point list than in the starting-point list but really it enters both. Suppose the i.s.a. is, 'We have 10,000 life insurance salesmen and some of these in rural areas (Australia) cannot earn a living from commission.' This might lead to the idea of the salesmen selling other things or selling their skill and acting as general purpose financial broker for loans, mortgages and other matters – a sort of money-doctor. Although an i.s.a. is often posed as a problem I would like to emphasize that it need not be. A brilliant salesman employed by a management consulting organization can constitute an i.s.a.: 'How can we most effectively employ this man's talents?' This is not really a problem because it could easily be solved by terminating the person's employment.

The practical procedure is simple. Identify an i.s.a. and then use it as a starting point. As usual the problem is to work at a fertile level of generality. An i.s.a. which states, 'How can we make more profits?' is much too general. An i.s.a. which states, 'How can we reduce costs in the customer service area?' is usable.

Provocation

Provocation is part of lateral thinking. It is an attempt to switch our thinking channel by taking a provocative jump. The process will be considered in more detail in the section on the treatment of ideas. Provocation is, however, a useful way of getting a starting point. Normally one idea follows logically from another but when using provocation this is not necessary – in fact: 'There may not be a reason for saying something until after it has been said.' The provocation opens up a new idea and this idea then justifies the provocation that was made.

A builder in London was having difficulty in getting people to go and look at his houses. He heard me talk briefly on the radio about lateral thinking and provocation. As a result he said to himself, 'Suppose I took my houses to go and see the people?' That was the provocative starting point. As a result he built a full-scale house on a barge in the Thames and then towed the house up and down the river anchoring at spots which people could easily reach. Within three months he had had 26,000 visitors to the house.

There are many ways of setting up a provocation and the simplest is to take the existing situation and reverse it. The food-processing department of a major company were used to taking the fish bones out of the fish. As a provocation they decided to try to take the fish away from the bones. They developed a process for doing this and it is said reduced their costs by £1.5 million.

In practice the provocation is often preceded by the word 'po' which is derived from suppose, hypothesis, possible and poetry and can be regarded as meaning 'provocative operation'. For example, in an ailing restaurant we might say: 'Po the customers served other customers'. This might lead to the idea that each day of the week the restaurant would be leased out to a different family who would do the cooking and serving. They might regard this as training for running a full-scale restaurant or they might only be able to run a restaurant one day a week. The proprietor would charge a flat fee and a percentage of the take.

There is no way of telling where a provocation will lead. The provocation provides the starting point and ideas that develop are followed. All the time there is an attempt to shape the idea into a practical opportunity. The process has three stages:

'Let's set up a provocation.'
'Where does the provocation lead?'
'How can we transform this into a practical idea?'

There is no situation in which a provocation cannot be used. The difficulty may lie in setting up a provocative provocation. There is a tendency to play safe and to set up as a provocation a weak solution. With a true provocation the person setting it up must have no idea how it could lead to a useful idea. For instance we might say of a bank: 'Po no customers can take out any money.' This might lead to the notion of information transaction points which could be open at all times to telephone interrogation and EFT.

Transfer

This is really a special form of provocation. We look at an unconnected operation and see how we can transfer the methods and processes to our own operation. We could look at a laundry and then try to see how the laundry process could be transferred to running a private hospital. We might look more closely at how different materials are separated out for different treatment. We might look at batching procedures and at quality control. We might look at customer satisfaction and the way complaints are dealt with. In each instance we mentally transfer the process to the hospital and look to see what opportunities emerge. From the batching idea we might think of setting up special months at the hospital: one month for varicose veins, one month for nose jobs, one month for renal diagnosis, one month for diabetic overviews and so on. During that month the appropriate teams of specialists would be on hand.

Most executives live in the world of their own business and know relatively little of what happens in other areas. And yet it may happen that in one of those other areas a procedure has had to be developed (because the need was greater there) which could be applied directly to another business area. Even if a procedure is not directly transferable it may serve to stimulate new thinking about an area.

As a starting point procedure the transfer operation is easy to use. You fix your attention on some other industry and then move mentally through its operations noting at each stage what transfer or provocative value they may have. The other industry may be chosen at random or because it seems to be parallel in operation to one's own. For example, there might be some parallelism between the church and advertising in so far as both deal with communication and belief. Alternatively the chicken farming industry would be a random choice for transfer to the advertising industry. It might lead to the concept of a steady and sustained diet of the right ingredients – waiting for the customer to be in a 'laying mood' rather than pursuing his mood of the moment.

The treatment of ideas

Once the starting point has been chosen ideas should begin to develop. This will not happen with every starting point which is why a check-list of starting points has been provided. The executive goes through them trying each in turn and spending some time with it to see what ideas do develop. When an idea does develop it should be followed and prodded. Sometimes it may be a matter of running the idea forward to see what would happen. At other times it may be a matter of extracting the principle to see how this could be applied in a more practical manner. These processes will be described in the section on the treatment of ideas – because an idea may arise from one's own thinking or from the thinking of someone else.

It is important to keep in mind that one is looking for benefits and hence for opportunities. This is the 'atmosphere' within which ideas are pursued. Nevertheless the idea must be allowed to develop according to its own nature. If the idea is killed too quickly because no benefits are seen at once (or grave faults are only too obvious) then many potentially valuable ideas are going to be killed. Also, as mentioned before, executives should be wary of the killer phrase, 'the same as', for a potentially new idea is easily dismissed if attention is paid only to its resemblance to an old idea rather than to its difference from that idea.

'With a problem we can define, in advance, the desired destination or end-point of our thinking.'

End-point check-list

In the moving-out type of thinking we start at a point and then move out with our thinking. When an idea has developed we see if that idea can be transformed into a profitable opportunity. When we start out we have no idea where we are going to end up except that we will only accept a final idea that we can show to be worthwhile. In the moving-in type of thinking we know the destination or end-point in advance and our thinking is concerned with finding our way there. The moving-in type of thinking is very similar to problem-solving but the concept is wider because it involves finding problems as well as solving them. With ordinary problem-solving we can ask: 'What is the problem?' With moving-in thinking we might say: 'What problem can we create here and then how can we solve it?'

The difference between having a starting point and an end point for our opportunity-thinking may be illustrated with an example. Suppose we use as a starting point the operating asset of a cigarette smoker that he can indicate something about himself through smoking. The next stage is to consider what he might indicate. It might be his class, his status, his self-image. What else? Perhaps it could be his mood. To some extent this is done already by the way in which the smoker puffs on the cigarette. Perhaps we could formalize this by having mood cigarettes (red for temper, green for tranquillity, rose for love, blue for icy decision) and the smoker would choose the cigarette he wanted in order to let those around him know of his mood. Or the idea might be refined by strongly associating different brands with different images – rather like the zodiac signs – or perhaps the cigarette could be a zodiac indicator. There are now several different directions which might be taken.

In the moving-in approach we might say: 'We have the problem of increasing brand definition.' For this we might go to ideas of advertising style and packaging, size and ingredients and the usual methods of differentiating a brand. We would certainly come up with a useful answer but it would be unlikely to be as novel as the ones produced by the starting-point approach. It may, however be easier to assess.

Much of what is written in this section on problem-solving is not novel. The section is not meant to be a treatise on problem-solving. Problem-solving is included because it is part of opportunity search and there would have been a gap if it had been left out.

Idea-sensitive areas

Idea-sensitive areas have been described in Part II and have also been mentioned in the starting-point check-list. An i.s.a. may be either a starting point ('We have the ability to mould plastic more cheaply than anyone else, how can we use the asset?') or an end point ('We have a very high cost of distribution, how can we reduce that?'). Within the idea-sensitive area of the high distribution costs we might define certain problems and set about solving these or we might define an end point in more general terms: 'Can we find some novel, lower-cost, distribution channels?'

We can consider some examples of idea-sensitive areas.

'Can we reduce the very high cost of seminar publicity?'

'There is a bottle-neck in the paint shop.'

'If only we had a USP for our school supplies we could capture the major share of the market.'

'John Katz has had very useful experience in the banking world; how can we make better use of him?'

'An increase in motivation of our sales force would make a big difference to our survival.'

'How can we keep the computer analysts we have?'

An i.s.a. should not be defined in the same way as a problem. For example, the i.s.a. of the high cost of seminar publicity should not really be defined as: 'How can we reduce the high cost of seminar publicity?' but rather as: 'The high cost of seminar publicity is an i.s.a.' From the latter definition we can think about reducing costs but we could also think in terms of making more profitable use of the incurred cost, by offering seminar packages for example. Within an i.s.a. several different problem definitions, objectives and starting points can be tried. To repeat: an idea-sensitive area is an area in which an idea may have considerable benefits. In short, an i.s.a. is by definition an opportunity area. The temptation to turn it into a single problem definition should be avoided.

The 'something' method

The 'something' method is a rather basic process that underlies much of our thinking. In this method we define our end point by defining the characteristics the final idea should have. For example, in looking for a mail order product we might say: 'We need "something" that is small in size, not easily damaged, easy to illustrate, with a high profit margin and with a naturally focused market.' We then set about looking for the 'something'.

The end point of moving-in thinking can be defined with differing degrees of precision. We might say: 'There is something wrong with our sales department.' That is really an i.s.a Or we might say: 'We must find a way to tempt Joe Smith away from his present job and ask him to take over our sales department.' That is the definition of a problem. Or we might say: 'We need someone who has had a lot of experience in this field, who is under the age of forty, who is good at motivating people, who understands merchandising and who is not averse to getting out on the road.' That is an example of the 'something' method for the characteristics are defined in advance.

In one of my books* I once suggested that we might give the special name 'requiron' to a something that we could define only by the characteristics it would have when we found it. By using the 'something' method we really create a search-type problem. The danger is that we may miss something which would have solved the problem because the missed thing may not have all the characteristics which we set out in advance. If we decide that our sales manager has to be under forty we may miss a very competent man who was in fact fifty. As with an interview the trick is to know what one wants but to be ready to assess someone or something who does not quite fit the supposed requirements.

The words 'something', 'someone', 'some way', 'a device', 'a method', 'a means', 'mechanism', 'a procedure', 'a person' and 'an

* *Practical Thinking*, published by Jonathan Cape and Penguin Books, London.

idea' are all general purpose terms that are interchangeable with 'something'. Rather more specific terms include words like 'a product' or 'an incentive'. On the whole it is better to avoid those. It is better to say, 'We need some way of motivating our salesmen other than by money', than to say, 'We need to look at salesmen's incentives other than money.' This is because the more specific the definition the more it locks out. For example a pep talk by the chairman or even a threat of redundancy might motivate the salesmen and yet neither of these could properly be called an incentive.

It is in order to be quite deliberate about the 'something' method. An executive could say to himself or to his colleagues: 'How would you define the "something" we need here?' If so desired the term 'something, quotes' could be used in conversation in order to indicate the special nature of the word 'something' by suggesting it is in quotation marks.

As suggested, the 'something' method is already a natural part of our thinking but it can be well worthwhile to be more deliberate about it. It is also worth practising it from time to time in an attempt to focus more sharply generally stated desires.

Market gaps

Looking for market gaps is a very traditional type of opportunity search and it still remains a very useful method. The philosophical distinction between a gap and a need is not always clear, for a genuine gap implies an unsatisfied need. In practice, however, a gap occurs when the need is being satisfied in some way but a gap in supply can be discerned. The distinction is probably not worth making except that by looking for gaps separately from needs we get two bites at the cherry.

The classic type of gap is the 'in-between' gap where two things are being done but there is a gap in between. A classic example is the 'Mastermind' game that we mentioned earlier. Because it was marketed by Invicta Ltd in the UK the price could be lower than if anyone else had been involved – this is because Invicta are heavily involved in plastic moulding and indeed some of the moulds used for the game had long been used for education products. The result was that the game reached the market in a unique price position. It was marketed at about £1. At a lower price range there were any number of small, pocket-type games which were too cheap to be given as a Christmas present. At a higher price range (£3–4) were more substantial games which involved a definite buying decision and were too expensive to give as casual presents. The Invicta game was substantial enough to be given as a present and yet cheap enough to be added on to other purchases.

The holiday industry is continually finding market gaps. In between the sun-and-sea young people's holiday and the expensive do-it-yourself holiday for older people is the 'cultural package gap' for people who want the price and convenience of the package trip but do not want to lie on the beach. There may still be other gaps. In Europe (but not in the USA) there is a gap for the family who want to go abroad but do not want to take the children. Some combination of holiday camp and overseas trip might serve the purpose: the children stay at a camp and the parents go abroad. In the USA a house-sitter service combined with travel arrangements might have a market. 'Combination-gaps' are useful areas for opportunity search. Two things might be done separately but bringing them together creates a new opportunity – such as, a holiday and organized shopping service in London for overseas visitors; a combined gardening and house maintenance contract; or a good shop and take-away food service.

Doing something no one else wants to do has always provided good opportunities. The new business of 'waste management' or city refuse handling is an example. I remember a medical friend of mine who concentrated on statistics at an early age. He found no trouble getting jobs in the best hospitals because the medical staff there were very bad at the statistics now required for medical publications. Government departments also need medical statistics. So the person in question has now built up a largish empire within his hospital.

Sometimes you can spot a gap which no one has thought of. Two young men noticed that the open display cabinets for frozen food items in supermarkets had no covers. So they devised a sort of roller blind cover with magnetic strip edges which could be rolled down over the display cabinets at night or at week-ends. It was shown that covering the cabinets saved up to twenty-eight per cent on the electricity fuel bills. Was this foreseeing a need which no one else had seen or was it a gap in the equipment supply to supermarkets? It does not matter.

I was once asked by the man who ran the Swedish Government research and technical bureau to suggest a source of 'seed' ideas for technical innovation. I suggested he went and looked through the bankruptcy files. A company may go bankrupt for various reasons: because the idea is ahead of its time; because a market gap has been correctly identified but poorly tackled; because the idea is wonderful but the financial management was poor; because it did not have the resources to ride out the development and market development costs; because it is so successful that the cash-flow problem created by expansion cannot be solved. In many cases the opportunity idea remains sound even though the organization has gone bankrupt. So there is a ready-made catalogue of ideas.

In the much used Lane Cove park in Sydney there is a short stretch of river. A friend of mine was told of an investment opportunity in a paddle-boat on this river. He snapped up the opportunity because he could see the entertainment gap: a passive form of activity for older people, an experience activity for children. The venture has been doing well.

Then there are 'transfer-gaps' where we transfer a marketing method from one field to another. Disposable pens to disposable lighters to disposable razors (the Bic company). The gap is seen as the lack of that marketing method in a particular field. In the UK because of the tax structure the leasing of cars is now quite common. Perhaps there are other fields the leasing concept can be applied to. Rental is another method that might be more widely applied. It might be possible for example to organize a camera rental service with safeguards against theft for holidays or weekends. At the moment you either have your own camera or use a photographer (apart from the limited booths). I would see a scheme in which you rented a camera, film and developing service as a package for an afternoon. Instant cameras would make it even easier.

The opposite of finding a genuine gap is 'falling between two stools'. A book which is not serious enough to be a scientific work and yet too complex to be a popular work falls between two stools. It falls into a gap where there is no market. A restaurant that is too expensive to be cheap and yet not good enough to be a luxury restaurant also falls between two stools. And yet a restaurant which provides good but simple food at a low price in simple but pleasant surroundings may fill a real gap. The important point about gap-finding is that it must be possible to define the gap crisply: 'An eating place for people who like good cooking but cannot afford high prices'.

Needs

The Babycham story is one of of the classics of need satisfaction in the UK. Women were beginning to go into pubs with their boy-friends. They did not like the taste of beer and it was still considered unfeminine to grasp large glasses of beer. It was difficult to sit and drink spirits all evening (for the pub was an evening's entertainment not a pre-dinner drink) and in any case it was expensive. To ask for an orange or tomato juice seemed feeble. So there was a need for a new 'dainty' mildly alcoholic drink especially for women. And that was where Babycham came in as a perry-based drink sold in elegant small bottles with heavy promotional backing. It provided the needed answer at the moment when the question was asked: 'And what can I order for you?' It could also be seen as filling a gap in the drinks market.

The revived popularity of discos in the USA in 1977 indicates a new need. The need is not for somewhere to dance or drink or take your lover but for an exotic experience or for a stage on which one can perform. It is also the need for somewhere to go in the evening beyond having a meal at a restaurant (especially as so many people are on diets). It is the need for a party at which there is no host and you do not need to wait to be invited. You choose the disco that is 'in' with your friends and you can be sure to see them there – just as you might at a party.

There is probably an unsatisfied need for 'experience' holidays. They would be rather like a prolonged fancy dress party. Instead of changing your surroundings by going to an exotic place you would drive to a large country house and then put on costume and assume a role for two weeks or so. The change of context would provide the experience and adventure, together with the other people there.

The success of the Disney parks in California and Florida has led some entrepreneurs to invest in 'theme' parks. They see in the USA a need for exotic experience. The USA is rather uniform in culture. It needs a lot of travel to get to somewhere exotic such as Europe or the East. This sort of travel is not possible – and too expensive – with a family of children and too risky for some people. So the 'foreign experience' places are created as theme parks and the themes are related to such TV idioms as space travel.

Some needs are obvious but others only become apparent when a means of satisfying them has surfaced. No one would have predicted that there was a 'need' for CB radios in the USA. Yet their appearance led to a huge boom in the market and suddenly everyone had a need for a CB radio. The same thing may happen with plug-in TV games or with home computers. One way to look for needs is to go through a person's activities minute by minute throughout the day. Another way is to consider basic needs – not just for food, clothing and housing but also for company, for entertainment, for individualization, for skill, for meeting people, for status and all the other psychological needs.

We can look at the success of some enterprise and then try to see what need it satisfied. Can that need be satisfied in another way? Instead of looking directly at the needs of people we can look at the needs demonstrated by their buying behaviour. What need does the Weight Watchers' organization satisfy? Is it the actual loss of weight or the encouragement or the social environment or. the provision of an achievement target? Can these needs be satisfied outside the weight-loss area?

Indirect needs or ancillary needs are an important area for opportunity search. The North Sea oil development creates a need for helicopter services, for drilling-mud and for catering supply services. One person made a fortune by perceiving the need for special underwater piping and developing the technology to supply that need. Just as trends were listed in the starting-point check-list so the needs that are created by trends can be considered here. The growth of mini-computers might create a need for advisers, brokers, service engineers or a second-hand market. The growth of the fast food market in the USA might create a need for new types of food (for instance squabs), food psychologists, instant car valet services, cooking courses, waste utilization contracts and new types of instant entertainment.

We identify gaps and we identify needs. The end point of our thinking is then the satisfaction of the need or the filling of the gap. We can define this end point in general terms: 'How can we satisfy the need for an individual to express his personality in the area of automobiles?' Or we can use the 'something' method: 'We need something that a person can do to his car, without any special skill on his part, which indicates his personality to the world in a way which cannot be easily imitated by others and which does not alter the trade-in value of the car.' It is this ability to define what we want to end up with that places gaps and needs in the end-point rather than the starting-point check-list.

Objectives

If we know what we want to do that constitutes an end-point for our thinking. Challenging and altering an objective may provide an opportunity. Finding quicker or cheaper ways of achieving an objective would also provide an opportunity. Setting up an objective is itself a definition of an opportunity: 'We want to enter the ladies' tights market', 'We want a fifteen per cent share of the truck hire business', 'We want to increase our output per employee by twelve per cent this year', 'We want to increase our passenger load by ten per cent this year' and 'Our objective is to maintain our dominant position in the biological pre-wash market.'

Sometimes we can go directly towards an objective. At other times it may be possible to move towards the objectives by a route which actually opens up new opportunities on the way. We may want to launch a new range of office furniture and in designing this we may evolve a new fabrication procedure which can be used elsewhere or even licensed. This is the sort of thing that happened to the Pilkington glass company when they evolved the float glass method to cut the costs of grinding plate glass. The licence fees from the method now contribute substantially to their profits.

In the 'something' method we define the desired end point by the qualities it will possess. In defining objectives we do something similar, except that we define the end point by describing the position we shall be in. The difficulty lies in making sure that the shorter-term objectives are not satisfied at the expense of the longer-term. Would it be acceptable to achieve the objective of

increasing a share of the car market by four per cent by introducing an innovation which increased the life of a car by fifty per
cent? The answer is not simple because a more durable car might
seem to cut down on repeat orders but the ready second-hand value
might actually increase trade-in activity.

Should objectives be changed half-way along? There may have
been a shift in outside circumstances that makes this inevitable
(the internal troubles in Cyprus would have halted development
of tourism there). At other times it seems that the objective is
unreasonable or can only be achieved at great cost. Should the
opportunity thinking be directed at finding ways of getting there
or at changing the objective? What happens if a new opportunity
opens up half-way along the route to the objective? On the one
hand there is the danger of pursuing butterfly-fashion every new
opportunity that seems to appear, on the other there is the danger
of obstinacy. Are the reasons behind the original choice of objective still valid? Can it be shown that the original thinking was
faulty? Are the reasons valid and the thinking correct but a new
opportunity overshadows the old one (a company with long-term
objectives in the mini-computer field may be tempted by sudden
technological changes in the micro-processor field)? The reasons
for changing an objective are no different from those which
prompt any change of destination: it is no longer worth getting
there or there is a better place to go.

A declared objective may stifle an opportunity. The declared
objective of staying in the mass car market may prevent the emerg-
ence of a new market segment: the executive car market (contrast
Ford UK and British Leyland).

There is a lot of opportunity thinking that can take place in
connection with objectives. The thinking involved in attaining
objectives includes planning and problem-solving and their
methodology.

Wishful thinking

This is related to provocation, the 'something' method and objectives. An objective should be sound and reasonable but if we go
beyond that to an objective which is fanciful and 'wishful thinking' then we are using the principle of provocation. 'Wouldn't it

be nice if we could keep our order book full by building a unique type of ship which other yards could not imitate,' would be an example of wishful thinking. Once the fantasy objective has been stated, in general 'something' terms, then we can start thinking towards it. Occasionally, having thought the unthinkable it becomes thinkable in the same way as Margaret Thatcher's unthinkable bid for leadership of the British Conservative party suddenly became fact. More often the thinking that takes place towards this fantasy objective will turn up useful opportunity ideas on the way even though the fantasy remains a fantasy.

'Wouldn't it be nice if we could carry out that operation with one man instead of two.' 'Wouldn't it be nice if we could mould dozens at once instead of doing them singly.' 'Wouldn't it be nice if we could predict the price of coffee for twelve months ahead.' 'Wouldn't it be nice if we could tie productivity to wages in a more direct fashion.'

The value of wishful thinking as an end point is that once we have an end point we can start working backwards from it or forwards to try to reach it. It provides a target. In a sense it creates a problem which we then set about solving.

As in many other instances, the value of the expressed wishful thinking depends quite a lot on the level of generality with which it is expressed. 'Wouldn't it be nice if we could treble our profits this year' is wishful thinking, but at so general a level that it does not lead our thinking towards a specific objective. 'Wouldn't it be nice if we did not have to print a run of five thousand at a time but could print only what we needed but at the same cost' is genuine wishful thinking and defines an i.s.a. On the other hand too detailed a specification just ends up as a problem definition: 'Wouldn't it be nice if we could afford another customer service engineer' as distinct from, 'Wouldn't it be nice if we could increase the effectiveness of our customer service operation.'

'Wouldn't it be nice if all my customers became selling agents on my behalf' could lead to concepts of pyramid selling or the Avon cosmetics type operation. It could also, indirectly, lead to the idea of selling kits and so allowing the buyer to be his own manufacturer – from the extracted principle that the purchaser helps the seller in some way additional to just buying.

Defects

The correction of defects is an obvious opportunity area. In this sense 'defect' has a wide meaning. It may be an obvious mechanical defect like the faulty cooling pump in a certain make of car. It may be a defect in customer appeal – a lack of branding in a near-commodity market. It may be a defect of image. It may be a reliability defect which makes too great a demand on customer services. It may be a pricing defect which keeps the product out of its right market. It may be a defect in the organization of work which allows a bottle-neck at some point. Whatever the nature of the defect, it can be focused upon and defined as a problem or an i.s.a. Once this end point has been established then thinking can be directed towards it.

It may seem that dealing with defects is pretty straightforward. But this is not always so. It is easy to see that a faulty cooling pump should be corrected so that it functions properly. The correction of the defect is towards an obvious state of satisfaction just like the removal of pain is towards a state of no-pain. But with the pricing defect the solution is not so obvious. We could try to reduce the price in order to enter the lower price market or we could try to increase the product value or image in order to stay in the existing market or even move into a higher-priced market. A defect implies an assumption about what things should be. It is in questioning these assumptions as well as in remedying the defect that opportunities may be found. Should we just remedy the mechanical defect or should we alter the design so that the defect does not arise (problem-avoidance as distinct from problem-solving)?

A defect often implies something missing – a gap. As usual it is much more difficult to focus upon something that is not there than upon something that is wrong. We can do it by comparison with other products or operations or we can do it by comparison with our own wishful thinking (what we would like to see). The trick is to use the 'opportunities' inherent in the existing situation. It is not so much a matter of defining a new objective and then seeing how the existing product can be used in reaching that objective; it is more a matter of seeing the inherent opportunities in the existing product and figuring out how they can be developed. For 'product' we can read 'procedure' or 'operation' or 'service'. What is the potential that can be developed?

Faults

In practice there is little distinction between defects and faults but it is worth making a distinction so that we can have two entries on our check-list, and hence two opportunities to focus our attention. So we can define a defect as 'something which falls short of expectations'. And we define a fault as 'something which is better removed, something which contributes negatively to the value of what we are doing'. The philosophers will quibble that removal of a defect will improve what we are doing but this is rather like converting anything we want to do to a problem: it is logically acceptable but practically limiting. If we are giving in a product much more value than the customer wants or is willing to pay for then that is a fault. If our advertising turns away certain potential customers even though it attracts others that is a fault. If a supervisor creates bad work relations that is a fault even though he may get the work done. If our financial planning involves high risks that is a fault. If we are dependent on an unreliable single supplier that is a fault. If our production process requires more stages than seem desirable that is a fault in procedure or in design.

The simple rule is:

'What does this product lack?' (defects).
'What would we like to do away with?' (faults).

It is best to make a deliberate list of defects and of faults and then to go through this list spending some thinking time at each entry. It is worth discussing such lists with others for what may appear to be an obvious fault to one person may not be a fault at all to another – for example, a brightly coloured range of ladies' shoes may seem vulgar to one person and fashionable to another; a large package-size might seem a selling advantage to one person but a disadvantage to another. All the time one is looking for opportunities: opportunities for improvement, opportunities for change, opportunities for changing the objective.

If we are looking at a telephone we might list under faults the twisting of the cord, the cumbrous shape of the handset, the need to pick something up and hold it. Under defects we might list the inability to read back the number that has been dialled (a simple liquid crystal or LED display might do here) and the lack of a signal that tells a caller that the person is at home but unwilling to answer the telephone (a switch which the person could activate when he wished in order to free himself from the phone without seeming to be out or occupying the line).

Quality improvements

Here we define a direction in advance and then see if we can improve what we are doing towards the direction indicated. There is no definite goal in terms of an ideal product or service that we would like to provide. There is only a direction. If we choose 'simplicity' as the direction we would see how we could simplify our product or service. We would continually be trying to do this. There would not be a point at which we would sit back and say: 'Now we have got there.'

The process is not unlike that of a nagging wife who is always complaining about her husband's untidiness. No matter how tidy he becomes there is always the need for him to become even tidier. Whether it is tidiness, punctuality, ambition or any other chosen direction there is continual pressure for improvement. In a way it is defect correction for by setting up a quality direction we can always pretend that what we have falls short.

Common quality directions include: customer appeal, cost-effectiveness, reliability, simplicity, efficiency, servicing costs, production efficiency, quality (in terms of apparent value), brand distinction and so on. These could be summarized as: cheaper, better, more saleable and less trouble. It is better, however, not to summarize but to consider each direction separately. For example, the term 'cheaper' includes cost-effectiveness, production efficiency, simplicity and design. We need these separate attention points rather than the summarizing label. In buying a house you might say: 'I like the house' but it would be more useful to say: 'I like the location, I like the appearance, I like the space and lay-out, I like the state of repair, I like the decoration, etc.' for then you know what has gone into the general term 'like'.

In Detroit the quality direction that has been chosen for design improvement in cars is that of weight reduction because this means a reduction in fuel consumption. It is estimated that by 1981 compacts will have been slimmed by about 1,000 pounds and that by 1985 the large cars will weigh only a bit more than today's subcompacts. In the course of this improvement there might be a significant shift to plastics.

Simplification is an attractive direction because it seems to imply a reduction in costs both of production and servicing and an increase in consumer appeal. Cost-reduction as such is an attractive direction in times of recession when sales slump. Sales appeal covers such things as brand image and brand distinction, packaging, design, merchandising and the other ingredients in marketing. How much resides in the actual product and how much in what is done to it (price, distribution, promotion) is not easy to determine when assessing sales appeal. But there always is a point at which the customer comes face to face with the product.

These quality directions provide quite specific end points for opportunity thinking. The end point is not 'simplicity' as such but a simplified product or procedure. The various thinking strategies we use to get there are problem-solving strategies, design strategies, improvement and modification strategies. A quality improvement focused on some operation can become an i.s.a. 'How can we simplify production of patterned carpets?'

As usual, a true opportunity is a balance between effort, risk and reward. If the cost of improvement is too high (in terms of tooling costs, wastages and existing stocks, consumer confusion) the excellence of the improvement does not constitute a real opportunity. One must always be aware of the danger of technology-push improvements in which improvements are judged only for themselves and not in the context of the market and the costs of production.

There also comes a point when pursuing the same direction of improvement gives diminishing returns. Cost-cutting exercises often show this. At first a huge reduction in costs is possible. Later only a minor reduction is possible and even that is often achieved by complicated changes in procedure. It may be more worthwhile to shift attention to another quality improvement direction – like job satisfaction.

Ideally, quality improvement thinking, like the nagging of a wife, should be a continuing process. This is ideal but somewhat impractical. The result is that specific exercises are undertaken now and again in order to focus attention on some needed area of improvement. The Opportunity Audit described in Part II of the book provides a firm structure for such exercises. There is a considerable danger in pretending, 'Oh, we are looking at quality improvement the whole time,' when this is not the case. The danger with that attitude is that no specific exercises are set up and the case for improvement goes by default until disaster in the market place makes it essential and then it is often too late. To wait until one is forced to think about something is always too late.

Problem-solving

By definition any problem is also an opportunity. A problem arises from our awareness that there is something we want because it would be to our advantage – and that is the definition of an opportunity. Whenever we have a problem we have an opportunity to solve it. Almost any of the items on the starting-point check-list or the end-point check-list can be transformed into a problem to be solved: 'To find a way of using this situation asset'; 'To reduce the high cost in this area (i.s.a.)'; 'To find a new market segmentation through "de-averaging" '; 'To simplify the production process for this product' and so on. But, as has been mentioned several times, there is little point in classifying everything that is desired as a problem to be solved. We can contrast the problems mentioned above with the time I received a telephone call from a large and well-known computer company to tell me that they were about to have a strike and could I talk with some of the management involved to see if some ideas could be generated. That sort of problem is more usefully described as a problem because a solution is demanded. In Los Angeles the ratio of empty to full seats in cars coming into the city at rush hour is four to one. If the occupancy could be increased to just two passengers a car there would be a saving of twenty-one million gallons of gasoline a day. That is a problem worth solving even though it does not have the urgency of the strike problem.

So in this section we will consider the problems that have been created by circumstance and thrust upon us rather than the problems that are created by our projected desires. The section is not, however, intended to be a treatise on problem-solving. The matter is included here for the sake of completeness in the matter of opportunity thinking.

We can consider some basic approaches to problem-solving.

Stock solutions: This is a matter of applying experience. We try to recognize the problem and having done so we search through our repertoire of stock solutions and find the one that fits the problem. Then we apply it and solve the problem. This is the sort of problem-solving that is used by doctors, lawyers, engineers, accountants and business executives. A doctor learns to recognize that shortness of breath, swelling of the ankles, a raised venous pressure and crepitations in the lungs suggest heart failure. The stock solution is a diuretic followed if necessary by a digitalis-type drug. The lawyer works in court to try to transform his brief into a typical case for which there is the stock solution provided by precedent. In management school the business executive learns, from case studies, to recognize some typical problems (such as cash-flow problems) and to apply the standard solution. This is the most common approach and to some extent the most useful since little thinking is involved and little doubt. The trouble arises when a problem is mistakenly identified as a classic problem and treated as such when it is different: for example, when economists treat a recession as being similar to the preceding recession and try the same remedies. There are also the problems which simply cannot be recognized as classic.

Constructed solutions: If there is no ready-made solution, we have to build one. We analyse that problem and break it down into its different components or sub-problems. We then try to find or develop a solution for each sub-problem. Finally these solutions are fitted together to give the overall solution. For instance, if there was a high degree of industrial unrest in a factory we could analyse this into working conditions, communication systems, the personalities involved, the structure involved, job satisfaction and historical factors. In each of these areas we would look for an inadequacy or an actual problem. These sub-problems we would tackle by applying a solution from experience – our own or other people's – or from common sense. If we wanted an incentive, common sense would suggest more money or more leisure. Much of our thinking is directed to breaking down problems into sub-problems which can be solved by the application of 'common sense'. Common-sense solutions are not infallible – for instance, experience shows that in many situations more money does not increase job satisfaction. The major process involved in constructed solutions is analysis in order to create sub-problems for which stock solutions can be found.

Working backwards: We take the desired solution and then work backwards from it towards our starting point. When we have reached our starting point the problem is solved. The best way to work out a winning strategy in the 'L-game', which I invented, is to take a winning position and then to see which positions could lead to it and then to see which positions could lead to the positions that could lead to the winning position (in other words, the winning position minus one, minus two and so on). Let us take the Los Angeles car-sharing problem. The desired end point might be that a motorist who would normally have driven into town finds that he can move about more freely if he leaves his car outside. How would he move about more freely? Through an increased taxi service. But that would be expensive. Not necessarily, because when he parked in a perimeter park he would get – in exchange for his car – a free taxi warrant valid for that day. The warrants would be paid for by a very high charge on inner-city car parks and tolls on entry roads. For example a $10 parking fee would give the equivalent in free taxi rides to someone else. It is important when using the working backwards procedure to work backwards from the desired end state and not from a proposed solution.

Re-definition of the problem: Here we challenge the problem itself. Instead of accepting the problem and solving it, we question whether we are looking at the right problem: 'Is this really the question we should be asking?'; 'Why do we want to solve this problem?'; 'What do we really want to do?' Too often we assume that our first perception of the problem is the correct one and that all we have to do is to solve it. For example, we could define the Los Angeles car-sharing problem in any of the following ways:

'To encourage people to share cars.'

'To make it advantageous for people not to drive into town in their own cars.'

'To save gasoline and diminish traffic congestion.'

'To increase the seat occupancy in each car from 1.4 to 2.'

Each of these problem definitions might lead to a different solution. For instance, saving gasoline and diminishing traffic congestion might be achieved by having special city cars or even motorcycles which an out-of-town driver could obtain by exchanging his car at a car park on the perimeter. These small city cars would be allowed to park anywhere. In the problem of shopper resistance to the system of automatic read-out at the check-out counter (with the UPC marking on the goods) we might define the problem as follows: 'The shopper can see how the system is to the advantage of the store-owner but not how it is to the shopper's advantage.' The shopper would therefore resist the change. The notion that lower costs to the store-owner would lead to lower prices is not credible (even if it is true). When the problem is defined in this way we might find a solution in which some of the good were marked as before but alongside them were UPC marked goods which are guaranteed to be five-per-cent lower in price. The shopper could then choose whether to take a priced item or a UPC item. He would probably use the priced item as a price label and then take the UPC item. Whatever the problem there should be a lot of effort at problem re-definition before any attempt at solution. Someone might say: 'I need to dig a hole in the ground; my problem is to find a spade.' He might then set about looking for a spade. But the real problem is to dig a hole in the ground. Indeed we might go back further and find that the real need is for a hole in the ground and it might be possible to find a hole already dug by someone else. Or the purpose of the hole might be served in another way.

Provocation: The provocation method has been mentioned above. Provocation involves an apparently unreasonable step which is taken in order to get our ideas flowing in a different direction. With the pollution problem in rivers we might say as a provocation: 'Po the factory ought to be downstream of itself.' From that apparently mad idea comes the sober notion that we could legislate that the factory's input should always be downstream of its output so it would at least get a sample of its own pollution and hence make more effort to clean up its effluent. Provocation is much used in lateral thinking. There is for example the use of a random word as a trigger. In considering the huge teacher-training problem in Nigeria (an increase from 150,000 to 450,000 primary teachers within five years is necessary) the random word 'tadpole' was used. This suggested the principle of a 'tail'? The idea would happen if teachers were equipped with a 'tail'? The idea then arises that the tail would consist of apprentice teachers who would follow around the real teacher, sit in on all his classes, take over an hour at a time, or even a day – and eventually branch out as teachers in their own right. Provocation is one of the lateral thinking methods of problem-solving.

Upstream problem avoidance: Instead of solving the problem we move upstream and take a route which does not allow the problem to develop. This procedure is said to be much favoured by NASA. Instead of improving a faulty component the effort is directed towards changing the procedure so the component is not needed in the first place. For instance, if the oil on bicycle chains is a problem because it dirties trouser legs we could try to encase the chain or we could move upstream by using a rubber band drive which avoided the need for oil. There may be a certain mental pride in overcoming the challenge of a problem but in many cases it makes more sense to avoid the problem by taking another route. After all, if you know a particular road to be flooded you would seek an alternative route rather than try to solve the problems of getting your car through the flood. We have to be careful, however, that problem avoidance does not create other problems or prove to be more expensive than the problem itself – many suggested methods for avoiding the problem of shoplifting would cost more to operate than is lost through shoplifting itself. In general the problem-avoiding procedure is simple. We say to ourselves: 'Let us go back upstream and see how this problem arose in the first place, let us then see if there is an alternative route we could take.'

To summarize, problem-solving requires a clear understanding of the objective, an appreciation of the context and of priorities, an ability to analyse the problem, a capacity to look at the problem in several different ways (lateral thinking), and a stock of experience upon which to draw.

Although problem-solving is an important part of the opportunity search exercise an executive should be aware of the danger of confining his opportunity-seeking to problem-solving. It would be easy to take this line because problems are concrete and staring one in the face whereas other opportunities do not exist until they have been discovered. Since there will always be enough problems to occupy fully an executive's thinking he will need to make an effort to go through the starting-point and end-point check-lists in order to develop other opportunities.

'Like a new born baby a new idea must, at first, be nourished by care and indulgent attention.'

The treatment of ideas

Having once focused on a starting point, ideas usually start to emerge. The two starting-point check-lists provided in preceding sections ought to give rise to some ideas about opportunities. The next stage – and perhaps the most important – is the treatment of these ideas. Very rarely is a new idea born in the full glory of its potential. At first an idea may be weak, dull or even impractical. Like an infant, the new idea needs proper handling if it is to develop its potential. It may be a matter of cosseting one's own ideas or it may be a matter of nourishing the ideas of others.

Paradoxically the best way to encourage a positive attitude towards emerging ideas is to develop confidence in the ruthlessness of one's final judgement. Many executives kill an apparently unpromising idea at birth because they do not want to waste time on it or because they fear they might be led astray by it. An executive who has confidence in the ruthlessness of his ultimate judgement can afford to nourish new ideas because he knows that in the end the idea will be thrown out if it cannot prove itself. To be afraid to play around with a new idea actually betrays a lack of confidence in judgement rather than the exercise of realism.

It is not easy to sit down and pluck a brilliant idea out of the empty air. It is much more practical to take a thought and to work upon it so as to form it into a useful new idea. This treatment of ideas is perhaps the most important part of creativity. In this section I shall indicate some of the problems and processes involved.

The killer phrase

There is one phrase which kills instantly at birth an untold number of potentially valuable ideas. This killer phrase is the expression 'the same as ...' A person comes up with an idea and immediately another person pounces on the idea and says: 'That is the same as ...' This killer phrase has the following connotations:

> The idea is not new and therefore not worthy of attention.
> It is similar to something that is already being done.
> It is the same as something that has been tried without success.
> It is the same as something a competitor is doing.
> It is not worthy to be considered as a creative effort.
> It is less interesting than something which really is new.
> It is a 'put-down' for anyone pretending to be creative.

The result is that the idea is dismissed and gets no more attention. If it does get attention it is henceforth treated exactly as if it were the old idea (with which it had something in common) and the value of the new slant is completely lost. In either case the idea is virtually killed.

The tragedy is that if we are so inclined we can show that any new idea whatsoever is similar to an old idea. We can do this by focusing only on those aspects which are similar. We can do it by rephrasing the idea so that it seems more similar. We can do this by moving to a higher level of generality which includes both ideas (we can say for instance there is a similarity between a recording group and a ship-building operation because both involve heavy forward expenditure on the basis of market hunch). It is not unlike the man who said that he did not want to buy a book 'because he already had one at home'. Showing how something new is indeed similar to something well known is one of the most powerful, and useful, functions of the human mind. The process enables us to use past experience to understand present circumstances and it also enables us to group and classify things.

I once carried out an investigation into kidney function that turned up some rather useful results. Whenever I talked about this research work the listeners would invariably ask how I ever got to do the investigation because someone else had done a similar piece of work with completely negative results. The truth was that I had not known about this other work and so my investigation was done slightly differently and this slight difference in approach led to very different results.

The truth is that if we are so inclined we can either find a similarity in two things which are apparently very different or find a difference between two things which are apparently similar. As in many other aspects of creativity it is this attitude which is crucial. The trouble is that we need to use both attitudes. When a new idea seems similar to an old one we need to focus on the crucial points of difference. When several apparently different ideas seem to work in a field we need to see what principle they have in common.

The answer to the killer phrase is as follows: 'Yes, in some respects this new idea is similar to the old one you mention but I invite you to join me in focusing on the points of difference in order to see if we can develop a new idea.' The proposer of the idea should also make an effort to point out the differences.

In the me-too market a slight difference in the idea may be vital. So it should be in the exploration of any proposed new idea.

There is a danger, however, that this attitude of accepting ideas as worth exploring even if they do not seem new may result in people putting forward old ideas instead of making an effort to find new ones. The appropriate response here is for the listener to say: 'That seems to be exactly the same as what we are already doing – could you help me focus on the difference that you see in this idea?'

Function extraction

This is an extremely important part of thinking and without an ability to think at a function level creativity and design are virtually impossible. Function extraction involves taking a concrete example and extracting from it the 'function' or 'general principle'. I shall be using the words 'function' and 'principle' interchangeably. Function extraction is related to the 'something' method that was described in a preceding section. It is a matter of dealing with processes rather than with things: 'What is the process here?'; 'What is happening here?'; 'What function is this thing performing?'

In my seminars I often invite participants to go through an exercise in function extraction. It seems to be very difficult unless one has made a habit of thinking in function terms. One difficulty is to find the most fertile level of function – this difficulty of choosing the most appropriate level of generality has been mentioned again and again in this book. If we say that the function of an insurance company is to make profits for the shareholders we are extracting a function that is common to all other corporations with shareholders. If we say that an insurance company is there to provide a framework for the re-distribution of risks, then we have a more fertile function level. We might also say that insurance provides a means whereby most policy holders can buy off fear (this applies to accident insurance and to those who do not actually suffer an accident but only fear one). From this last description of function we might develop the idea of a basic insurance premium which the policy-holders can top up for short periods according to the fluctuations in their own assessment of risk.

One of the easiest ways of developing a new idea is to extract the function from the idea and then to see how else this function could be carried out. For example, if someone suggests that taxis could have 'ignorant' drivers a listener might extract from this the function question: 'Is there a need for a taxi-driver to be as knowledgeable as a London cabbie (who has to pass a very strict test)?' This might be altered to: 'Is there a need for all drivers to be equally knowledgeable?' From this we might develop the idea of 'learner' taxis which might bear a large question mark on the roof and would be used only by those who knew exactly how to get to where they wanted to go. In this example the term 'principle' would be more appropriate than 'function'.

At a meeting someone suggests that the brown eggs should be separated from the white eggs and sold separately. The principle here is that they are visually different and, it is suspected, the housewife will treat them differently. It may be possible to sell the brown eggs at a premium, otherwise the cost of separation would be pointless unless it was a market-share situation. If housewives are willing to pay a premium for eggs just because they are brown should a company take advantage of this gullibility? In terms of business ethics the answer must be no – unless you subscribe to the ethic of 'what you can get away with'. But we can continue to develop the principle further. The principle has now become one of 'brand distinction'. Perhaps special eggs from special chickens fed in a special way could be marketed at a premium as 'breakfast eggs'. Consumers might be willing to pay for the extra attention to get better-tasting eggs if the eggs were going to be eaten directly as distinct from being put into cakes and the like. Those who could afford it might buy 'breakfast eggs' for all purposes. The brand distinction principle could also lead to the idea of 'day-old eggs' with the emphasis on time and a higher price to cover wastage.

In the section on symbols it will be seen that there is a symbol to indicate 'function extraction' and another symbol to indicate 'function incorporation'. From even the most unpromising idea it may be possible to extract an important function or principle which can then be incorporated in a practical idea.

The PMI

The first of the sixty thinking lessons that we have developed for use in the school curriculum is concerned with the PMI. The lesson has proved most effective in thousands of schools. PMI stands for Plus, Minus and Interesting. Perhaps the commonest fault in thinking is 'instant judgement'. An idea is proposed and the listener instantly judges whether or not he likes it. His thinking is then directed to supporting and rationalizing this instant judgement. Indeed, the more skilled he is at thinking the less chance will he ever have of exploring the idea because his support of the instant judgement will be complete enough. So the PMI device requires the children to look first for the Plus points and then for the Minus points and finally for points of Interest.

A group of thirty twelve-year-olds were asked if they liked the idea of every pupil being given a weekly wage for going to school. All thirty indicated that the idea was wonderful for they could then buy comics, chewing gum and other goodies. After doing a PMI on their own – in groups of four – all but one of the thirty completely reversed their decision. The PMI is so simple a device that every adult claims to do it instinctively but experiment after experiment shows that when a group of executives are forced to do a PMI their ultimate decision is different. The truth is that people may tend to do a sort of PMI (pros and cons, etc.) when they are in doubt. But they do not do this when it is clear that they like or dislike the idea. And this is precisely where the PMI is most necessary.

In practice the PMI means that if a person does not like an idea he is nevertheless forced to spend some time looking for the plus points and the interesting points. It also means that if a person does like an idea he is forced to make himself aware of the negative points. An idea emerges and someone indicates why he does not like it. Someone else in the group asks each group member to take the idea and do a PMI on it. An individual working on his own can force himself to do a PMI on an idea whenever he finds that his instinctive reaction is so strongly positive or negative that the opposite point of view is likely to be neglected

It is surprising how a simplistic device like the PMI can be effective. It works by formalizing and making objective a process that is usually emotional. Anyone who prides himself on his thinking will make an effort to do an efficient PMI, whereas previously he would pride himself on supporting his instant judgement.

Provocation and stepping stones

Provocation and lateral thinking have been mentioned at different times throughout this book. I must repeat here that this is not a book on lateral thinking, for the many techniques and processes of lateral thinking are described elsewhere. Nevertheless, the search for opportunities is helped by some of the principles of lateral thinking and in particular the value of stepping stones.

Normally we treat a suggested idea as something to be judged. Do we like the idea or not? Do we like what it would lead to or not? We judge whether the idea would work. We judge whether the idea would be practical for us. Even if we have a positive attitude of mind or are doing a PMI we are nevertheless making judgements.

The 'stepping stone' process means that we make no attempt whatsoever to judge an idea. We use the idea purely as a mental stepping stone to get to a new idea. The purpose of a stepping stone in a stream is to allow us to get across to pastures new. We step on to the stepping stone only to step off it again. We do not even have to keep our balance on the stepping stone if we move off smartly enough.

In the advertising medium example above, the suggestion that the 'town crier' should be brought back could have been judged as a serious idea. There could have been a discussion about cost-effectiveness, type of message, noise levels in cities, environmental pollution (noise) and the like. Perhaps there might even be some merit in the idea. In fact the idea was not judged at all but used as a stepping stone. From the idea was extracted the principle or function that the town crier, unlike most advertising media, could not be turned off. This led quickly to the idea of injecting 'commercial breaks' every twenty seconds or so into the conversation on public telephones or special advertising telephones. The town crier concept served only as a stepping stone.

Once the stepping stone procedure has been understood it opens up huge creative possibilities. It makes it possible to suggest ideas which seem ridiculous or which are deliberately provocative because they go against hallowed principles. In the treatment of ideas it makes it possible to work with any idea whatsoever. However unpromising the idea may seem it can always be tried as a stepping stone to lead to another. The new idea reached via the stepping stone does not need to resemble the stepping stone in any way. The provocation, 'drinking glasses should have a hole in the bottom' would lead to the idea that the drinker would have to keep his finger over the hole and so could not put down and lose his glass at a party. This might lead to the product idea of self-adhesive labels for glasses at a party, either with the party-giver's crest and motto, like bookplates, or an advertising message for promotion parties.

Since even the daftest idea can lead somewhere useful – the idea of shooting down aeroplanes with a radio beam led directly to radar – the stepping stone procedure ensures that an infant idea gets at least some attention. The onus shifts to the listener who must now try to use the idea effectively as a stepping stone. The stepping stone procedure also means that someone can protect himself as he puts forward an idea by saying: 'I am putting this forward as a deliberately provocative idea.' This is especially useful to senior executives who are often reluctant to put forward ideas lest they should seem less creative than their seniority would warrant. Provocation puts the task of responding on to the listener.

Tailoring an idea

This is a very important part of the treatment of an idea. In the early days of brainstorming the intention was to have an effervescence of ideas which could then be screened and judged. This works quite well in the advertising world – for which brainstorming was devised – but much less well outside this world. If we bring our screening criteria to the output of a brainstorming session we might find that none of the blue-sky ideas are of any practical value and so creativity gets a bad name. My own view is that generating an idea involves creativity but tailoring that idea so that it becomes practicable involves just as much creativity. Instead of screening blue-sky ideas I prefer to define the 'reception area' for ideas and then to tailor ideas to see if they can be brought into this reception area.

Tailoring may involve simple modification to an idea to get rid of some obvious disadvantages. As an illustration, the idea of having a permanent price reduction 'sale' department in big stores might lead to loss of credibility in what was offered in this department. The idea could be modified to allow access to this department only through sales vouchers obtained by buying elsewhere in the store (a sort of internal trading stamps scheme). Tailoring may involve a change in scale. Sometimes an idea may seem too expensive and yet a change of scale can make the idea feasible. Often tailoring involves extracting the principle of an idea and then incorporating this in a more practical form. For example, the discount principle can be operated either by cutting or by preserving the price and including services that would normally be charged in addition. Sometimes the tailoring seems to involve a transformation of the idea. For instance, instead of offering an insurance service with the sale of deep-freezers there may be the provision of food vouchers for stocking the freezer. This idea may itself be modified so that the vouchers will increase by a fixed interest rate if unused and can themselves be used for the purchase of other items in the future from the seller of the freezer (a sort of inflation-proofed future discount).

The packaging of cheap camera kits in large polystyrene-filled boxes was a good idea because it opened up the gift and birthday present market which seems to demand large 'boxes of air' to satisfy the giver's sense of contribution. The idea may also help display, storage and the sale of more accessories. How could an individual retailer tailor that idea to suit his own purposes? Obviously he could not get involved in the heavy tooling costs of packaging. Focusing on the gift interface he might set up a camera introduction club. A customer would buy a gift token which would entitle the receiver to attend a two-hour camera introduction session in which different equipment was described. The person attending could then choose whatever camera and accessories he wanted to make up the price of the voucher. The difference in cost would be made up by the sale of films. The price need not appear on the voucher.

The difference between tailoring and screening can be expressed quite succinctly. 'Is this idea of any use to us?' is replaced by, 'Can we tailor this idea to suit our situation?' In tailoring we cut the coat to fit both the cloth that is available (the opportunity-user) and the wearer (the market).

Instruction symbols for thinking

Each of the symbols shown in Figure 13 and described here formalizes a simple thinking operation. The value of the symbols is the value of formality. By means of the symbols we can give a formal instruction to ourselves or to others, to carry out a particular thinking operation. The symbols may be inscribed in the margin of a report or Opportunity Audit or they may be scribbled on a pad during an idea session. The symbols may be used on task-sheets that are circulated to invite applied thinking on an identified problem (or i.s.a.). The symbols may be used on an overhead projector. The symbols serve to focus attention on an operation in the same way as we might focus attention on an area. The operations themselves are all quite easy to carry out but because something is easy to do does not mean that it always gets done – in the absence of a specific request. The symbols may also become a communicating shorthand amongst a group of thinkers.

Each symbol is named in Figure 13 and described below under that name.

No entry: This is similar to the traffic sign forbidding entry to a street. The idea is the same. We may at times wish to forbid the use of a particular track or idea. We want to do this because we know that the thinker will find it so easy to take this track that he is unlikely to look for any other. So we use the no-entry sign to block that track. When used in a report it urges the person to come up with an alternative. At other times the forbidden idea track is spelled out following the no-entry sign. For example, in considering retail inducements the no-entry sign may be used followed by the words: 'price-cutting or discount inducements.'

Build upon: the instruction here is to build upon the idea and to develop it into something valuable. Used in the margin of a report it indicates that the reader finds interest and potential in the idea and would like this worked upon. 'Build upon' is synonymous with 'work upon'. The instruction to build upon is quite distinct from the use of a stepping stone since when an idea is to be built upon the final idea must include what was attractive in the initial idea.

Make practical: The symbol suggests the process of bringing a blue-sky idea down to earth by a series of transformations. This is a similar process to tailoring except that the objective is general practicality. In the margin of a report it indicates that the reader is not satisfied that the idea is practical in its present form but that he is interested in it.

Use as a stepping stone: This evocative symbol which illustrates a stepping stone action may be used before a provocation to indicate that a provocation is intended (it would serve the same purpose as

no entry

examine the
basic assumptions

build upon

focus

make practical

challenge

use as a
stepping-stone

expand

extract
the function

contract

incorporate
the function

show
evidence

Figure 13

the new word 'po'). It may also be used in the margin of a report or indeed written against any piece of literature as an instruction to the reader to use the indicated idea to generate others. On a task-sheet or during an idea session the symbol may be affixed to any idea that arises in order to focus attention upon its provocative use. Used with a question mark it can suggest: 'Are you putting this forward seriously or as a stepping stone?'

Extract the function: The instruction is to extract the function or the principle from what follows the symbol. There is no one correct function to be extracted. Different people might extract different functions. It is the effort to extract a function that is requested. Several alternative functions or principles should be offered as the answer rather than just one.

Incorporate the function: Here the general principle is to be fleshed out in a concrete example or procedure. In a way this is another instruction 'to come down to earth'. It is sometimes possible to talk in philosophical and general terms without ever putting forward a definite idea. The symbol urges a concrete incorporation of the principle. The extract function symbol and the incorporate function symbol may be used together to indicate that the function should be extracted and then immediately incorporated in another idea. It indicates: 'I like the principle but not the way it is used, can you use the same principle in a better way?'

Examine the basic assumptions: The term 'assumption' includes perceptions. The instruction is to go back and examine the way the situation is being looked at. Are the starting concepts the only ones possible? What is being taken for granted? What premises have already been accepted? As the symbol indicates, it means 'Go back and examine the base-line before building on it.'

Focus: This symbol must be followed by whatever is to be focused upon. It is necessary that this be spelled out very precisely. When the symbol is used in the margin of a report or piece of literature it is advisable to underline what is to be focused upon or to write it out against the symbol. A focus should be as precise as possible. This does not mean that a focus need be upon a detail. For example it is legitimate to ask for a focus on 'profitability' or on 'convenience'.

Challenge: This is an extension of the focus symbol. It means: 'Focus on a concept, challenge its uniqueness and come up with some alternatives.' A challenge to uniqueness is a challenge to inevitability as has been explained earlier in the book: 'Is it the only possible way of doing this?' The challenge symbol may be used specifically with an indicated concept. But it may also be used in a more comprehensive sense to indicate a general area in which the person receiving the instruction is asked to pick out his own concepts for challenge.

Expand: A general instruction which asks for more 'writing' about the issue. It may mean more elaboration, more information, more details or anything else. It means: 'Please expand upon this.' For example, in reading a report a senior executive may be excited by an idea that is tucked away in the discussion of some other idea. The instruction would request the next reader to give more attention to the point – to expand it.

Contract: This is another general instruction which has an opposite effect of the 'expand' instruction. It means: 'Come to a conclusion' or 'summarize this' or 'pick out what really matters.' In more colloquial terms it means: 'What does all this boil down to?'

Show evidence: If this symbol was used in the margin then the statement for which evidence was required would be underlined. The symbol should not be used in a critical fashion to suggest that something is mere speculation. It should be used constructively to allow the responder to show the support he has for a statement he has put forward. It means: 'I am interested in this, tell me why you think this.'

Other formal symbols of a like nature are available but the ones given here are the more useful in the treatment of ideas. They do take some getting used to but can become a useful focusing device. The person at whom the symbol is directed should of course understand it. He would be expected to have a copy of this book or at least a symbol sheet explaining each one.*

* *Lateral Thinking for Management,* published by McGraw-Hill in the UK and the American Management Association in the USA.

The DPA rating

Where an idea is concerned with a new way of doing something the DPA rating can provide a convenient device for allowing people to express their view. 'D' stands for 'difference': how different is the new suggestion? 'P' stands for practical: how practical is the new suggestion? 'A' stands for advantages: what advantages does the new suggestion offer? The rating is given out of a maximum of ten points or a hundred. An idea may be rated ten out of ten for difference if it really is novel. But it may get only two out of ten for practicality and only three out of ten for advantage. Another idea may get a high rating both for difference and for practicality but may offer no special advantages over the existing method. Packaging the three aspects of consideration together ensures that each gets some attention. It also emphasizes that novelty or difference as such do not create an opportunity for change.

Spell it out

This is a request that a person may make of himself or of another. It is surprisingly easy to talk about an idea in a general way and yet never spell it out in concrete terms. One can talk grandly about incentives, inducements, job satisfaction, but be unable to spell out what these will involve in practice. Vague ideas evaporate when an attempt is made to spell them out either in writing or verbally.

I do not want to suggest that ideas cannot be held in a general or even a vague form. But I do want to suggest that to spell out an idea in concrete terms is a useful way of treating it and forcing its further development. There comes a time when an idea has to be made concrete in order that the gaps and deficiencies can be seen. To state that a service will be advertised leaves matters at a general level. To state exactly how and where and at what cost it will be advertised may make it obvious that some cheaper method of promoting the service must be devised. Is the new service one that a segment of the market will always find attractive or one that anyone will find attractive but only at a certain time in their lives? Spelling something out forces such considerations. The concrete details that are given when an idea is spelled out need not decide the final form of the idea.

What is requested is not a plan of action but consideration of the idea at a concrete level. Publishers are fond of saying to an author who has an idea for a wonderful book: 'Exactly who do you think will be interested in buying this book?' Many a new product venture would never be undertaken if the details (and costs) of distribution had been spelled out at the idea stage.

As with some other procedures mentioned in this section, the spell-it-out procedure is not meant to be used in a critical or destructive manner. It is meant to help the development of the idea. Throughout this section the basic philosophy has been the development of an idea as far as it will go – then comes the evaluation.

Information available and information required

Another of the thinking lessons in the schools programme requires pupils to consider carefully what information is available and what is missing in any situation. The process is condensed to read 'information-in and information-out' and this condensation is itself abbreviated to give the initials FI–FO. But there is no need to add this mnemonic device.

Consideration of the information available and the information needed is related to risk and uncertainty. These matters will be dealt with in a later section. Clarification of what is known and what is not yet known is, however, part of the treatment of an idea. To know clearly what information is still needed is an important part of the treatment of an idea. It is different from mere ignorance. A person who knows that he has to find out the current price of paper is in a different position from someone who has ignored that price even though neither of them knows the answer.

It can be useful to halt the consideration of an idea in order to ask what is known and what needs to be known. Once a crucial area of ignorance has been defined it may lead to a modification of the idea. If for instance the behaviour of a certain plastic at the required temperature range is not known and cannot be easily ascertained, the design may have to be altered to allow the use of metal.

Satisfy and define

There are two types of requests which a listener may make of someone who is proposing an idea. The first request is: 'Satisfy me.' The listener may ask to be satisfied as to the evidence, the reasoning, the background, the estimated probabilities and the projected scenario concerning the idea. He is asking to share the idea environment. He wants to be able to see things as clearly as the person proposing the idea.

The second type of request is: 'Define for me.' The listener asks the proposer of the idea to define the objective, the advantage, the problems, the gaps and the uncertainties. The listener wants to be sure that the proposer knows what he is looking for even if he has not yet found it. In the 'satisfy' request the listener wants to know what the proposer can see. In the 'define' request the listener wants to know in which direction the proposer is looking even if there is nothing to see at the moment.

Any effective thinker should be able to use on his own thinking the requests that are useful when used on the thinking of others. He should be able to detach himself from his own thinking in order to treat it objectively.

'An opportunity is a mixture of uncertainty and action. The more we are in control of the uncertainty the more effective will the action be.'

If-box maps

The if-box map is a simple notation for mapping out on paper an opportunity in such a way that we separate the action from the uncertainty. The value of any notation is two-fold: first, a notation forces us to clarify our thoughts in order to express them in the notation; second, we exteriorize our thinking so that we can then examine it and pay attention to different aspects of it. By forcing us to deal in concrete terms an if-box map is not unlike the process of 'spelling it out' discussed in the preceding section. When you are forced to write something down you are forced to make a commitment and a decision – you may then decide that it is the wrong decision. In mathematics the value of notation is that the symbols used then acquire a life of their own according to the rules of the game of numbers. Another advantage of a visible notation is that it provides a common ground for discussion: an if-box map can be looked at and discussed by a group of people. An if-box map provides something to work upon in our consideration of an opportunity; we can note the gaps and deficiencies; we can make alterations; we can suggest by-passes or alternative routes; and we can focus attention upon the uncertainties.

The main purpose of an if-box map is to separate action which is in our control from uncertainty which is not. The if-box map has only two elements: action-channels and if-boxes.

Action-channels

An action-channel is a course of action from which we are only separated by a decision. Once we have made the decision to take the action then we move smoothly along the action-channel. If you are looking at a selection of pocket calculators in a shop window you are only separated from them by a buying decision. Once you have made the decision, the action-channel of entering the shop and buying the calculator follows smoothly. We must assume that the decision is rational and that you only make the buying decision if you have the money.

You examine a holiday brochure and then decide which destination you want to visit. The action-channel of making the booking, travelling there and having the holiday is then open to you and you proceed along it.

An action-channel is an action that is in your power to take. For example, if you are a salesman it is in your power to knock on a door or to make a telephone call. The response to your sales pitch is not within your power. So it would be wrong for a salesman to say that 'going out and selling a vacuum cleaner' is an action-channel. The correct action-channel is 'going out and attempting to sell a vacuum cleaner'. The salesman may know from experience that he is very unlikely not to sell a vacuum cleaner to someone so the uncertainty may be very small yet the response of the buyer is not within his control and hence cannot be part of the action-channel.

An action-channel may involve setting out to do research in an area or to look for some information. The result of the search is not part of the action-channel. The simplest test of an action-channel is to ask the question: 'If I decide to take this action what will definitely follow?'

If-boxes

If I decide to take the action-channel of crossing the road, what will follow? We may argue that there is uncertainty because I may get run over or faint or have a heart attack. In that sense of the word almost everything is uncertain: there may be an earthquake tomorrow; the president of the USA may be assassinated; an epidemic of swine influenza may strike, etc. For practical purposes we have to ignore this sort of uncertainty (though we can insure against it). We have to assume that our factory will still be standing tomorrow and that the sun will rise as usual. So if we decide to cross the road we have to assume that we will succeed.

If, however, I telephone someone and ask him to lend me some money I cannot be sure of his response. So my telephoning is an action-channel but an if-box intervenes before the outcome. An if-box is a device for crystallizing uncertainty. We can make a decision to advertise a product and the mechanics of advertising will ensure that the advertisement appears, but the response to the advertisement (of a new product) is uncertain so we place an if-box there.

The word 'if' has a pretty clear usage:

If we can find the right man for the job.
If we can get raw material at this price.
If we can solve this problem.
If the trend continues.
If the response is favourable.
If we can find the information we need.

In an 'if' situation we can usually define the desired or favourable outcome in either general terms (like the 'something method') or in specific terms: 'If we can persuade Jim Smith to head our sales department' or 'If the head-hunters can send us someone with a background of experience in the textile industry and a knowledge of Japanese.'

In a way the if-box is a sort of junction box. The switch is in the open position until the uncertainty has been removed. The if-box is then followed by another action-channel which is then followed by another if-box and so on. If there was not uncertainty then one action-channel would follow another and we should be able to reach our objective simply by deciding to take action. Usually this is not possible because we are held up by uncertainties or if-boxes. If-boxes may contain a variety of contents including the following:

Needed item: If we had a 'something' to fulfill these defined needs. It could be a person, a product, a material or a type of situation. Once the 'something' has been defined, an effort can be made to find it.

Problem solution: If we had a solution to this problem. Straightforward problem-solving. Once the problem has been solved, action can proceed again.

Search: If we could find what we are looking for. This is usually a matter of information or availability or something. The thing itself already exists but it is a matter of finding it. Market research falls into this bracket on the supposition that people know what they want and we need only tap this knowledge.

Response: If the response to our action is favourable. This would cover the response to advertising, sales effort, investment or any situation where an action is taken with an intended outcome but the outcome depends on other people.

Circumstance: If the trend continues or if these circumstances arise. The set of circumstances can be envisaged precisely but whether the circumstances will occur is a matter of uncertainty.

Protective: If this does not happen. 'We shall have a very profitable run with the calculators if competitors do not enter the field at once and start a price war.' In contrast to the other types of if-box this one would contain something that was not wanted.

Another example might be a change in the law regarding a particular type of product.

Unknown: We really have no idea what will happen. Here the response is totally unknown. In practice one creates some possible alternative outcomes and considers the likelihood of each. Nevertheless the actual outcome may be quite different.

In using an if-box the desired (or favourable) outcome has to be defined in advance. Alternative outcomes can be considered but since it is an opportunity-mapping device rather than a decision device, the emphasis should always be on the most favourable, sought-for, outcome. If you for example were to consider whether there was an opportunity in individual custom-painting of standard automobile models you could put down action-channels involving setting up the mechanics of the system, advertising, publicity stunts, samples and so on. Then would come the if-box of the response. The desired outcome would be a heavy response. If there was no response there would be no opportunity or the idea would have to be modified. For instance the idea might be changed to painting company livery on cars, or personalized artistic efforts ('My car is a Poltz, what is yours?').

The test of an if-box is as follows: 'Can I be reasonably certain about the outcome of this action?' If there is uncertainty then there is an if-box.

Constructing if-box maps

I must emphasize again that the if-box map is a device for exploring opportunities – not a general planning tool. There are five stages in the construction of the map and each will be considered in turn:

The most favourable scenario: The proposer of the idea sets forth in general terms how he sees the opportunity and what he sees as happening under the most favourable circumstances. At this stage it must be the most favourable scenario because it is the uncertainties present in this most favourable scenario that are to be considered. We can take the example of someone who suggests that there is an opportunity in selling out-of-fashion clothes. He states his favourable scenario as follows:

'High-fashion stores and boutiquès can never be seen to be selling stock that is out of fashion. Their ordering can never be so exact that they buy exactly what they are going to sell. In any case, the manufacturers are likely to have a stock of unsold garments. The idea is to buy up this out-of-fashion stock and to sell it in special shops called 'Second Sell' at a low price. This low price will be credible because people will believe that with out-of-fashion goods the material value is still high. I would expect the stock to be bought by people who did not feel the need to be at the height of fashion, people who were price-conscious and people who were themselves capable of altering the garments, such as removing the flare from flared trousers.'

Action stages: The next step is to take the favourable scenario and to break it down into practical action stages which are listed one under the other. For the example given above the proposed stages might be as follows:

1. Obtain a small supply of this out-of-fashion stock.
2. Hire or lease a shop for a short time and put in stock.
3. Advertise the new concept.
4. If the idea seems to work, obtain larger stocks and take over on a more permanent basis a larger shop.
5. Franchise the idea to shops in provincial towns.

Modified stages: The preliminary list of stages is examined. It may be found that one stage should be split up into several stages. By way of illustration, stage 4 in the example used involves looking for a larger supply, arranging finance, looking for and operating a larger shop. Examination of the first list of stages may also show that stages have been left out. For example, there is a stage missing before stage 1: There would have to be some exploration to see whether such stocks really did exist and what the fashion houses felt about them (perhaps they were disposed of quite adequately in periodic sales).

The modified list might read as follows:

1. Contact a few fashion houses and explore both the availability of the stock and their willingness to dispose of it in this way at low prices.

2. If the response is favourable, look for a shop that might be leased for a short period of time.
3. If the search is successful and the shop can be leased at a reasonable cost, stock it with garments and advertise.
4. If the public respond do a full survey of the availability of stock on a long-term basis.
5. If the outcome of the survey is satisfactory look for more permanent premises and financial backing.
6. If the outcome is favourable make arrangements for the stock and set up shop and advertise.
7. If turnover was satisfactory do a market survey on buyers to see whether or not they came from out of town.
8. If survey response was promising explore franchise operation.

If-box map: The modified stages list can now be turned directly into an if-box map by separating the action-channels from the if-box uncertainties. The result is shown in Figure 14. Once the map is drawn we can comment upon it. For instance the exploration of the long-term availability of stock seems to come quite late. If all else has been satisfactory but the outcome to if-box D is unsatisfactory, the whole opportunity disappears. Perhaps this exploration should have been done at A. The same might be said for the exploration of financial backing except that it is easier to obtain such backing if the success of a pilot scheme can be pointed to.

If we look at if-box B we can reduce the uncertainty by setting up alternatives such as a market stall, a stall in another shop, a joint venture with someone who is already running a not-so-successful shop. That way we increase our chances of finding some means of selling the garments.

By examining the map we can also see that the crucial if-box is C. If there is no response from the public the opportunity does not exist. But what happens if response is moderate? A risk decision must now be made. Is there any reason for supposing that it takes time for such a concept to catch on? How long can the trial period last? A possible action-channel is to survey the buyers to see why they have come.

Another person might put forward a different if-box map altogether. He might suggest the one shown in Figure 15. Here there is a commissioned market survey and if the result is strongly

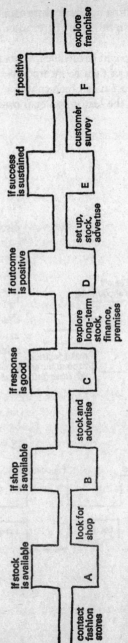

Figure 14

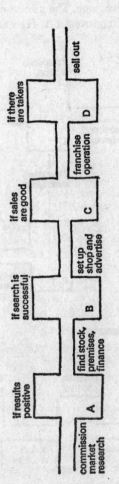

Figure 15

positive the move is directed into setting up the venture on a large scale. But is market research reliable in this type of operation?

Final if-box map: The first if-box map will be modified, altered and annotated. All these improvements can then be incorporated in a final if-box map. The process of evolution can then continue with further improvements. For example the first if-box map could be

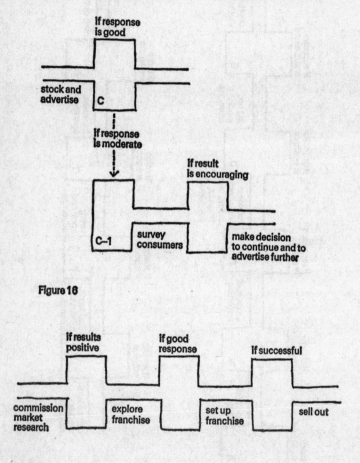

Figure 16

Figure 17

modified by the inclusion of an alternative path if the response to if-box C was only moderate. This modification is shown in Figure 16.

Similarly the second if-box map could be radically altered by realizing that boxes B and C could be ommitted as shown in Figure 17.

If the most favourable outcome is not to be obtained it is a matter for evaluation to decide whether a lesser outcome still constitutes an opportunity. If alternative outcomes are to be considered then the alternative outcome from the if-box is indicated by an if-box on another line as shown in Figure 16. A new track is thus started for each alternative outcome. That new track is followed through separately even if it might seem to re-join the main track again. It is treated as a separate opportunity. There is thus no branching in an if-box map.

Influences which are likely to affect the outcome of an if-box (either way) are listed above the box as shown in Figure 18.

In general all matters relating to the if-box are written above the track and all matters relating to the action-channels below the track.

In drawing an if-box map the size of the box may be made to vary visually with the estimated degree of uncertainty as shown in Figure 19.

The construction stages can be summarized:

1. Most favourable scenario.
2. Action stages list.
3. Modified action stages list.
4. If-box map.
5. Final if-box map.

'An opportunity may be an opportunity if you can hitch a ride – but not if you have to walk.'

Action structure for opportunity

The preceding section defined an action-channel as a channel which could be entered simply by making the decision to enter. In

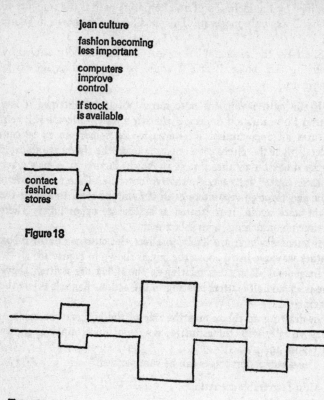

jean culture

fashion becoming
less important

computers
improve
control

if stock
is available

contact
fashion
stores   A

Figure 18

Figure 19

this section we shall contrast channels where you have to make all
the effort yourself and those in which you can 'hitch a ride' because the channel has its own energy.

One lumber company hauls its logs out of the forest, loads them
on to trucks, takes them to the railhead, transfers them to flat cars
and finally transfers to barges again on the coast. Another lumber
company just drops its logs into the river and picks them out the
other end. This second lumber company does not have to make all
the effort – it plugs into an existing action structure.

One author meets an effective literary agent at a cocktail
party. He finds out which books are selling and writes a book on

214

these lines. The agent negotiates a huge price with a publisher. The publisher takes the book, polishes it up a bit, puts it through its production routine, gives it the publicity build-up and distributes it through its usual channels. The author sits back and enjoys the royalties. Another author writes a book which no one wants to publish, so he arranges printing and binding himself. He takes the book around himself from bookshop to bookshop. The first author has plunged into a powerful action structure whereas the second author is having to make all the effort.

Channels of effort

The flowing river and the publisher's established channels provide the effort once the idea has been plugged into the system. In considering an opportunity it is important to pay attention to the action structure that may be required. Many an inventor has had great fun designing a new board game that is going to out-Monopoly 'Monopoly'. The game is designed and even produced. Then comes the trouble. The cost of distribution and advertising is so high that the project never gets any further. There is no suitable channel of effort – the action structure is inappropriate. There is however, one chance for this games-designer and this will be considered under the heading of 'trigger'. Channels of effort are very often distribution or communication channels. If they exist it is no great effort to plug a new idea into the system. If they do not exist the potential of the idea would have to be great enough to justify the risks of setting up special channels for it.

In a complex society the existence of effective channels of effort is often more important for the success of an opportunity than is the new idea itself. The term 'market muscle' means that a company with powerful marketing channels can make a success of a product which is not itself so wonderful.

Delegation

Many brilliant executives would be much less effective in a smaller company. In a large company what is required of them is thinking and decision-making. The decision is then passed to someone who takes action or passes it to someone else to take action. Successful delegation is one of the most powerful tools of any organization.

We can contrast the action of an electric power line or water conduit with the action of a human nerve. Power flows through the electric line and water flows through the conduit only if there is a head of pressure at one end. This head of pressure drives the water through the pipe (voltage in the case of electricity). In a human nerve the impulse travels because at each moment the nerve itself produces the energy for it to move further. The input energy need only be enough to start it off. The impulse is then self-energizing. Similarly with effective delegations each link in the chain is self-energizing and not just a passive channel for the energy that is put into it.

The existence of effective delegation makes an effective action structure for opportunity. Without it an opportunity is likely to die because it would be unusual for everyone to be as enthused about it as the originator.

Fashions, trends and bandwagons

The opportunity-spotter plugs into the energy of a fashion or bandwagon and gets carried along with it. He may decide that pollution is going to be a bandwagon and so he sets up a pollution consulting service. Riding a fashion trend can be very effective because the trend both provides the publicity for the service and creates a need for it. Many successful opportunity-takers have paid more attention to action structures such as these than to the basic idea itself. The opportunist who can ride a trend is very like the lumber company that can drop its logs into the river: there is publicity for the product, retailers are happy to stock it because it moves fast, consumers are happy to buy it.

Tapping existing energy

Many companies have set out to tap the energy of housewives who cannot leave home because of having to look after children. Often the work provided tends to be rather low paid: stuffing envelopes, painting toy soldiers and the like. One enterprising estate agent in Cambridge arranged with a bed-ridden girl for her to be his telephone answering service. It provided variety in her life and ensured that there was always a living voice at the end of the telephone.

The Avon cosmetics distribution system made very effective use of the energy and motivation of housewives – making stockists and saleswomen of them. The Tupperware concept was somewhat similar.

A great deal of charitable work gets done because people do have unused energy and do want a sense of purpose. A simple objective or organizing framework can often put this energy to work – just as hydro-electricity is energy obtained by providing a simple structure to use energy that would otherwise be ignored.

Trigger

The Queen lights a ceremonial match and triggers off a mammoth firework display. The bomb-aimer presses a switch and releases twenty tons of bombs from a B-52 flying at 40,000 feet. In both cases the output is totally out of proportion to the input. All opportunity seekers love trigger situations where the right input at the right time can trigger a response quite out of proportion to their efforts.

Once someone shows that something can be done an avalanche of action may be triggered off. The problem for the initiator is to be sure he keeps part of the action.

'Monopoly' and 'Scrabble' are two immensely successful games. Yet initially both were rejected by all the manufacturers they were offered to. So the designer made up the games himself and placed them in toy shops. The response was very good and this proved enough to trigger off the whole phenomenon of each game. It is possible for an innovator to try one thing after another in the hope of triggering off a huge response. But the response will depend on a conglomeration of circumstances and not just on the value of the idea. For instance, a person repeating the 'Monopoly' story with a parallel game today would have much less chance of success because distributors and the public are mainly influenced by what they see on television and the innovator would have no access to that channel of communication.

Amplification

If a lot of people are doing your work for you, your efforts are amplified. An obscure writer who becomes a cult figure finds that there are so many high-priests commenting upon his work and upon each others' commentaries that his influence is magnified quite out of proportion to his efforts. The various pyramid-selling schemes and rackets were based on the huge power of amplification. If everyone who receives the message becomes a spreader of the message then it gets around a lot quicker.

In considering an opportunity it is useful to see whether there are any amplification possibilities in the action structure of that opportunity. Public relations is an effort to involve the amplifying power of the media – at no cost.

The success of most insurance companies depends on the amplifying effect of all its salesmen motivated by the generous commissions they receive. Thus there are said to be 250,000 life insurance salesmen in the United States.

Amplification is worth a lot of attention. If it is as effective for a pharmaceutical representative to talk to thirty doctors brought together for a free dinner as it would have been for him to call on each one separately, the number of representatives could be reduced very considerably – along with wages and expenses.

Positive feedback

Positive feedback is one way of achieving amplification. A publisher makes a promotion effort with a book. The book gets on to the best-seller list. Because it is there bookshops want to stock it and readers want to buy it. That keeps it on the best-seller list. High sales make more money available for promotion so the publicity effort is increased which further increases readership. A scandal involving a person gives that person publicity value so the next thing the person does gets publicized, and so the process goes on until it reaches the point when a number of people are very well known simply for being well known.

There is nothing 'positive' about positive feedback because it can also work in a very destructive way. It simply means that the effect is fed back to add to the input (as distinct from negative feedback where the effect is fed back to cancel out the input). Increased wage demands put up prices which in turn lead to further wage demands in a positive feedback cycle. Price-cutting with pocket calculators leads to lower profit margins and a need for higher volume sales which in turn leads to a further cut in price. The trick is to get positive feedback working positively in your favour.

A variation of positive feedback is the repeat customer: once he has bought your product he is more likely to buy from you again. Here his purchase feeds back to increase his willingness to buy. This is not quite the same as the captive customer who must buy your razor blades because no other make fits his razor (if you are successful enough someone else will come along to take part of your captive market by producing a blade that fits – and at a price which does not include your development costs).

Contact channels

In some areas contact channels are vital. It may be a matter of knowing the person who makes the decisions or knowing the person who knows the mechanics of the situation. It may be a matter of knowing the person who has the information or who knows where it can be found. Many non-executive directors of large corporations are there because they are the custodians of important contact channels. It is not a matter of inside information or slush funds but of the vital importance of knowing at the right time. Without such knowledge expensive mistakes can be made. The coming together of different fragments of knowledge can itself create opportunities. Knowing the mechanics of a particular market can affect product design (for example, knowing that toys are bought by buyers in the January and February fairs for the following Christmas – so a new toy must be rather similar to the one which has sold so successfully the December before the January).

Contact channels are part of the action structure of an opportunity and should be considered as such.

'Whenever we are dealing with the future we are dealing with risk and uncertainty and whenever any change is proposed that risk and uncertainty is greatly increased.'

Dealing with risk and uncertainty

The brain is a history library that has to run in the future tense. Almost all our thinking activity is directed towards dealing with the future since all actions taken are directed towards bringing about an effect which is not yet present. Yet the brain can only make observations of the moment and recall experience of the past. Even what we see at the moment is conditioned by the perceptions of the past. Our habit of analysis has been developed in order to break down unfamiliar chunks. We seek to discover scientific truths so that we may predict what will happen and how we can make things happen with a practical degree of certainty. We are forever extrapolating the past in order to prepare the future into which we are always moving.

It is not surprising that much of business is dealing with risk and uncertainty because all of business is dealing with the future. When we concern ourselves with opportunity we are dealing with greater risk and uncertainty because we have to do much more than predict that an already existing business will go on being successful (the minimal prediction anyone has to make – and it is increasingly difficult to make).

As an illustration of dealing with uncertainty we can take the difficult position of a garment manufacturer who has to predict this season's fashion colour. If he gets it wrong it can mean that his whole output may be difficult to sell. Some years ago a well-known maker of jeans predicted that flared legs would be in fashion – but it turned out that straight legs became the fashion and the loss was huge. Let us consider some possible mechanisms of prediction. (I am not suggesting that these are the actual mechanisms.)

Sensitivity: Some people might have an acute fashion sensitivity or 'nose' and they can sense, for example, what the colour is going to be. Such people may not be able rationally to explain their choice because it is a matter of subtle observation and heard whispers. Those who are bad at it drop out – there is no market for a poor soothsayer – and so by natural selection those who survive do have this 'nose' (as with wine-tasting and tobacco-blending).

Cycles: There may be natural cycles or progressions of colour so that one colour is usually followed by another in order to get sufficient contrast or mood change. Knowledge of such cycles will narrow the range of options. This would be somewhat similar to skirts going up and down in cycles because once they are down there is no way to change except by going up again.

Self-fulfilling: The sugestion here is that the colour is actually chosen by a few fashion writers or textile-makers and then through an unconscious whispering campaign this becomes the colour of the season. So it is not a matter of predicting what people will want but finding out what the people in the trade are 'arriving at' as the colour. This is like sensing the mood of a stock market.

Observation: This means being a little behind anyone else and waiting to see what happens. It is a sort of second-in-the-field stance. It is not always possible when manufacture and ordering have to precede sales or fashion publicity by several months. Observation must then be applied to what competitors are doing.

We can now look at the various methods we use in order to reduce risk and uncertainty.

Analysis: This is not as useful as it would seem. Through analysis we seek to treat each component of what we are doing and each component of the market as a factor with a likely mode of action. When we put all these actions together we hope to work out the prognosis. Financial analysts use this method or pretend to use it. It works well enough in a scientific situation but less well when each part cannot be clearly defined. The problem is that subtle outside influences may be neglected and also two separate types of action may, when combined, lead to a third type that is not predictable from the first two. In spite of all this we have to attempt an analysis in order to satisfy ourselves.

Recognition: With analysis we may seek to break down a new situation into an assembly of known situations whose behaviour we recognize. A very experienced person may have the ability to recognize a situation which every one else would consider to be novel. An experienced person would also recognize a trend or the type of reception a new idea was receiving. Recognition is valuable because if it is accurate it leads to sound prediction – just as a doctor recognizing chicken-pox or measles can predict the outcome. There is of course the danger, mentioned earlier in the book, of false recognition where a new situation is falsely treated as a recognizable one just because it has some features in common – like a doctor mistaking polio for hysterical paralysis.

Comparison: This is by far the most used and most useful method. We can compare the new product to something already existing in the field or in the experience of our company. We can look at what has happened abroad. We can look back in history and compare what we are doing with what has happened before. Comparison is much less certain than recognition because there may be only points of similarity and we have to decide whether these are important points. Will the film on killer whales be as successfully received as was *Jaws*? Is the point of comparison that both are about sea monsters or that sharks have a special terror? Or is it that people go to a cinema to be frightened in mass company – something that they cannot get in front of a television set? Most of our thinking is comparison thinking. But in order to use comparisons we may have to use analysis first to isolate points of comparison. We may also have to use lateral thinking to generate new concepts before comparing one thing with another.

Hunch: As described in the example of choosing next season's fashion colour, some people would work on hunch or their exquisite sensitivity to a situation. This might mean that the complex computer of their mind has taken in a large number of factors and put these together in a special way to give the hunch that is not open to rational description. In a self-fulfilling situation (for example a company with effective marketing skill) the hunch can be made to work because of the effort put behind it. A publisher may find or actually create a best-seller whilst believing that he has found it.

Trends: You observe the trend, you plug your idea into the trend and then you predict the success of your idea from your prediction of the trend. Here you have the advantage that a lot of other people are analysing the trend along with you. Indeed if enough of them are involved it may become a self-fulfilling system. The beauty of such a system is that you make it happen rather than wait for it to happen.

Market research: Market research can be used to give a factual state of the market: how many people have two cars; how many households do not yet have a refrigerator or deep-freezer. There is no quarrelling with such findings. The interpretation put on them may be open to debate. Are the families without deep-freezers potential future buyers or those families whose eating habits have decided them against a deep-freezer? Even so, are such habits likely to change with better education?

Market research as to what people have done in the past also provides facts: how many people took a holiday in Spain and how many stayed in England. But the extrapolation from such facts is again difficult. The Spanish peseta may be devalued, thus increasing the attraction of a holiday in Spain. Tourists may visit Cornwall in increasing numbers but they may choose to go camping or take their tents on self-catering holidays. Extrapolations are usually based on the assumption that things may change but by only a small percentage because the time course of change is slow (everyone is not going to buy a caravan overnight).

Market research as to declared intentions or desires is the most unreliable of all. Everyone knows about the famous Edsel car which was meant to combine all the desirable features people said they wanted in an automobile. There is a big difference between saying what one might want and actually buying it if it were available – everyone who would like to buy a Rolls-Royce is not a potential consumer of such a car. Furthermore, the combination of desirable features does not add up to a super-desirable end-product. You may want an economic car and you may want a car that looks glamorous but you may not want a glamorous-looking car that is economical: you might prefer an economical car to look economical and so take you outside the glamour stakes.

It is easy to pick faults in market research because in general it is so useful. The main point is to ask the right questions and to realize that it is your interpretation of the results that matters.

Test runs: Instead of predicting you try it out. You advertise your product in a small area and see what response there is. The Tyne-Tees television area in the United Kingdom has been such a favourite that housewives have almost developed a special attitude to test products. A test run should be more effective than any other means of prediction because it actually creates a mini-future which can be observed. The difficulty is that the novelty of the trial may ensure more attention than would be sustained if it were a full run. For example, it is said that there are 15,000 people in London who would buy the first issue of any new publication. But they would not buy subsequent issues. A person may also like something if it is thrust under his nose but not enough to seek it out if it is on the shelves amongst other competing brands.

Nevertheless the test run remains one of the most effective ways of reducing risk and uncertainty – and in addition motivating extra effort or even obtaining financial backing. People react better to actual than to promised success.

Extrapolation: The L-game I designed was once marketed, over Christmas, in the Allentown area of Philadelphia. Through good publicity and placement in major stores, 20,000 copies of the game were sold within two weeks in a population area of about 300,000. If one were to multiply up that success the results would be staggering. But to repeat that success on a national scale would involve a very heavy investment in publicity and marketing and that would only be possible for a large company and any large company would have so many other products that the focused attention required would not be possible.

Extrapolation and scaling up are full of dangers. And the dangers can work both ways. A service or product tested on a local level may be a failure but when promoted nationally may be a success (this might happen with a fast-food chain).

Feasibility study: This is a cross between an analysis and an if-box map. We consider a favourable scenario and then work out what is actually involved. We might for instance find that to cover the costs of tooling, a new kitchen cooker would need to sell 20,000 units a year and to do so it would need either a price advantage or heavy advertising. To be a worthwhile opportunity a market of about 50,000 units would be necessary. So the question changes.

Instead of, 'Is this a good design?' it becomes, 'No matter how good a design this is, do we think we can sell 50,000 a year?' So a feasibility study shapes the risk and uncertainties so that we can react to them precisely. Instead of asking whether consumers will like the new cooker, the manufacturers must ask whether 50,000 of them are going to like it. It is no use arguing that the market will grow over the years if there is not enough cash-flow to keep the company going that long.

Spell it out: A feasibility study is a precise form of the exercise of spelling something out. What are the risks and what are the uncertainties? What is the exposure and what is the fall-back position? Spelling out something may reveal that even if the response is excellent the market size is too small and the cost of reaching it too high. Spelling out something may show that an attempt to estimate customer satisfaction is pointless if there is no satisfactory way of bringing the service to the attention of potential customers. The more precisely risks can be defined the more they can be by-passed, tailored or reduced.

Wide targets, narrow targets and nearby targets: If you aim at the bull you may easily miss. If you are content just to hit the dartboard you are much more likely to be successful. That was the thinking of Dimitri Comino when he founded the very successful Dexion company. The slotted angle steel product had so many possible uses that the target was very wide. If you aim to produce a specialist product like an underwater pipe valve you will have the whole market to yourself so long as your product is the best – but if it is not you may find yourself with no market at all.

The widening of the target in order to reduce the risk is not contrary to the principle of market segmentation. In fact market segmentation is really a form of target widening: we find that market in which everyone is a potential buyer of our product.

A nearby target is not the same as a wide target: it means being ungreedy. If we aim for only a tiny share of the market the risk of getting that is reduced. If we do not rely on a price advantage we may not need high volume sales. If something can be done in small stages the risk is obviously less than if it has to be done all at once. A fast food chain can grow with success. Investment in a new car design may involve a huge capital outlay – the car cannot be altered year by year. In the step-by-step process there is, however, the danger that once the market has been opened up someone else may come in and take the big pickings.

Perhaps the ideal philosophy is to have a high degree of timidity but a plan for progressively reducing that timidity.

Degree of innovation: There is a story of the television producer who thumped the table at a planning meeting and declared: 'What we really need are some brand new platitudes.' In other words something which seems new enough to be called an innovation but is really old enough to be predictable in its outcome. Tobacco companies know very well the effect on their market share of introducing a new brand because they do it all the time. When the smoking substitute materials, like NSM and Cytrel, were launched in the United Kingdom in the early summer of 1977 no fewer than eleven new brands were launched at about the same time. A new TV series or a new cigarette are variations on a theme and the degree of innovation may not be very high. The risks are consequently lower but they can still be considerable. Many a new TV series costing millions of dollars has failed dismally, and at the time of writing the cigarettes containing tobacco substitutes are not conspicuously successful.

Doing something totally new – like introducing the Philips–MCA video disc system – has higher risks inasmuch as the market is untested. A distinction must be made between a product which is good but the value of which can only be seen after purchase and use, and a product where the use is well known and the new features are evident in advance. For example a new health-diagnosis calculator (sensing outputs from the body such as pulse rates and temperature and respiratory rate) is bound to involve more risks than an ordinary calculator with the additional feature of a permanent programmable memory. It is not unlike a new game which you may recognize as wonderful after you have bought it, learned the rules and played for about a week. Contrast that with a model-building kit where the value is obvious at once. The difficulty is that those working with the innovation know too much about it – in the same way as an author may be the worst person to put a title to his book since his title is a summary whereas what is needed is an enticement.

Whether or not we like it consumers, and the world in general, base their behaviour on their experience. So the more an innovation connects up with this experience the less is the risk. That is what is meant by degrees of innovation.

Cumulative effects: When there is a string of 'ifs' in a row and the chance of success in each case is estimated at about even odds, the eventual chance of success is only one in sixteen ($\frac{1}{2} \times \frac{1}{2} \times \frac{1}{2} \times \frac{1}{2} = \frac{1}{16}$). But if the risks are in parallel ('We would be content if this happened or if this happened or if this happened',) then the chances of success are quite high. This difference between sequential 'ifs' and parallel 'ifs' is important. When a number of things must go right the 'ifs' are sequential; when any one of a number of alternative 'ifs' will do then they are parallel.

A difficulty arises when there is an area of uncertainty but there are a number of factors or pointers which tend to reduce the uncertainty. Yet there is no single factor large enough to reduce the uncertainty on its own. Do a series of minor pointers add up to a major pointer or not? The answer is that in some circumstances they do but in others they do not. By way of illustration a rise in inflation, a falling stock market, industrial unrest in South Africa, a good grain harvest in Russia, political uncertainty in the middle East, a weak government in India might all suggest a rise in the price of gold. On the other hand the fact that red is a nice colour, that people cannot afford expensive Christmas presents, that people are used to buying diaries, that people like novelty cannot be taken as an indication that a new red diary will be a winner. Any number of damp matches are not as good as one dry match. A number of small reasons, each of which is valid in itself, can reduce uncertainty. A number of half reasons can never amount to a full one. If we are trying to predict what will happen then every clue helps. If we are trying to ensure that something does happen then we need strong, full reasons.

Risk and reward: No one gets a medal for taking unnecessary risks. An effective innovator gets the odds on his side. He makes an attempt to reduce the risks as much as possible. It does not follow that the higher the risk the higher the reward. We must not let a puritan ethic convince us that there can be no rewards without risk or that risk successfully survived earns a reward. The man who dashes across the road in front of the traffic is no better off at the end than the man who waits for a gap or moves along to the crossing.

A dangerous way to regard uncertainty is to behave as if there are only two possibilities: it will or it won't happen. This excludes all sorts of variations and also gives the impression that the chances are even. A man seeking to borrow money from the bank could say, 'Either I get the money or I don't.' In fact he might get only part of what he wants, or only on certain conditions, or if he presents his case in one way but not if he presents it in another. It is, however, permissible to say, 'At the worst this is what might happen', In between there is a spectrum of possibilities.

It was Peter Drucker who said that the biggest risk was to take no risks at all. If we assume that we do not need to look for opportunities; if we assume that the world outside will not change; if we assume that our competitors will also stand still; if we assume that continuity alone will see us through – we might be taking rather a big risk. Uncertainty is perhaps the only certainty we have. We cannot shy away from uncertainty and cannot hope to remove it entirely, but we can learn to cope with it.

'If the benefits cannot be spelled out clearly and precisely there is no opportunity. There may be a calculated risk involved in achieving the benefits but the benefits must be clearly perceived.'

Evaluation

At last we come to what many readers will feel to be the most important aspect of opportunity search. I do not agree with this view. In the end the success or failure of a company will depend on how adroit it is at opening up good opportunities and avoiding mistakes. But this is like saying that in the end the safety of a car will depend on how good the brakes are – the brakes alone will not propel a car. Our lives depend on our ability to avoid poisonous food but this ability will not itself provide the food that we need to survive. So evaluating skill is essential but it must be allied to a skill in generating and developing opportunities in the first place. I have no doubt in my own mind that the evaluating skill of executives is far greater than their opportunity-generating skill. The usual habit is to wade in immediately with this evaluating skill as soon as a glimmer of an opportunity appears. That is why I have devoted so much of this third part of the book to the development of opportunities and only this section to their evaluation.

In this section I do not intend to go in detail into methods of critical path analysis, cost analysis or cash-flow profiles. I must assume that costing and planning techniques will be available to senior executives who have to evaluate opportunities. What I do intend to do is lay out a simple conceptual framework within which opportunities can be considered. There is nothing unusual or exotic about this framework – it is designed to be usable rather than impressive. The more clearly we can see something the more appropriate will our judgement be. By defining the ways in which we can look at the opportunity we can arrive at a better evaluation.

Spell out the benefits

Earlier in this book it was said that with a problem we look for the solution and with an opportunity we look for the benefits. If we cannot see and define the benefits there is no opportunity. We may have doubts about our ability to achieve the benefits (because of uncertainty and risk factors) but we must, nevertheless, be able to spell them out. Hitherto we have accepted that an idea may usefully be held in a general or amorphous form since from this may spring a new idea in an unexpected direction. Hitherto we have adopted a positive thinking attitude and looked for those aspects of an idea that seemed promising, ignoring the deficiencies. But now we have to be specific and ruthlessly honest. The idea has been nourished and given a chance to develop – now it has to appear before the judgement board.

In spelling out the benefits individual egos, motivations and political desires may have to be assessed. The new head of a marketing division may for instance wish to adopt a new marketing style because he wants to show his action initiative as soon as possible. It is valid to accept a direction of effort solely because it will motivate a moribund division. Once we can accept a ruthless honesty in such matters – and accepted that this sort of benefit is valid – we are freed to consider the other benefits more objectively. Otherwise we may be inclined to colour our assessment of the other benefits by our unexpressed suspicion of the place of the hoped-for benefits.

Benefits should be expressed in as precise terms as possible. A new product may be very well received by the public. That may be a benefit for the company image. But will they buy the product? At what price? How many units? A new play may be very well received by the critics who are looking for something to write about – but few people may go to see the play because they are looking for entertainment. Where the benefits are put forward as contributing to the progressive, innovative image of the company there should be an attempt to spell this out more precisely. Does the company wish to indicate that it is already into a new field of technology or that it is willing to try new ideas? Perhaps the benefit is the direct one of corporate advertising – to keep the name before both the buying and the investing public. Many a new product has been announced for the direct benefit of preserving a stock market quotation. There is, however, some doubt about the ethics of announcing a new product ahead of time in order to deter consumers from buying a rival product. I am concerned here, however, with a ruthless objectivity in spelling out the exact nature of the benefit expected from the opportunity.

Multiple benefits may be present but a listed mass of lesser benefits may hide the absence of a major one. If a major benefit is present this tends to get diluted by the addition of every conceivable other benefit so these should be firmly separated from the main benefits. Do a number of minor benefits add up to a major benefit? The answer must be no – as it was with the addition of minor pointers in a direction. As was stated there, a number of damp matches do not add up to a usable match.

It would be unusual for benefits to arrive in a single package at a defined time. There will usually be a profile of arrival depending on development, production, the market and the behaviour of competitors. As far as possible the expectations should be spelled out because they add to the precision of definition of the benefits

A fast-food chain may for instance decide to spend rather more on its style and decor than seems warranted at the moment but the benefit is that if the chain becomes countrywide the style will be necessary to attract customers who know the chain.

Approval and rejection

Approval or rejection of an opportunity should also be spelled out. In life we often try too hard to place something either in a box generally labelled 'good' or one labelled 'bad'. Then we react to the label. With opportunities the specific reason for approval or rejection should replace the general label. For example, the Opportunity Team may decide that the opportunity is a good one but that there is a better one to which resources can be directed. Or it may be decided that the opportunity is real but that it does not 'fit' the particular organization. There is, however, a danger in this 'not fitting' reason for rejection since it can so easily be applied to any suggested opportunity and can therefore be used to kill any suggestion of change. In the old business parable the stagecoach manufacturer could reject the opportunity to get into motor cars on the basis that he was in the stagecoach not the transportation business. But reasons such as this do at least mean that the opportunity gets a fair assessment on its merits. Too often an opportunity is rejected on the general ground 'that it will never work' when the real reason is that someone has other motives for not liking the opportunity -- and in fact it would work. It is far better to be able to say: 'I believe this opportunity would work but nevertheless I do not want to get involved in it for the following reason.' Unfortunately this other reason may not be expressible (it may for example involve one partner asking help from someone he hates, or allowing a rival to increase the importance of his department at the expense of yours).

A person who puts forward an opportunity proposal has a right to know exactly why it is being rejected. If more information is required then it must be specified. A person who accepts an opportunity proposal has the duty to spell out to himself and to his colleagues his exact reason for doing so.

Benefits

In looking at the benefits we can adopt a very simple check-list approach.

What are the benefits? The answer to this question may include: increased profit margin; reduced production costs; reduced cost of some departments; increased market share; less absenteeism; higher productivity; increased retailer acceptance of product; retention of consumers; increased occupancy of hotel or aeroplane, etc., etc.

How do the benefits arise? They do not materialize out of the air. Where are they expected to come from? It may be a matter of reducing the production cost but keeping the price the same. Selling two rolls of toilet paper instead of one at a time will not actually increase the consumption of toilet paper but it may reduce packing and handling costs. It may also make it possible to offer price reductions which could not be offered on a single roll because of the low price. It may initially increase the market share but competitor catch-up is very easy.

How large are the benefits? This is a very important question because the scale of the opportunity may decide whether or not it is worth pursuing. An opportunity may be excellently worked out and very practical but if the expected benefits are small it may not be worth the effort. The volume of the market and the profit margins must be considered in as much detail as possible.

On what do the benefits depend? The benefits may depend on the workers responding in the expected manner to an incentive wage rise. Or the benefits may depend on the continuation of the existing anti-pollution legislation. Or the benefits may depend on the continued difference in costs between having an office in Philadelphia and one in New York.

In what way may the benefits fall short of expectation? Market penetration might for instance be far less than expected. Cost of production might be higher than anticipated and so the price advantage of a me-too product might be shaved. A competitor may get into the field faster than expected. The question asks for the areas of possible shortfall.

What are the assumptions? There may be an assumption that a trend will continue or that a change is due. There may be an assumption that the publicity given to the fuel crisis will lead buyers to prefer smaller cars (for themselves that is, not for the rest of the nation). There may be an assumption that there is room for another producer in a particular field. There may be an assumption that dissatisfaction with an existing product is widespread and hence offers a market for a better product. Again it is a matter of defining the assumptions rather than attacking them.

What problems are likely to be met? This question covers much of the previous discussion. It offers an opportunity to focus upon and list all the difficulties that may arise in the course of pursuing the benefits. For example, a delayed FDA approval of a new pharmaceutical in the USA may be a very serious problem. Technical problems may arise, such as the problem Rolls-Royce had with its hyfil turbine blades.

We can try applying all these test questions to an actual suggested opportunity: flying punch cards to the Philippines to have them punched up more cheaply than in the USA.

What are the benefits? A proportion of the saving in costs to the card-user will accrue to the organizer of the service.

How do the benefits arise? From a difference in wages – or availability of labour – between the USA and the Philippines.

How large are the benefits? This depends on accurate assessment of transport and labour costs and also on the size of the card-user market, i.e. those who do not do the work in-house.

On what do the benefits depend? On continuation of cost differentials, cost of transport, quality of the work.

In what way may the benefits fall short of expectations? Potential USA users might be afraid of upsetting their unions, the Philippine workers may increase their prices, the quality of the work may not be good enough for many purposes.

What are the assumptions? Basically a continuation of the existing price and legislative framework. Also an assumption that the cost saving would be attractive to USA card-users.

What problems are likely to be met? Customs and excise problems in the USA or the Philippines, poor quality of work in general or on one occasion, union problems.

On the whole the opportunity seems a good one because if at any time it turns sour the whole operation can be stopped without any loss of invested capital. The benefits can also be accurately costed.

The time profile

The time profile is inseparable from any consideration of opportunities. It is a long-term or a short-term opportunity? What sort of lead can be expected over competitors? Is it for this season's fashion shows or next? How long will the negative cash-flow period last before returns start coming in? How long a time is likely to be needed for research and development? Will the full benefits come through in months, years or decades? What is the opportunity life-cycle (on the analogy of a product life-cycle)? The time profile may be related to matters outside the control of the organization (for example the length of time an anti-trust suit may be drawn out) but most favourable and least favourable guesses should be attempted.

The choice of one opportunity over another may depend entirely on the time profiles. So spelling these out is as important as spelling out the benefits. Benefits that might arrive too late to save a company are not really benefits.

Goodness of fit

As was suggested earlier in this section, the way an opportunity fits a particular organization is important but difficult to assess. On one hand there is the danger of excessive conservatism which rejects anything new and on the other there can be an over-optimism which assumed that a well-managed organization can tackle anything. When the Rank Organisation got into office copiers by arranging a market-deal with Xerox there was no way in which it could be said that this new opportunity fitted Rank. And yet the result was an enormous success. On the other hand, the ventures of RCA, Xerox and General Electric into computers have all ended in failure.

The following are possible questions to assess goodness of fit:

Does the opportunity fit the type of manager we have? In the end the success of an enterprise depends on its managers. If they are conservative and safe, an opportunity that requires dash and salesmanship might be inappropriate.

Does the opportunity fit our cash-flow situation? Some organizations, like the K-mart discount stores, might have a huge cashflow and can therefore accept opportunities which other organizations cannot. It does not mean that an organization with a healthy cash-flow should accept an opportunity which initially mops up cash-flow but it is in a position to do so if it wishes (it may prefer to keep the same type of cash-flow in its new ventures).

Does the opportunity fit our market strengths? Know-how and distribution channels are difficult to build up. Once they are there, new products can be fed through them. Retailers also accept new products more readily from someone in a particular field.

Does the opportunity fit production and research facilities? It is possible to contract out both production and research. But if there is underused capacity then the actual cost will be less than for an organization without this capacity.

Does the opportunity fit our style of thinking? An organization like Perstorp A B in Sweden prefers to sell to other industrial users than to consumers. Every organization has its own framework for thinking. Know-how of this sort can be an asset but it can also sometimes be a prison – because it becomes self-perpetuating.

The context of judgement of an opportunity is vital but very difficult to alter. As an illustration, the first typewriter was regarded only as an aid to writing for blind people who could not see to write properly. The ball-point pen was originally seen as a writing instrument for aeroplane pilots at altitudes where ink-flow is interfered with. The Xerox process was originally seen as an aid to printing and not as an office-copier mechanism. The startling history of ideas that have been turned down and gone on to become huge successes (like Western Union rejecting Alexander Graham

Bell's telephone patents) illustrates this difficulty of projecting contexts into the future. For many years the makers of video-cassette equipment have been predicting a big break-through in which video-cassettes would achieve the popularity of gramophone discs. But it has never happened and investments like EVR have come to nothing. Judging discontinuities is notoriously difficult because once something has happened it may, itself, create a new context for its acceptance.

In considering goodness of fit the basic question is whether the opportunity is one which especially fits the organization (making use of assets and serving needs) or one that would be open to any organization that happened to think of it. In between are the opportunities that would be open to any organization with enough cash and management resources. If an opportunity does fit a particular organization, that opportunity would seem to have priority unless the organization is in danger of stagnating within its established outlook. On the other hand if the benefits offered by the 'open' opportunity are huge (as with Rank Xerox) it should be seriously considered, especially when some protection is available through licensing arrangements. What would not make sense is an open opportunity without protection because the considerable amount of initial work required may just open the market for someone with advantages in that field.

Again, it is well worth spelling out in detail why an idea is thought to fit and why it is thought not to. It is surprising how often firmly held convictions evaporate when subjected to the 'spell it out' test.

Investment

In the pursuit of any opportunity there is going to have to be an investment of money, time, people, effort and attention. Obviously the investment has to be considered against the expected benefits and against alternative use of the resources. Even if the intention is only to pursue the opportunity to a test-bed stage or an 'information-complete' stage the investment needed for the full pursuit of the opportunity must be considered. Otherwise the initial investment may reach a satisfactory first stage at which point it is found that full implementation is too costly. It is best to say: 'We are only committed to the first exploratory step but if this is successful what investment would we need to continue with the opportunity?'

In terms of cost there will be exploratory costs, start-up costs, support costs and fire-fighting costs. It is worth identifying the points at which cost estimates are very likely to be underestimates and where unforeseen circumstances, may lead to a sharp rise in costs (for example, delayed planning permission may mean delayed construction on a site and hence increased building costs).

Resource allocation is very much part of a manager's basic function and the exercise of this skill needs to be applied to opportunity investment. Are the resources available? Can they be obtained? What are the alternative uses? The effects of dilution, distraction and diversion should not be underestimated. It may be possible in terms of time, money and people to pursue several projects but mental energy and motivation may not be spread so easily. Many people work much better if they are single-minded. Attention is a resource like any other.

In considering the availability of resources and resource allocation it is worth getting parallel and independent assessments from members of the Opportunity Team. These parallel assessments can then be put together and compared. The manager whose division is going to be responsible for developing the opportunity must also make an independent assessment. The parallel assessment can then become the basis for a group discussion. If the whole assessment is done on a group basis from the beginning then the person who seems to have most knowledge in the area will dominate the discussion and use the other members of the group to endorse his views.

Test-beds

An opportunity is dealing with the future in one way or another. The risk and uncertainty are dealt with by analysis and comparison and above all by test situations. The possibility of setting up a test-bed and the cost of this need to be considered when the opportunity is evaluated. The test may be a market research test, an information test, a scientific test, a production test or anything else. Is it possible? What will it show? How long will it take to reach the test? What will it cost? Will the results be reliable and applicable outside the test situation? Tests can be misleading either way: a successful test can still be followed by failure and a good idea may still fail a test – this happens especially when a product has to be around long enough to create its own climate of acceptance.

A sort of mental test-bed involves defining the ideal version of the suggested opportunity and then working to see if this can be achieved. Preliminary suggestions regarding the production of a new mobile radio might be followed by tight specifications: technical, size, weight, and price. The design team would be told: 'If you can achieve these specifications then we can go ahead'. This constitutes a design test by specifications. It can be applied to an opportunity: 'If you can work the opportunity into this precise form – then we can go ahead.'

Cut-offs

There must be a pre-planned point at which a project can be abandoned. Otherwise, from moment to moment, it will always seem to make more sense to put in a little more effort and money in order to avoid waisting what has already been invested and because the feeling is that success must be just around the corner. The cut-offs should be considered in advance when the opportunity is being evaluated. Cut-offs may be operated in many different ways.

Target cut-off: Certain targets are set. If these targets cannot be achieved as planned, the project is abandoned. They may be design, research, recruitment, or planning permission targets. Westinghouse, for instance, abandoned a massive investment project in California because they. had obtained only four out of fifty or so permits demanded – after several years of effort.

Cost cut-off: A cost limit is set and when the money has been exhausted the project comes to an end. Unforeseen circumstances and poor planning can play havoc. If a project turns out better than expected or worse than expected the cost can be increased. Margins can of course be built in by the decision-makers even if not revealed to the executors of the plan.

Time cut-off: Sometimes time is vital (for example with the development of a me-too product in a new market). If something has not been achieved by a certain date then it may not be worth pursuing the project further. More generally time is taken as an index of effort: 'We have been working on this project for all this time and we have not got anywhere so I suggest we drop it.'

Test response cut-off: A test-bed is set up and if the project fails to pass the test satisfactorily it is abandoned. The terms of what constitutes success or failure should be precisely defined in advance.

Disaster cut-off: If things go badly wrong in terms of research (a promising lead peters out), legislation (new pollution demands), personnel (loss of a key person), competitors' activity (price-cut or better product, cash-flow problems, etc.

Review cut-off: The building into the programme of specified review stages with the abandonment of the project if at any stage the benefits no longer seem sufficient to justify the investment.

Difficulties

Although a consideration of the difficulties and problems has entered into every other aspect of the evaluation it is well worth while considering them again under the specific heading of 'difficulties'. Difficulties include problems, gaps, uncertainties, known risks, resource limitation and managerial requirements. There may be difficulties which will have to be lived with. There may be difficulties which can only be identified and so made visible. There may be difficulties which cannot be overcome but which can be avoided through choice of a different route.

When an opportunity presents no difficulties it usually means that it has not been examined in sufficient detail. A properly evaluated opportunity will be accompanied by its list of difficulties and it will also be shown how these are going to be tackled. Yet again it is a matter of focus and spelling things out.

Scenario

A scenario is a script for the future. It is like writing a film script and hoping that future events will follow it. A scenario is wishful thinking. A scenario is also what the opportunity-proposer expects to happen. If events will not follow your script, it must describe what events will themselves do. For a good opportunity the wishful thinking scenario and the expected results scenario should coincide.

Should the scenario be set at the most optimistic or the most pessimistic level? The answer is that it should be set at the most favourable or optimistic level. If the opportunity does not look good even at this level it is clearly worthless. As suggested in the section on the if-box maps, the assumptions and risk involved in the most favourable scenario can then be examined in detail. 'On what does this claim rest?' 'Do you really expect to get this response at this point?' 'Why do you say this?' 'How much will it cost to get this effect?' A favourable scenario still has to be realistic. For example, estimates of sales or market penetration have to be reasonable. In this respect a 'favourable' scenario is one in which all things work out as expected. It does not mean setting the actual values or extent of effects at the maximum level (for instance market penetration at the two-per-cent not at the fifty-per-cent level).

Once the most favourable scenario has been spelled out in detail and possibly mapped, three other scenarios can be derived from it. There is the worst possible scenario and two intermediate ones. These refer to the extent of what happens rather than to the nature. After all, if we take the most favourable scenario and at every point of doubt (every if-box) we plug in the negative then we get a pretty bad scenario. But if we are looking at the response to an advertising campaign we can look at four levels:

Excellent: The extent of what we hope for is at the best or most optimistic. Everyone wants to buy the product (still with a reasonable estimation).

Moderate: Here the response is good but far less than our most favourable projections.

Poor: The response is poor and may well indicate that the project is not viable or at least that the approach has been wrong. The difference between a moderate response and a poor one is that with a moderate response the opportunity can go forward but the benefits have to be re-assessed in line with the results. A poor response makes change or abandonment inevitable.

Disaster: The response is so bad that the opportunity is abandoned at once.

With each of these four levels of response or four scenarios the cost and action plan can be considered. It is no different from the best-case, worst-case approach to a situation. A next step would be planned for each of the four levels. So whichever scenario works out the planners know where they are (what it has cost them) and what they are going to do next. Such considerations are part of the evaluation of an opportunity and not just part of the planning. The answer to the question, 'What would we do if things turned out less well than we hope?' may well determine whether an opportunity is worth pursuing in the first place.

Comparison

There are organizations which claim that their problem is never one of generating opportunities but one of selecting from the mass of opportunities that are continually presenting themselves to the active management. Evaluating whether or not an opportunity is worth pursuing is different from choosing which of a number of attractive opportunities is the best.

There are three stages in the comparison process:

Pre-definition: The Opportunity Team define, in advance, as precisely as possible the sort of opportunity that would be most worthwhile. They define their criteria of choice and acceptance in as specific terms as possible (cash-flow profile, resource use, market know-how, development potential, risk level, time scale, etc.).

Individual assessment: Each opportunity is taken separately and assessed in its own right. This is done on the lines suggested throughout this section. There is no attempt at this stage to bring in the pre-definition that has already been set up. The question is: 'Is this really a valid opportunity?' The next stage of the individual assessment is to apply the pre-definition criteria in order to see whether the opportunity is valid for the organization and what they think they want. At this stage an effort may be made to

241

see whether an attractive opportunity can be made to fit the criteria and whether these need changing. This is the reason for first assessing the opportunity on its own merits.

Comparison: Those opportunities that survive the assessment at two levels are now placed in competition with each other. An effort is made to see the relative value of each on a single criterion at a time: benefits, goodness of fit, risk, potential, difficulties. As usual there should be as much specific spelling out as possible.

In the end all decisions are emotional but the reasons for the decision must be spelled out. Thus an emotional decision to choose a technology-based opportunity may be founded on the excitement of new technology, not on a market need. Once this is revealed it may alter the decision.

Value

In the end what matters is the value of an opportunity. The value is the relationship between the benefits on one hand and the effort and risk on the other. As a sort of clarification we can write the following:

$$\text{Value} = \frac{\text{Benefit}}{\text{Effort} \times \text{Risk}}$$

$$\text{Effort} = \frac{\text{Cost} \times \text{Inertia}}{\text{Resources} \times \text{Method}}$$

$$\text{Risk} = \frac{\text{Novelty} \times \text{'if-count'}}{\text{Experience}}$$

$$\text{Inertia} = \frac{\text{Complacency} \times \text{Opposition}}{\text{Motivation} \times \text{Need}}$$

The evaluation of any specific opportunity should also include a consideration of the need for opportunities as such. For example, a consumer products company may reject every opportunity offered on the grounds of uncertain market reception. Yet in the long run such a company has to find new products because of the relatively short life-cycle of its existing lines. This is a factor which must be taken into account in the evaluation. The people evaluating opportunities must be aware of the overall need of the company for opportunities in addition to their assessment of each suggested opportunity. This does not mean that a worthless opportunity should be pursued but it does mean that an effort may have to be made to spell out why an opportunity is not good enough and to indicate that it should be improved. There is obviously a difference in the evaluation attitude between a corporation where new ideas are the very life-blood (for instance in electronics) and one where they are something of a luxury.

We can therefore end the book with two questions:

Do we need opportunities?
What are we doing about it?

'Words are concept handles. We sometimes need a new word or expression in order to deal comfortably with a complex idea.'

Summary of Terms

Almost all the expressions used in this book will be familiar to anyone involved in the active world of business. A few novel expressions have been introduced in order to focus attention on concepts that would be awkward to handle in any other way. It is also sometimes useful to make strange what is familiar in order for it to get the attention it deserves. Many of the expressions described in this summary list are not novel at all and involve ordinary words used in an ordinary way. They are included here so that I may clarify and focus their meaning so that a reader is not led astray by an apparently familiar word which I have used in a special way.

In addition the formal terms used for the systematic Opportunity Search Exercise are given at the end of the list. The list is not alphabetical but follows the introduction of the words into the book.

Hindsight: Looking back from the vantage point of history. An idea may become obvious only after it has been found. An opportunity may be staring us in the face only after we have succeeded in seeing it. The steps leading up to a disaster may be visible only in retrospect. The ingredients of a success may be discernible only at a later date. Once you have got to the top of a mountain it may be easy to see the best way up. Something which may be easy to see in hindsight may have been invisible at the time. An obvious idea may have required hard thinking.

Lateral thinking: The type of thinking concerned with the way we look at the world. It involves moving 'sideways' to change perceptions instead of moving forward and using the established ones. You cannot dig a hole in a different place by digging the same hole deeper. Lateral thinking involves escaping from fixed ideas and fixed channels of thought. Ideas reached by lateral thinking may be obvious in hindsight.

Important and urgent: What is urgent requires immediate attention: answering the telephone, turning off a tap or putting out a fire. What is important may be important for the success or failure of an organization but it may not seem urgent at any particular moment. Solving minor day-to-day problems may be urgent but looking for opportunities is important. Urgent matters tend to get all the attention and important matters get squeezed out unless thinking time is deliberately allocated to them.

Technology-push innovation: The momentum for the innovation is derived from a technical development (physical, mechanical, chemical, etc.). The innovation is developed to its full intrinsic potential and then everyone looks around to see how it could be sold and to find a commercial use for it.

Market-pull innovation: Innovation that has been developed to fit a specific market need. The innovation is 'pulled' from the company by the needs of the market. The need is perceived first and the innovation designed to fill that need.

Minding the store: Being so busy with moment to moment housekeeping that there is no time to think of more important matters. The store cannot be left unattended and similarly there is no way of stepping aside from the usual daily chores.

Reactive and projective thinking: A reactive thinker just reacts to whatever hits him or is placed in front of him. A projective thinker looks ahead and sets up in his mind models of what he would like to see happen.

Problem-solving and problem-finding: When a problem stares us in the face we set about solving it. We may even spend time clarifying and re-defining a confusing problem. With problem-finding we set out deliberately to look for problems. We search for things that could be improved or for new things that need doing. By perceiving such needs we create for ourselves the problem of satisfying those needs. We do not wait for problems to arise – we set out to look for opportunities.

Blocked by openness: Because the straight road is so obvious and easy to follow we move fast along it and may go straight past an important alternative turning without even realizing it is there.

The problem of no problem: By shrinking one's horizons to what is already being done it is possible to show that there is nothing left to achieve.

Train-driver-style executive: The executive who likes to operate as efficiently as he can the existing system: sticking to the established tracks and running things to schedule.

Doctor-style executive: The executive who thinks in terms of problem-solving and who tackles the problems that arise in order to protect and restore the good health of the organization.

The farmer-style executive: The executive who seeks to get the most out his own patch. He invests in the organization in the hope that it will be improved, thus yielding a higher output.

The fisherman-style executive: The executive entrepreneur who equips himself with skill which he then brings to any new situation. He cannot foretell exactly what is going to happen but he reduces the risk by careful preparation, the use of experience and good mental equipment. He looks for big pay-offs.

An opportunity-negative structure: An organizational structure in which it does not make sense for an executive to look for opportunities since the penalties of failure are much greater than the rewards of success. A structure in which risk-taking is frowned upon. It can also refer to a structure which lacks the encouragement of mechanisms for opportunity development – even if there is a proclaimed interest in opportunities.

Riding the cycle: The feeling that profits can be made simply by riding the ups and downs of the business cycle. When there is a boom you make profits and when there is a recession you struggle to survive. This seems to be enough without any need to look for development opportunities as such. A somewhat fatalistic approach.

Opportunity war: The fear that any innovation will be matched and even surpassed by a competitor and that in the end neither side will be any better off. The fear that opportunity development might have made the same characteristics as a price-cutting war.

Escape benefits and achievement benefits: Escape benefits are obtained by escaping from an unsatisfactory situation such as escaping the attention of mosquitoes. Achievement benefits are obtained by achieving a desired situation – like getting a glass of beer.

Break-off point: The point at which an executive terminates his thinking about an opportunity. There are a number of standard break-off phrases many of which are valid and all of which can be used as an excuse to avoid further thought.

The opportunity dilemma: Every individual opportunity involves risk, effort, investment and hassle of all sorts. It is difficult to justify innovation in any particular instance. And yet if opportunities are not developed an organization stagnates and dies. The dilemma is that opportunities in particular are not worthwhile, but in general they are vital.

Idea-sensitive area (i.s.a.): An area in which a new idea could make a significant difference. An area which is crying out for a new idea. The definition of an area as an i.s.a. means that it is worth spending time trying to generate ideas in that area. The general term i.s.a. may include a high-cost area, a specific problem area, a further development area and even an emotional target area (where the justification is that someone is emotionally involved in the area).

246

Sticking point: A matter that is recognized as likely to offer uncertainty, delay, difficulty, friction, confusion or people problems. A sticking point may be foreseen in a plan or an idea. An attempt may be made to pick out, in advance, the likely sticking points.

Provocation: A fundamental thinking process that is especially useful in lateral thinking and in generating new ideas. We may need a provocation to jolt us out of our established channels of thought. A provocation is only justified by the new ideas it leads to: 'There may not be a reason for saying something until after it has been said.'

Po: A new language device that serves as an indicator to show that a statement is being put forward as a provocation. The word is derived from suppose, hypothesis, possible and poetry but is most easily remembered as standing for Provocative Operation.

Moving-in and moving-out: If we use a starting point for our thinking and then set off on a voyage of mental exploration we are using the moving-out method. A check list of possible starting points is given and from each one there may be a moving-out operation. But if we know our destination in advance then all we have to do is to find our way there and we are using the moving-in method. A check-list of end-points or destinations is given.

Intrinsic assets: All the owned assets that go to make up the organization: money, plant, know-how, research, licences etc. Personnel may also be included.

Operating assets: Assets that arise directly from the particular way in which something is done. An operating asset means an asset that arises in the course of the operation. The operation itself may not be worth while but there may be hitherto unnoticed operating assets which can be exploited.

Situation assets: Assets that arise from the circumstances of the moment. Assets that arise from the situation that exists at any particular time – usually in the outside world. There may be a legal, political, technical or economic change in circumstances that create a situation asset. Where an hotel is located is an intrinsic asset. A relaxation of government control on business expenses may offer a situation asset.

Left behind: Whenever there is a significant development in a particular direction there is automatically a development away from an area that is 'left behind'. The more powerful the development the more extensive what is left behind. The expression may apply to activity or even to thinking.

Synergy: The coming together of complementary activities to create a new benefit. Sometimes the separate activities have no value until they are combined. At other times the value of the combination exceeds the separate values of the components.

Variable value: Value is in the eye of the user. The same thing may have little value for one user and a high value for another. One man's waste is another man's treasure.

'De-averaging': The opposite of averaging. We work backwards from the average in order to find the variety that has gone into it. We work backwards from the average shopper or the average reader in order to see the different types of shopper or reader.

Me-too: Setting out to do what someone else is already doing. Offering a product or service that is similar to one that is already being offered. Cashing in on the success of an existing operation through imitation.

The 'something' method: Spelling out in advance the functions and properties of what is required. We define in advance how 'something' will behave and what it will do. Then we set out to find what the defined 'something' could be.

Upstream problem avoidance: Moving upstream from the problem and seeing whether it can be avoided by taking a different route. Avoiding a problem instead of solving it. Moving back to the time before the problem ever arose and looking for alternative lines of procedure.

'The same as': The killer phrase that is used to squash any new idea by suggesting that it is not new at all and hence has already been tried and is not worth considering. Focusing on the similarity between the proposed new idea and an old idea instead of on the difference.

Function extraction: Abstracting from a concrete example the general principle or function that is seen to be operating. Looking at the functional bones of a situation rather than at the flesh of detail. It may be a matter of extracting the function from an example or of incorporating a function in a practical example.

PMI: A simple device for ensuring that the initial positive or negative reaction to a proposal does not preclude consideration of the other aspects. Doing a PMI involves listing the Plus points, the Minus points and the interesting points of the presented idea. The main use of the device is to protect against instant dismissal of an idea when the first impression is unfavourable.

Stepping stone: One of the methods of provocation and part of lateral thinking technique. Instead of being judged, an idea is used as a stepping stone to a new idea. The purpose of the stepping stone is movement not judgement. The final idea must be useful but the stepping stone may be wrong or even deliberately fantastic. The word 'po' may be used to indicate that a stepping stone is intended.

Tailoring an idea: Instead of the criteria of judgement being applied directly in the screening of proposals, the criteria are used to define an area of acceptance. An idea is then modified, changed and transformed to see if it can be made to fall into that area of acceptance. Tailoring involves cutting one's coat to suit the cloth available.

DPA rating: A quick rating can be applied to any suggested innovation and in particular a new way of doing something. How different is it (D)? How practical is it (P)? What advantage does it offer (A)? A rating out of ten or a hundred is given for each of these characteristics. For example: 'On a scale of ten I would give this a DPA rating of 3, 7 and 1.'

Spell it out: An instruction to oneself or to others to spell out a suggestion in detail and in concrete terms. It indicates that the time has come to get away from a general concept and to convert it into a specific proposal. The emphasis is on concrete elaboration. Weak points, gaps and assumptions may only become obvious when an idea has been 'spelled out'.

FI–FO: An abbreviation of 'information-in' and 'information-out'.

It becomes a shorthand way of asking that the information available be spelled out and also the information that is needed but is not available. It puts the emphasis on clear definition of the areas of ignorance. Like most shorthand devices there is no need to use it unless it seems convenient. 'Do a FI–FO on this for me, please.'

If-box map: A visual mapping of opportunities that makes it possible to see at a glance the stages and the risks. Once a map has been drawn it becomes possible to direct attention to any part of the opportunity. Weaknesses can be attended to and alternatives considered. A mapped opportunity may be modified, improved, condensed or extended.

Action channel: One of the two basic elements of an if-box map. An action channel is an established channel through which your action can flow once you have made the decision to enter the channel. When your action depends on no one else then it is only a decision away. An action channel defines the action steps that you can take without any uncertainty.

If-box: Just as the action channel describes action that can be taken, so the if-box condenses the uncertain outcome of an action and puts it all together at one place. The hoped-for outcome is defined in advance and when an 'if' is placed against the outcome an if-box is formed. An if-box forms a sort of switch box. The switch is in an open position until the uncertainty has been resolved. When the outcome is known the switch is closed and we proceed through the box to the next action channel.

Wide targets, narrow targets and nearby targets: With a wide target the aim does not need to be so precise. A new product may have several different markets so if any one of them does not come up to expectations the product may still be a success. With a narrow target there is a specific aim and if this misses the outcome is failure. With a nearby target what is aimed for is modest and easy to achieve. A nearby target is unambitious.

Time profile: The time profile of an opportunity seeks to lay out on a time scale the profile of investment, effort and reward over the years of development and implementation. A time profile is usually essential for evaluation purposes.

Goodness of fit: How well does the suggested opportunity fit the organization to which it is being presented? Both the opportunity and the organization may be effective in their own right but there may be a poor fit. Goodness of fit involves an assessment of assets, personnel, know-how, experience, philosophy and other factors including the personalities of the decision-makers.

Cut-off: The pre-determined point at which an opportunity project is to be abandoned. The cut-off may be set up in terms of money, time, test response or reward. There may be a cut-off because a defined target has not been reached or because too much money has been spent. A cut-off may also be operated as a result of a review decision or because of unexpected mishaps.

Scenario: A view of the future run almost as a movie-scene within one's head. Each part of the scenario is described in detail. It is just like writing a script for the future – in the hope that the future will stick to the provided script. The scenario may describe what we hope will happen with an opportunity. It may also describe what we think will happen. There are usually several alternative scenarios.

Best-case and worst-case: Consideration of the most favourable outcome (if all things go as hoped) constitutes the 'best-case' view. Consideration of the least favourable scenario (if nothing happens as hoped and if all the expected disasters come about) constitutes the 'worst-case' view. In between the two extremes lie moderate success and relative failure. Knowing the worst case in advance allows contingency plans to be made and also allows one to assess whether the rewards of the opportunity are substantial enough.

The opportunity search exercise (Opex): The overall name given to the systematic and deliberate search for opportunities that is advocated in this book. It includes various elements such as the Opportunity Audit and the Opportunity Team. For ease of reference the abbreviation Opex may be used.

Opportunity Audit: A formal reporting exercise in which chosen executives spend time looking for the opportunities that they perceive in their own opportunity space and also outside it. There is a formal reporting procedure with specified headings.

Opportunity Manager: The person who is given responsibility for opportunity action in an organization. He would be responsible for running the Opportunity Search Exercise. His duties would involve running the Opportunity Audit and setting up the Opportunity Team. Outside this framework he would be responsible for coordinating all opportunity search and development. His role would involve harvesting, stimulating, focusing, liaising and generally acting as the central figure in opportunity thinking. His role is, however, more that of organizer than director. He is there to set up the framework rather than to generate opportunities.

Opportunity Team: A small permanent group, the membership of which may rotate, with the responsibility of assessing, coordinating, directing and helping opportunity development. The team is at the receiving end of the Opportunity Audit forms but also acts as coordinator of ongoing activity and may set up its own initiatives. The team provides help for specific projects and monitors progress.

Opportunity Task Force: A specific task force set up by the Opportunity team to explore and develop a defined opportunity that seems too large to be handled by a single executive.

Opportunity space: An opportunity space is the action space, the responsibility space and the decision space of an executive. If an opportunity falls within an executive's responsibility space he can do something about it. In the Opportunity Audit an executive is asked to define his opportunity space in order to have a framework within which to look for opportunities.

General opportunities: In the Opportunity Audit the executive is asked to put forward at least three 'general opportunities' for consideration.

Specific opportunity objective: In his Audit return the executive is asked to choose a specific opportunity objective that he would like to tackle. He may request help in tackling it. He will be expected to make progress reports.

FOR THE BEST IN PAPERBACKS, LOOK FOR THE 🐧

In every corner of the world, on every subject under the sun, Penguin represents quality and variety – the very best in publishing today.

For complete information about books available from Penguin – including Puffins, Penguin Classics and Arkana – and how to order them, write to us at the appropriate address below. Please note that for copyright reasons the selection of books varies from country to country.

In the United Kingdom: Please write to *Dept E.P., Penguin Books Ltd, Harmondsworth, Middlesex, UB7 0DA.*

If you have any difficulty in obtaining a title, please send your order with the correct money, plus ten per cent for postage and packaging, to *PO Box No 11, West Drayton, Middlesex*

In the United States: Please write to *Dept BA, Penguin, 299 Murray Hill Parkway, East Rutherford, New Jersey 07073*

In Canada: Please write to *Penguin Books Canada Ltd, 2801 John Street, Markham, Ontario L3R 1B4*

In Australia: Please write to the *Marketing Department, Penguin Books Australia Ltd, P.O. Box 257, Ringwood, Victoria 3134*

In New Zealand: Please write to the *Marketing Department, Penguin Books (NZ) Ltd, Private Bag, Takapuna, Auckland 9*

In India: Please write to *Penguin Overseas Ltd, 706 Eros Apartments, 56 Nehru Place, New Delhi, 110019*

In the Netherlands: Please write to *Penguin Books Netherlands B.V., Postbus 195, NL–1380AD Weesp*

In West Germany: Please write to *Penguin Books Ltd, Friedrichstrasse 10–12, D–6000 Frankfurt/Main 1*

In Spain: Please write to *Alhambra Longman S.A., Fernandez de la Hoz 9, E–28010 Madrid*

In Italy: Please write to *Penguin Italia s.r.l., Via Como 4, I-20096 Pioltello (Milano)*

In France: Please write to *Penguin Books Ltd, 39 Rue de Montmorency, F-75003 Paris*

In Japan: Please write to *Longman Penguin Japan Co Ltd, Yamaguchi Building, 2–12–9 Kanda Jimbocho, Chiyoda-Ku, Tokyo 101*

BY THE SAME AUTHOR

I Am Right – You Are Wrong

In this book Dr Edward de Bono puts forward a direct challenge to what he calls the rock logic of Western thinking. Rock logic is based on rigid categories, absolutes, argument and adversarial point scoring. Instead he proposes the water logic of perception. Drawing on our understanding of the brain as a self-organizing information system, Dr de Bono shows that perception is the key to more constructive thinking and the serious creativity of design.

The Happiness Purpose

Lucid, entertaining and provocative as always, Edward de Bono presents his blueprint for the disciplined pursuit of happiness which, in his opinion, is the legitimate purpose of life. Self-respect, dignity, self-importance and humour occupy an important place in his scheme, and in this practical manual he shows how to utilize these assets as tools for mental and spiritual betterment.

Edward de Bono's Masterthinker's Handbook

It is never enough just to want to think or to exhort someone to think. What are the steps? What is to be done? Avoiding error and winning arguments is only a tiny part of thinking. The main enemies of thinking are confusion, inertia and not knowing what to do next. The 'Body' framework designed by Edward de Bono overcomes these problems.

Wordpower

Could you make an *educated guess* at the *downside-risk* of a *marketing strategy*? Are you in the right *ball-game*, and faced with a crisis could you find an *ad hoc* solution? These are just a few of the 265 specialized words – or 'thinking chunks' – that Dr de Bono defines here in terms of their usage to help the reader use them as tools of expression.

The Use of Lateral Thinking

This book is a textbook of creativity. It shows how the habit of lateral think-ing can be encouraged, how new ideas can be generated. Edward de Bono has worked out special techniques for doing this, in groups or alone, and the result is a triumph of entertaining education.

Practical Thinking

How is it that in an argument both sides are always right? How is it that no one ever makes a mistake on purpose but that mistakes get made? These are some of the questions that Edward de Bono answers in this book. His theme is everyday thinking, how the mind actually works – not how philosophers think it should work.

The Mechanism of Mind

In this fascinating and provocative book Dr de Bono illustrates with simple analogies the mind's tendency to create and consolidate rigid pat-terns, to build myths, to polarize and divide, and then relates these mech-anisms to the various modes of thinking – natural, logical, mathematical and lateral.

The Five-Day Course in Thinking

This book offers a series of simple but intriguing problems in thinking that require no special knowledge and no mathematics. The problems are designed to let the reader find out about his own personal style of think-ing, its weaknesses and strengths, and the methods, latent in himself, that he never uses. Being right is not always important – an error can often lead to the right decision.

also published

Po: Beyond Yes and No
Lateral Thinking for Management
Conflicts: A Better Way to Resolve Them
Children Solve Problems
Atlas of Management Thinking
Future Positive
Teaching Thinking
Six Thinking Hats
Lateral Thinking